I Rode With Heroes

Volume 1

I Rode With Heroes

Volume I

A lifetime of riding with Heroes as we chased down hundreds of outlaws, bandits, pirates, and crooks, and brought them to justice.

Fred G. Macdonald III

Walkiah Bluff Publishing LLC

All photos are courtesy of the author except where otherwise noted.

Print Book Interior Design and Formatting by Lynda K. Stinson

Walkiah Bluff Publishing LLC

Macdonald, Fred, Author
I Rode With Heroes, Volume I
ISBN: 978-1-7340888-0-9
eISBN: 978-1-7340888-2-3

Background Map Imagery:

© 2020 Conquest Maps LLC

www.ConquestMaps.com

I dedicate this book to my family…

To my beautiful Wife, Best Friend, Courageous Partner, and Hero
Gayle
who has been by my side as we…
rode many rivers
…for more than forty years
To My Son Chad and Daughter-in-Law Bonnie
To my Daughter Freddye and Son-in-Law Bobby
To my grandchildren for whom this effort was made…
To Manry, Gracie, Piper, and Tucker
To Ethan, Emma, Layla and
To Kensley Elizabeth

May God bless each of your hearts with some piece of
knowledge or wisdom
from the pages of this book, which will benefit each of you as you
ride along all of your rivers
throughout your life's journey!
May you always ride wisely, cautiously, courageously, and safely
with *your* cherished Partners and Heroes by *your* side!!!

From my heart to yours,
with the deepest of love,
Fred, Daddy, Papa Mac, Papa

The Cowboy Lawman

Life's a long winding river
That we ride our life through
With currents and eddies
And an occasional slough

As I've ridden my river
It's been wide and it's been long
I've entertained some strange feelings
They've been persistent and strong

They're dreams of the past
And in lands far away
With Bandits and Outlaws
Often going astray

In some visions quite vivid
I see a whole different me
A lone Cowboy Lawman
Stands where I should be

In these brief recollections
Though most subtle and dim
I know the lawman I'm seeing
I know... 'cause I'm him

As I ponder my history
And things that might have been
I wonder... just 'cause one life has ended
Could not another begin

When a Cowboy's life has ended
And he wakes on the other side
Is it so hard to imagine
He'd be assigned another ride

And now riding a new river
He keeps making his way
But he acknowledges right quickly
It's just another Cowboy kinda day

So as the new rides continue
Along rivers near and far
Our Cowboys are always changing
Some ride horses, some ride cars

Whether a Marshal, a Ranger
Or a Cop on a beat
Our Lawman changes badges
And wears different boots on his feet

But in his heart he's a Cowboy
No matter where he's at
Because being a true Cowboy
Doesn't always require the same hat

With the highest Cowboy standards
He continues on his way
And rides down his own river
Day after day

But when this Lawman's trail has ended
And he wakes again on the other side
He awaits his next assignment
Another Cowboy River to ride

By riding these rivers
Many lessons are learned
But one keeps repeating
Around every turn

While chasing Bandits and Outlaws
These Lawmen always find
That being a true Cowboy
Is a pure state of mind!

By: Fred G. Macdonald III

December 2019

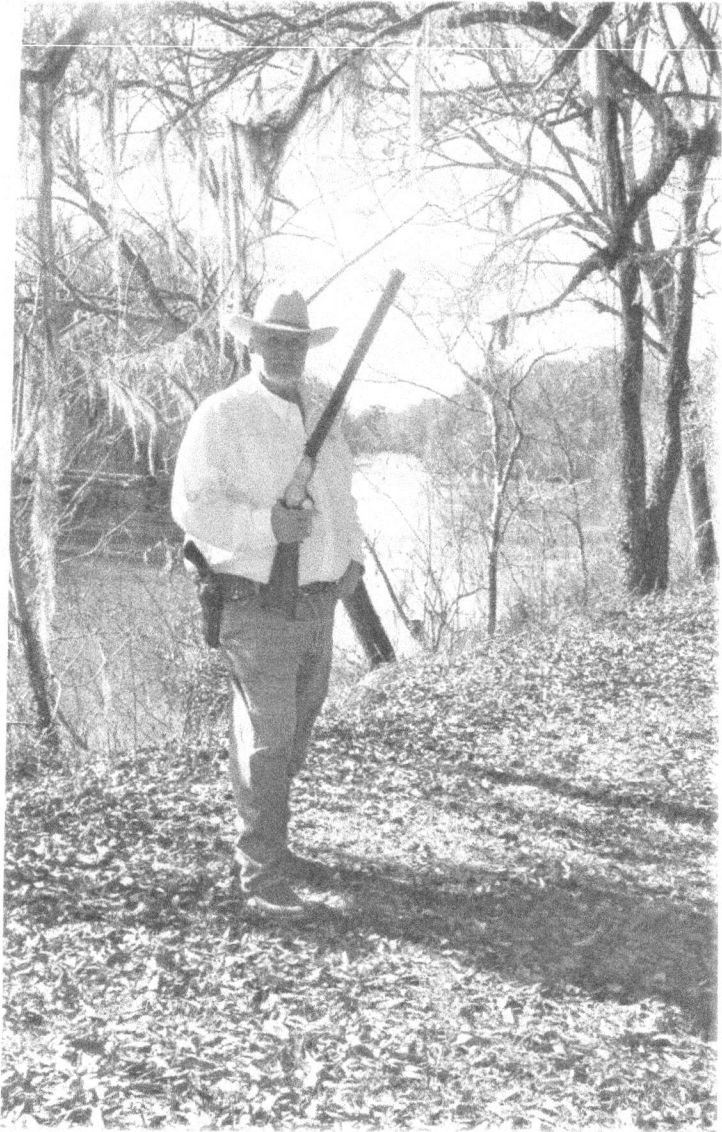

On the river's edge at Walkiah Bluff
From hunting and fishing,
to a ride along many rivers that was to become...
My life in Law Enforcement

Table of Contents

Section IV

"Working for the MBN"   79

Section V

"The Gulfport Office"   98

Section VI

"Working For The Picayune Police Department"   165

I Rode With Heroes
By Fred G. Macdonald III

Introduction

Since the beginning of Law Enforcement in America, the pages of our country's history have been highlighted by famous "Peace Keepers". Most were noted for an outstanding act of courage and in some cases, a series of such events that yielded a level of notoriety or fame that almost everyone in America for decades to come, would at least recognize that Officer's name.

The "rest of the story" is that hundreds if not thousands of Officers routinely have performed the same duties as the "famous" Peace Keepers, including similar acts of courage and bravery, but these Lawmen remain unknown and unremembered in the pages of our Nation's history. Yet collectively and often individually, these professionals represent some of the most valuable resources and assets in the history of these United States. Each day across our country, these unnoticed Heroes go to work on the streets of America and selflessly and bravely enforce our nation's laws among and on behalf of an often ungrateful population.

This ungratefulness is not entirely due to any negative attitude toward our Law Enforcement Officers, but most often due to an "unknowing" population. These Heroes constantly perform acts of bravery by successfully and safely resolving extremely hazardous situations while apprehending hundreds of violent and extremely dangerous armed felons each day. They arrest these individuals so professionally and so meticulously that most often there is no noticeable "force" employed. Consequently, these situations are resolved with minimal impact to the community. No one is injured, not the Officers,

Citizens in the area, and when compliant, not even the "bad guy", so no one even notices. Most often the circle of awareness that the event even occurred is very limited.

These Heroes are highly trained, intelligent, community and family oriented citizens who in many instances "live next door". Because they do their job so well and so professionally, most communities simply take them for granted. They do not seek fame or notoriety. Quite the opposite, they simply do their job each day because they love their families, believe in their communities, and are committed to protecting the American way of life. These *Peace Keepers* are by definition…

American Patriots and True American Heroes!

Throughout this book, I will refer to some of these Peace Keepers by name and give a brief glimpse of why I believe they are in fact Heroes. Others will be represented only by their part in a situation or event in which I witnessed their participation. Many of these are Heroes with whom I have had close personal and professional relationships and have known for many years. Some, I met only briefly during the course of specific investigations or activities. In either case, they individually impacted my life and career in a way that was meaningful. Each Hero holds a very special place in my heart and in the fabric of my life.

Expletives Deleted

Although I speak normally through a highly unfiltered mouth, I purposely chose to delete all, or most, expletives from my book. I managed my mouth and pen in this manner entirely to insure that my grandchildren, children, and others of tender nature, might read the book and not be shocked or embarrassed by Papa's language. My greatest wish in writing this book is that my life and career might be chronicled in a way that my children and grandchildren can have the story and possibly be positively impacted by some of my experiences and the "life lessons" that I learned from them.

In reading the book, the reader should know, without any doubt, that there was *never* a shortage of expletives, and colorful language! We were boys and men engaged in activities and conversations that constantly needed, in our minds, a strong "bite" to our verbiage to insure that our feelings were understood and appreciated. Very frequently strong words of utter amazement, shock, excitement, or fear would simply "occur" and be inadvertently or intentionally projected from my mouth or the mouths of others during the events described within the stories in the book. In writing the book, I made every effort to inject into each story, the amazement, shock, excitement, and fear that was present at the moment, but allow the individual reader to insert the extra "bite" from their own imagination.

As one reads the book, please feel free to mentally insert all expletives and other colorful language necessary to convey any emphasis, inflection, drama, or humor that, in the reader's mind, will make each story "complete"!

It's The Whole Truth,
and Nothing But the Truth...

The Best I Can Remember!

In writing this book, I have made every possible effort as a human being, to assemble each story herein honestly and accurately regarding time, space, and persons present. I have exhausted every resource at my disposal to insure that each story is also factually correct!

As one reads the book and the stories, it should immediately become obvious that many of these are "snapshots" of historic events that occurred nearly a half century in the past. Due to the numerous moon phases which have passed since most of these events occurred, it should be understandable that in at least a few of my recollections, there may be a small number of facts, times, or locations that may be slightly out of focus or misaligned.

While a certain amount of literary license has been purchased to insure that I adequately emphasized the humor, amazement, or fear involved in some of the recounts, I assure the reader that all of the stories are real and based upon fact and actual events. In short, each story in the book is 100% accurate...

As I remember it!!!

In the unlikely circumstance that a reader were to have been present in one or more of these actual events described in the book, and that reader should take exception to my *accurate* depiction of facts, time, or space, then that reader should feel free to write a book and present that reader's "version" of the events.

I will be happy to recommend a publisher!

I sincerely hope that each reader will allow these stories to place them into the many circumstances depicted within the book in which many of America's greatest Heroes went regularly into harm's way to insure the safety of many unknowing fellow citizens each day, for many years! These and thousands of other Heroes all across our Nation are still *"on the line"* for America!

Most of their "Stories" will never be told!!!

Section I
"Learning to Ride"
with my earliest Heroes

A s a young boy growing up in the 1950's and 1960's, I was surrounded by exceptional role models, many of whom soon became my first Heroes. My father's father, after whom we were both named (Fred Gray Macdonald Sr.) cast a shadow that I often found myself standing in and trying to duplicate. He was a "Man's Man" in a day when that was a highly respected quality. He grew up in the early 1900's and quickly became an outdoorsman of the highest order. By the time I arrived as a twig on the family tree, Papa Mac, as the grandchildren all called him, was an entrepreneur who owned and operated the largest plywood manufacturing plant in the nation, was a well-known community leader and was highly respected in our hometown...

Picayune, Mississippi

Most noteworthy to the "youngest Fred", however, was that Papa Mac regularly hunted and fished in the northwest portion of our

*Papa Mac beside Caribou that he just
"Harvested" in Alaska on an early 1950's hunt.*

nation, and in Canada and Alaska. I can still remember frequent visits to his "den" at his home where we would sit and talk for hours about the many exciting circumstances surrounding his many adventures in what was then still the wilderness areas of North America. He would show me the weapons that he carried and used to harvest animals that I only knew from pictures, his stories, and the "Trophies" that would eventually show up after one of his hunts and be hung on a wall in his den or other area of prominence. As I grew older, he would allow me to "target practice" with the rifles, shotguns, and handguns that he carried on his hunts. Each of those weapons, the hunting stories associated with each, and being taught to handle and fire them safely and correctly still hold deep significance to me! They always will because of the love with which they were shared with me by one of the greatest Heroes of my life....

My "Papa Mac".

Alongside Papa Mac and always close enough to care for and watch over us all was his wife and my grandmother "Mama Nina".

Mama Nina

She was a treasure to each member of the family for many years as we all grew up in our small town. Mama Nina, like Papa Mac, was one of my greatest heroes. She was always available and willing to take time to explain events and answer the hundreds of spontaneous questions from a wide-eyed boy of the 1950's. She took me shopping with her for household needs at the "C & R Store", and to have her car filled up with fuel at the "Standard" gas station across from the Post Office while attendants (in uniform) filled her tank, checked her oil, and cleaned her windshield. This was in a time when the stores, gas station and the entire area looked unbelievably similar to scenes from "Mayberry". If we could step back into those activities again today with Mama Nina, you would expect Andy or Barney to walk around the corner at any moment and act like they were part of the family. As the years passed, Mama Nina became more and more loved and adored by me and the other grandchildren. She took me to acquire important items from the "Western Auto" store like fishing hooks, corks, and sinkers for my homemade fishing pole. Then she would transport me back to their home on Glenwood Avenue so that I could embark on my next fishing adventure in a small ever flowing ditch that created the southern border of their property in Picayune. As I fished and played along that ditch, I built memories with Mama Nina that I still cherish greatly today. Then and for many years to come, she would be a remarkable example of calmness and good judgement that I have tried to duplicate in many of the most trying situations of my life. Mama Nina was a critical hero to this country boy in my trajectory of maturing to become a man.   She was, and still is, much more of a "Role Model" than she ever could have known!

*Daddy Jim (far Right), Papa Mac (center
kneeling), and Crew on Wyoming Hunting trip
near Cody (1949)*

Another "large shadow" in our family was "Daddy Jim". James Calvin "Kid" Nichols was Mama Nina's dad. I met Daddy Jim several times in my younger years before he passed away as a result of a bout with cancer. Daddy Jim also was quite an outdoorsman and many of his adventures and life stories are found in a book written about him by his daughter Lucile titled *"The Candy Kid"*. Among those adventures were such details as him having been a "Blacksmith" for Buffalo Bill Cody in his young years and later being a prominent community leader in Cody, Wyoming. He owned the "Diamond Bar Ranch" outside Cody. With more than twenty thousand acres of deeded land on the ranch and more than 200,000 acres permanently leased from the government, he controlled over three hundred square miles of property near Yellowstone, where he raised cattle and conducted big game hunts that became the legends of my youth. He was the "Real Deal" and created one of those "shadows" mentioned earlier that I always wished that I could have grown up in much more than I ever had the opportunity to do.

During the late 1920's, Daddy Jim and some of his hunting partners planned, and embarked upon an African Safari. In that time period, this was no small feat! The actual trip, hunt, and return home lasted more than six months. He harvested numerous trophy animals, and like Papa Mac, those "Trophies" were displayed in his home in Cody, his offices in Chicago, and some are still displayed by family members to whom they were passed down. The family stories of his adventures, his bravery in the face of many difficult and dangerous events throughout his life, and his unwillingness to ever "give-up" became examples of courage that I have drawn from throughout my life. For always having been a part of how I have perceived and dealt with fear and danger, Daddy Jim is also one of my greatest Heroes!

Also casting a "shadow" from my mother's side of the family tree was my "Papa Weston". Weston Lott was my mom's step-father and the grandfather that along with my mother's mother "Mama Nannie"

comprised a team that watched over me frequently in my younger days.
Mama Nannie was the voice of reason
and regularly uttered proclamations and
admonishments to an often "worthy"
young Freddy that are still, almost
seventy years later, quoted by me to
make points that simply cannot be
explained more appropriately to a
"worthy recipient". For example…
"Boy… I'll knock you a winding…" What
more could possibly need to be said…?
The "visual image" of the potential
physical results of that admonishment is
enough to bring any young boy
promptly to attention with a
spontaneous "Yes Ma'am…"!

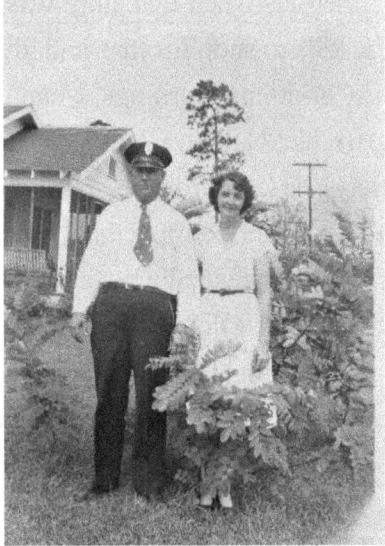

Papa Weston and Mama Nannie at their residence on 6th Avenue in Picayune

Mama Nannie was a rock! She could touch an injured knee
of a grandson who did not adhere to valuable instructions regarding
the riding of a bicycle for the first time with no "training wheels", and
make the pain vanish as though by magic. She could utter a few
simple words that along with a "Mama Nannie look", could convey

Mama Nannie in Western Auto just before her annual transformation into "Nannie Claus"

more needed information to the
recipient than a three dollar
paper back novel! She sang in
the Church choir on Sunday
morning and made sure that I,
along with other grandchildren
were present to hear the songs
and the sermon. She made the
best cornbread on the planet
and introduced me to the pure mortal ecstasy of tomato sandwiches.

She worked at the Western Auto store in Picayune, and at Christmas when that store was "The" town's biggest resource for all the kids to shop for toys and give Santa ideas for insuring the happiest of Christmas mornings, Mama Nannie was known by every child in town as "Nannie Claus". She was loved and respected by all! Her fiery, no-compromise, right-is-right, never give up personality has also been an example that I have called upon many times during trying circumstances. She has always been a source for, and example of true courage that I have tried to duplicate many times throughout my life!

Mama Nannie…... Hero!!!

Papa Weston, likewise, holds a place of respect in my memory of my youth that no one else could ever fill! He was soft spoken and a "man of few words", but whatever he said was worth listening to and remembering!!! My earliest memories of Papa Weston were of him as a Police Officer in our home town. I would come to realize in later years that he was a "Town Marshal" for six years starting late in the 1940's, and the second "Chief of Police" in our home town in the 1950's. These and other facts were items that could not be adequately appreciated by a boy of my age at that time.

I remember when I was only five or six years old, I sat in his police car with him and watched him test his new Police radio… the first radio ever installed in any Police Car in our small home town Police Department. This was quite an event, to say the least. Seeing how enthralled I was in the workings of the radio, its knobs, and the sounds emitted from its speaker, he brought me an old non-working tabletop AM radio to dissect and play with. Receiving the radio, I immediately started turning its knobs and dials and before long had asked for a screwdriver to disassemble my new treasure to see what "previously" had "made it work". He patiently watched and helped me "work on the radio".

The next day he went to work. When he got home that

afternoon, Mama Nannie met him at the door and told him he needed to come see what his grandson "had done". Wincing somewhat, and not knowing what to expect, he walked into his den to see me seated on the floor with the radio plugged in to a nearby power outlet. The radio was blaring some of those "oldies" that we listened to when they were new. I looked up and said "Look Papa Weston, I fixed it!" He had hooked me on radios and electronics forever!

I remember watching him get dressed to go on duty and admiring the meticulous manner in which he placed the items which adorned his uniform. From his badge and whistle, to his name tag and tie clip, he treated each item with respect and was always eager to explain the significance of each item to me.

Papa Weston (January 1950) Chief of Police with other Officers after arrest of two fugitives from Texas

He also demonstrated the proper and safe methods of caring for, handling, and wearing his service revolver. Papa Weston was left handed, and I remember him joking with me as he handed me items to inspect, that I was "holding everything backwards". He told me stories of arrests that he had made of dangerous individuals, and search warrants that he had conducted in which drugs and various other types of evidence had been seized and confiscated. He explained the process of arrest, incarceration, the bonding process, and the trial process. He was tireless in his determination to answer my every question about "being a Police Officer". Unknown to him or me at that time, Papa Weston's patience and loving explanations created the foundation and the interest that led me to a fifty-year Law Enforcement career and placed me on the path to my future. There has been no bigger Hero in my life than my Papa Weston!

All during my childhood and early adolescence, I was constantly in the company of my grandparents. I deeply loved and respected my mom and dad, but the lure of listening to Papa Weston's stories of his adventures as a Police Officer and Mama Nannie's "mater samiches" and such, kept me by their sides at every possible opportunity. Likewise my Papa Mac and Mama Nina drew me to their home whenever I could get an affirmative nod from Mom or Dad. With that "nod" of approval, I would be off to participate in one or more of the numerous activities that I had matured enough to "survive" at the time.

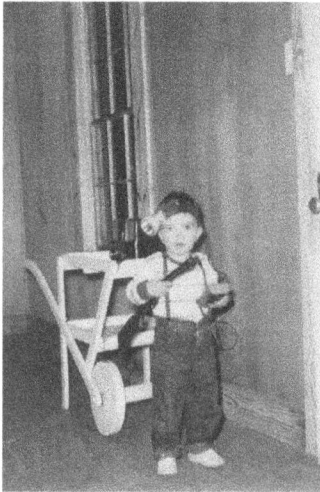

Freddy "going hunting" (1953)

Although Mama Nina and Papa Mac lived in town during my early years they had a remote "camp" along the Pearl River about six miles or so west of Picayune. It was at this camp, in my early youth, that I began to appreciate and truly love the outdoors. There I could "be a boy" in a setting that supported all my favorite activities. We hunted, fished, target practiced, and played in the mud along the river bank. We spent nights at the camp and enjoyed meals from the enormous rotisserie or barbeque pit where huge meals were cooked over an open fire on an enormous screened-in porch that completely encircled the camp. We lay in hammocks under the moon light and watched for shooting stars as if they were supposed to follow a schedule. I grew up believing, and I still believe that every child should be required to experience, and be taught to appreciate, the great outdoors. With a wonderful family watching over me constantly, I grew up! As I grew older, Papa Mac sold, purchased, and built several camps at different locations along the Pearl River.

By the time I was twelve years old, he and Mama Nina had purchased a large piece of property on the Pearl River in an area known as Walkiah Bluff. It was about nine miles west of town and became their home. A home that I would remember for all of my years. The home was on more than two hundred acres of land that ran for more than two miles along the East Pearl River which was the state line between Mississippi and Louisiana. Other than a yard that comprised about ten acres, and a few pastures

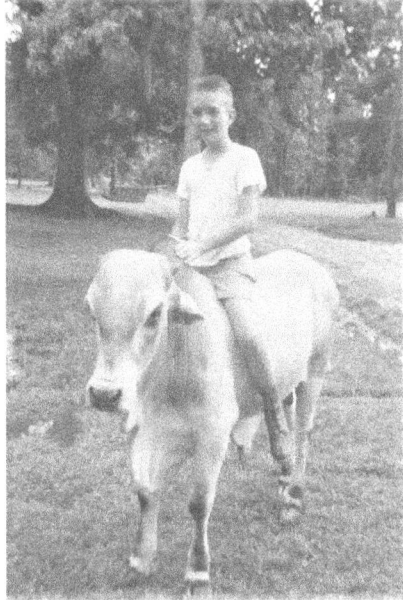

Freddy "riding a bull" on the banks of "Peaceful Pearl" (1961)

that accounted for another fifty or so acres, the rest of the property was mostly dense woods and swamp… the real deal. This portion of the property was home to just about every form of wildlife that was common to this part of the nation. From the largest of catfish species to the finest bluegill bream population anywhere, we fished for and caught ample amounts of fish to feed the family or whoever happened to be present at supper time. During the various hunting seasons, I constantly bagged my "limit" of squirrels, rabbits, dove, or whatever might be the desired meal du-jour. No matter what the season, I could always be found with firearms on my person or near, "very near" me. The swamp was filled with "critters" that would sting, bite or eat you if given the chance. From the time I was thirteen walking the muddy floors of a highly unpredictable swamp, I was, as many of my cowboy heroes would say, "well heeled". Along with learning to cast a spinning rod and consistently hit a six inch circle at fifty or more feet, I could draw my Colt frontier scout .22 caliber single action revolver and hit a coffee cup sized target from a hundred feet or more. With any other handgun, rifle, or shotgun, I was equally proficient and confident. These and other skills were developed only by thousands of proper repetitions of the skills. These repetitions included thousands of "casts" with the rod and reel, and thousands of rounds of various calibers of ammunition fired through a number of weapons. I found very early that one does not learn any skill by reading or talking about it. One learns the skill by casting the rod and reel and by shooting the guns! That's how it works. This hand-eye coordination and weapon proficiency served me well while hunting and fishing along the Pearl River. These same skills would serve me well in many dangerous circumstances for the rest of my life. They still serve me well, even today.

Over the next few years as I grew older, into my mid-teens, I logged hundreds of miles up and down the river on foot and in Papa Mac's twelve foot aluminum skiff powered by a Johnson 9.5 HP outboard motor. I was taught to drive by a patient but demanding Papa Mac who turned me loose on the property in his four door 1962 Chevy Impala, where I drove for hours back and forth between the house and the barn, a distance of just over a quarter of a mile. Staying with Papa Mac and Mama Nina at their house, I would drink coffee with them in the

Freddy III holding his twenty pound Northern Pike on the shores of Cree Lake, Saskatchewan in (1964)

early mornings and watch the sun come up through the windows of Mama Nina's kitchen and breakfast area. We would watch out over the river from our coffee nook and enjoy the first daylight glimpses of the snags that protruded from the waters along the edges of the river and watch as softshell turtles climbed onto the snags to begin "sunning" for the day. Great Blue Heron cranes were among our favorites to watch each morning as they walked in the water along the river's edge catching and eating small fish for their breakfast. These priceless scenes repeated themselves in that coffee nook with me and Mama Nina and Papa Mac until they are forever indelibly etched into this "ole country boy's" favorite memories. I still have the old green, highly worn, coffee mug in which Mama Nina served my special cups of coffee for many of my favorite mornings.

By the time I was about fifteen, I had my driver's license, and my first car. It was also about this time that Papa Mac had begun selling campsites on the extreme upper end of his property along the river. On one of these lots, he had built a camp and upon its completion, he allowed me to use the camp from which to stage my hunting and fishing adventures. From that time until I went to college, I virtually lived in this camp or another that he built on a nearby lot a couple of years later. Even upon my going to college, I returned most weekends and resided almost exclusively at "the camp". It was an

Filets from one lake trout....Shore lunch for 6 people

elevated camp house consisting of one large room with a kitchen in one corner and a small bathroom and storage room along the back wall. All the "bunks" were arranged around the walls of the big room and a few chairs and benches provided seating when the occupants were not sleeping. I often stayed alone at the camp, but frequently was accompanied by high school or college friends who would join me for fishing or hunting trips for the weekends. The camp became my home for several years and played a large role in my maturing and going out into the world on my own. Although I never kept it clean enough or "in order" as Papa Mac would have liked, it became one of the most important aspects of my "growing up" and a resource for me that Papa Mac could never have imagined. It helped me grow some mighty important "Wings"! Wings that I have always hoped that Mama Nina and Papa Mac would have been proud of if they were still here today.

Papa Mac and Mama Nina at Walkiah Bluff (1968)

As I grew up around my real life heroes, I also was constantly surrounded by my "TV Heroes". Television was still in its infancy and by today's standards, much of the programming was somewhat crude. However, many of the greatest shows ever to fill the screen are still being broadcast daily. They are still just as good today through much older eyes as they were some sixty plus years ago. Shows like *Gunsmoke*, *Bonanza*, *Lawman*, and *Tales of Wells Fargo* still project images and ideals that I cherished then and cherish now. Each show not only entertained but taught "life lessons" that I think every young person would be well served to watch and understand even today. Each show always portrayed the "Good Guys" and the "Bad Guys" having it out, and the "Good Guy" always won. The shows instilled a desire to "Be" the good guy, to always do the right thing, and always stand on the "Right Side" of every situation. The "Characters" of these and other similar shows projected the morals of our society at the time when our greatest heroes had made America the greatest Nation in the history of the world! They instilled a desire to be one of the "Good Guys" that would keep America great. All of these shows and many others, helped create a mindset for thousands of young men and women all across America. That mindset gave our country's youth an expectation of success and also one of winning against any adversary! It's that mindset that causes one to run toward the gunfire as others run away from the threat. It's the mindset and personality that has molded many of our nation's greatest heroes!

Throughout my early teenage years (the 1960's), I met and came to know most of the Law Enforcement Officers in our city and county as a result of my family's relationships with many of those

(L-R) Chief Kenny Bounds, Sheriff J.P. Walker, Officers Buddy Watts and John Bullock, and Chief Deputy Larkin Smith (1969)

Officers. My Dad was a city Councilman in our home town for over seventeen years, owned and managed a business, and also grew up there. He knew almost everyone in our area and was a highly respected leader of our community. As a result, I grew up around most of our city and county officials including Sheriffs, Deputies, Chiefs of Police, and City Police Officers. Several of these Law Enforcement officers became close friends of mine as a result. The Chief of Police by this time was Kenny Bounds. The Sheriff was J.P. Walker, and the Chief Deputy was Larkin Smith. All three of these men as well as most other Deputies and Officers "took me under their wings" when I expressed an interest in becoming a Law Enforcement Officer. They, like Papa Weston, would show me various pieces of equipment, tell me stories of arrests and other exciting official activities that they had participated in, and answered hundreds of un-filtered questions from a young unknowing "wannabe". They each handled it all with the patience of Job! These men created the foundation for my first "Law Enforcement Network". They were to remain highly valued friends, remarkable resources, and trusted confidants for many years to come!

Section II
Starting College and a Career

After graduating High School, I went to College at the University of Southern Mississippi in Hattiesburg. Having had significant interaction with Larkin Smith as above described, it was no surprise to me that he contacted me very soon after my arrival at USM. He explained that he had a close friend in the Hattiesburg area who was an investigator for the Mississippi Highway Patrol. Larkin went on to say that Bruce Rogers of the MHP was the Narcotics Investigator for the Patrol in the area and he was interested in meeting me and discussing the possibility of my working for the Patrol in an "undercover capacity".

Well…. After I caught my breath, and calmed down a bit, I met with Larkin and Bruce a few days later. During the meeting I talked with Larkin and Bruce for some time and learned that because of the high level of drug activity that was occurring on and around college campuses at the time, Bruce was eager to develop resources to combat the rapidly growing drug epidemic. Bruce explained that what he wanted me to do, if I was interested, was to infiltrate the drug dealers in the area of the University, and provide a covert resource for ongoing intelligence information with which the Patrol could combat the drug trafficking in the area.

Because I had always wanted to become a Law Enforcement Officer, this opportunity seemed like an unbelievable chance to get started down that path. Although not being an actual "Sworn Officer" (I was still quite a ways from the required twenty-one years of age for that), I would at least be working as an unsworn Agent for an Agency that more than thirty years into the future, I would actually "retire" from. After several subsequent meetings with Bruce, I agreed to go to work for him and the Patrol in this capacity.

So, I began my Law Enforcement career on September 14, 1968 on a country road outside Hattiesburg, Mississippi! It was like the old joke... *"Yesterday I couldn't spell Investigator, and today I are one".* Little could I know where that path would lead, the unbelievable adventures that lie ahead, or the numerous Heroes with whom it would bring me in contact!!!

I continued working for the Highway Patrol for several years while attending college and provided a resource for intelligence information regarding the illicit and illegal drug activities of students and others active on and around the USM campus. I also worked on the Gulf Coast for a summer after the devastating hurricane Camille struck the coastal area on August 17, 1969. There, while working as a foreman on a "clean-up crew", I provided the same resources as when I was at USM. I worked on the campus of Perkinston Junior College in Wiggins, Mississippi for a semester providing drug related intelligence resources all with and for the MHP.

While working for the Patrol, I was fortunate enough to meet and work with many of the Patrol's senior Investigators, and Troopers. Investigators like T.P. Naylor, Bobby Parker, and Joe Price, and Troopers like Johnny Fox and Bruce Breland, only to name a few, were constantly eager to share experience and offer support to a young "narc" who was long on "want-to", but short on experience. They were then and remain today, not only great heroes to me, but also some of our state's greatest Heroes!

Section III

New Orleans and the NOPD

In mid-1970, while visiting with Larkin Smith, Chief Kenny Bounds, and other Officers in the area of my hometown, Chief Bounds commented that he had seen an advertisement in the local newspaper, the "*Picayune Item*", stating that the New Orleans Police Department was recruiting new Officers for the department. He asked me if I thought I might be interested. I told him I didn't know, but that I had always wanted to be a "Detective" in a big city. He chuckled and remarked that he didn't know if they would start me off there but he was sure I could work my way up! He, Larkin and others present used my remark to "jest" with me for months after the exchange. In the months that followed, it came to be expected that each time I met with any of those present when the "Detective" comment was made, at least one of my "buddies" would ask, "Hey boy… you a Detective yet..?" I would always quip back just as seriously, "Nope but I'm working on it!"

As a result of Chief Bounds' guidance, however, I began a tedious and lengthy process that resulted in my applying for the position of Police Officer with the New Orleans Police Department. During the application process that took almost a year, I contacted a close friend and fellow student at USM named Jay Moore. Jay and I had attended USM together since our first day at college in 1968, and had also been Fraternity brothers. Jay was one of the few people who knew that I was working for the Highway Patrol during that time and had also expressed an interest in getting into Law Enforcement as a career. I explained to Jay that I was going to apply with NOPD and asked if he was interested in also applying. He said he was very interested and within a few days, we were both at City Hall in New

Orleans and had officially applied for the position of "Police Officer" with the city.

Throughout the hiring process, Chief Bounds, Larkin Smith, and Sheriff J.P. Walker supported me in every way possible. They offered moral support, acted as references on both mine and Jay Moore's applications, and the Sheriff and Larkin hired me as a Deputy with the Pearl River Sheriff's Office while waiting for the outcome of the application process. They would continue to be some of my strongest allies for many years to come. Larkin had a lengthy Law Enforcement career as Chief Deputy, Chief Investigator, Chief of Police, and Sheriff, and went on to be a U.S Congressman. J.P. Walker was a city Police Officer, a Deputy Sheriff and Sheriff for several terms. Chief Kenny Bounds was a Police Officer and Chief of Police for many years. Although they are all deceased now, they continued to be some of my closest friends and supporters throughout the remainder of their lives. Each of these men contributed greatly to the foundation of my Law Enforcement career and remain, even now, some of my greatest Heroes!!!

During the process of applying for and being evaluated for the position of Police Officer, there were numerous "tests" that we navigated through. The process was slow! We would take one test, and await the results of that test before advancing to the next stage. After being notified by NOPD personnel that we had passed a particular testing phase, we would be told when and where to report for the next test. There were basic civil service tests, I.Q. tests, Psychological evaluations, P.T tests, Physical exams including vision tests, hearing tests, etc.

We were given Polygraph exams and were interviewed by several senior ranking officials within the Department. It was very demanding and very comprehensive. After months of testing and driving back and forth to the NOPD, both Jay and I received word in early April of 1971 that we had been accepted as recruits with the New Orleans Police department. I was to report to the Department on April 28, 1971 to be officially sworn in.

Both Jay and I quickly made several more trips to New Orleans and located apartments to move into in the city. It was required that all Officers reside within the city. So we asked some of the Officers by whom we had been tested where they would suggest that we reside. They offered several suggestions and Jay and I chose an apartment complex in "New Orleans East" that placed us in a convenient location to return to Mississippi for visits, but also put us in an area from which we could travel to work comfortably. After obtaining an apartment and completing my "Move" to New Orleans East on April 27, I arrived at the NOPD personnel office early on the morning of April 28 and was promptly sworn in. Jay had made his move a few days before me and had already been sworn in on April 27.

As I finished my Oath, I noticed an Officer standing to my rear and upon turning around toward him, he asked my name and told me "the Chief wants to see you". Being the naïve rookie recruit that I was, I remember thinking, "how nice, the Chief must greet all the new guys". After following the Officer to the third floor "Detective Division", I learned that the "Chief" was none other than "Chief of Detectives" Henry Morris. Chief Morris was to become one of my greatest Heroes and continues to hold that position of respect to this day! In all my years in Law Enforcement, he stands out as one of the best examples of a "Good Guy" that I have ever had the honor to work for or beside. He was truly a "Hero's Hero"!

Upon reaching the Chief's office, I was met by Chief Morris and other members of his Staff who all cordially introduced themselves. The Chief informed me that he had been made aware that I had prior Law Enforcement experience. He went on to say that due to that experience, they wanted me to work in the Detective Bureau until the next Police Academy started. He and his Staff explained that I would have the opportunity to learn the workings of the Detective Bureau and observe Detectives conducting their investigations for several months until the academy started. They assured me that I would undoubtedly learn a lot that would help me throughout my career.

I was so tickled, I could hardly breathe. I knew that the Department would have to put me somewhere for the months before the academy started, but could never have imagined in my wildest dreams that they would put me in the Detective Bureau on my first day with the Department! I thought…" wait till I get back home!" And I couldn't wait until the next time they ask "You a Detective yet boy…?" ! I was going to make them loose THEIR breath!!!

Just as I was about to catch *my* breath, and thank the Chief for his offer, his phone rang. No, this was not the phone on his desk with all the separate buttons for different lines into his office. The phone that was ringing was a single line, rotary dial, black phone on a small table in the far corner behind his desk… behind the *"Chief's desk"*. The Chief walked calmly over and picked up his private phone and said "Hello, this is Morris"…

He slowly turned and with a look that I will never forget, said… "It's for you" and motioned for me to come behind his desk and answer his phone. Well… I lost my breath again! As I walked/stumbled to the phone, I'm wondering "who on earth could I possibly have annoyed within the thirty minutes *max* that I have been with the department that was important enough to have the Chief's private phone number"? As I walked to the phone, I must have looked like I had seen the proverbial "ghost". I felt like there was so little blood in my head, if someone had cut my throat, I wouldn't have bled a drop. I was breathless…!

I took the phone from an obviously amazed Chief and with a raspy voice said "Hello, this is Macdonald". To that the Chief gave an audible and very rare chuckle! Then to my shock and surprise on the other end of the line was James "Jay" D. Moore! As he was asking me how I was doing... I was sputtering "how the devil did you get this number and what the devil do you want?" Well, with the Chief and his Staff standing somewhat patiently on one side, Jay began to quickly explain in my ear on the other side. Since he had been "sworn in" a day earlier, he had already been recruited for undercover work within the Vice Squad while awaiting the next academy. After settling into the Vice Squad for almost a whole day, Jay had convinced the Vice Squad Commander, Sgt. Bob Frey, that he really should try to have me assigned to the Vice Squad instead of the Detective Bureau. The Commander agreed and had called the Chief's office for ole Jay to talk me into coming to the Vice Squad.

Now.... This was no small dilemma. Since I was about ten years old, I had dreamed of being a Detective in a "Big City". I had watched every TV program that had a Detective in it, and being a Detective was the "Holy Grail" of police work as I knew it at that time. I also knew that I had been successfully working undercover for a couple of years by that time. I felt that I would do well and be comfortable in that capacity in the Vice Squad also. I would also be working with Jay and that would mean that I would know at least one person upon whom I could "trust my backside".

So... after a couple of minutes that seemed like an eternity of standing in front of the Chief and his Staff, I gave him my answer. He was noticeably stunned when I opted to go to the Vice Squad instead of staying in the prestigious Detective Bureau while waiting to go to the academy. I thanked the Chief and each member of his Staff for their generous offer and explained my reasoning. I asked the Chief not to hold my decision against me if I later wanted to come back to the Detective Bureau. He shook my hand and told me that he would keep the offer open and wished me safety and good luck while in the Vice Squad. Little did either of us know that within two years, I would in fact be back as a Detective in the city wide "Robbery Unit" which was part of the "Offense Against Persons" division, and would remain in that position until I left the Department in late 1974.

A Recruit in the Vice Squad

Arriving at the Vice Squad, I had no idea what was in store for two young country boys! Over the next several months, I was afforded the opportunity to gain experience and work with Officers that most twenty-year veterans would have given an arm and leg for. We worked alongside seasoned officers who took us in and treated us like we had been "on the job" for years. They involved us in every type investigation that we could have imagined. We worked gambling, prostitution, gaming machines, horse track investigations and made arrests, executed search warrants, and testified in court to all the above. Night Court alone was an education in itself. I drew upon my experiences testifying in Judge Glancey's court in almost every court trial in which I testified for the remainder of my career. What a judge and what an experience!

Bill Derbyshire destroys illegal slot machines seized during a raid in The French Quarter of New Orleans (1973)

We were taught how to run surveillance in vehicles, on foot and from fixed locations. We were taught how to write reports of investigation that would stand up to the most aggressive scrutiny by the finest of attorneys. A report of investigation written under the tutelage of Sargent Dietz Lauman, was bullet proof. We learned from the best! Most importantly… we were taught how to think like a real investigator by some of the finest investigators with whom I ever worked. These were Officers like Bob Frey, Paul Melancon, Dietz Lauman, Dave Kent, Tommy Casey, Jimmy Preau, Rudy Melancon, Herbie Lund, David Henley, Billy Derbyshire, Richie Woodfork, Wayne Jusslin, and others. These men worked every day in the most dangerous of circumstances with a minimum of equipment and in conditions in which their closest "back-up" was never *close enough* to respond *quickly enough*. They worked long hours often without compensation to take dangerous felons off the streets in order to protect innocent citizens. Most of these men were known well by other Officers within the department for individual acts of extreme heroism.

Acts which included Paul Melancon, and Bob Frey dressing as Catholic Priests and successfully going into a heavily fortified housing complex known as the "Desire Project" to arrest numerous heavily armed suspects without any possibility of "Back-Up". Or similar acts of bravery that were performed by Dietz Lauman who taught us all how to write those "bullet proof" reports of investigation.

Dietz also had survived numerous deadly shootouts with armed felons actively engaged in committing violent crimes against citizens and upon Police Officers including himself. Dietz was so determined to protect us while we were involved in dangerous investigations in the French Quarter that he would walk along the heavily crowded street carrying his handgun in a brown paper bag *in his hand* to insure that he could deploy his weapon in time if our lives were to be threatened while conducting our undercover investigations.

These heroes also included men like Dave Kent who as the commander of the Vice Squad was able to manage a group of young Officers effectively enough to insure our safety during the infamous

"Howard Johnson Sniper Attack" which was to occur a couple of years later. As a group of young eager inexperienced Officers, we were blessed with these heroic tutors and mentors as our bosses and partners! They worked alongside us daily, instilling in us not only the competence, but also the confidence we needed to be successful and also to insure our safety. I appreciated these outstanding Officers contributions then and as the years passed they became and remain some of my most treasured Heroes!

Going to the Academy

Major
Sidney R. Terrebonne
Director
Bureau of Education
and Training

Top Row: Patrolman Jean F. Weiskopf, Patrolman Edward M. DiGiovanni, Sergeant Ted L. Brister.
Center: Lieutenant Victor L. Cimino
Bottom Row: Lieutenant Roger A. Baron, Sr., Assistant Director, Mrs. Eugenie Pagnac, Secretary, Lieutenant Melvyn K. Fourmaux

Academy Staff for the NOPD Police Academy (1971)

After a couple of months of working in the Vice Squad, I was informed that class number 55 of the NOPD Academy would begin on June 21, 1971. I was further informed that I was to attend that class. The academy was seventeen weeks in duration and would be conducted in the NOPD training buildings near City Park. On that sweltering hot and humid Monday morning in June, I arrived at the academy and started the program. It was well structured and very demanding both physically and mentally.

I was accompanied in the class by many fine young men including Rudy Melancon. Rudy who had also been assigned to the Vice Squad while waiting to attend the academy, was selected by our other classmates as the "Class Counselor" (or Class Leader), I was likewise selected as the "Assistant Class Counselor". During the Academy, we were taught classes by numerous highly qualified instructors. Men and women from many agencies, departments, and universities

Graduates

Richard P. Artigue	David R. Mc Cann
Alfred E. Asuncion	Rudy A. Melancon
Yves J. Benoit	Michael V. Mones, Sr.
Clifford D. Bland, Sr.	Luis F. Murillo
Lawrence M. Bourgeois	David C. Piazza
Alan L. Bowie	Miles M. Rogers, Jr.
Wilbert E. Brown, Jr.	William A. Schultz
Leigh W. Cole	Kenneth L. Solis
John M. Couvillon	Clarence R. Southern
Landris Dixon	Wayne J. Tamborella
James R. Dupuis, Jr.	Joseph L. Vaccaro
Hugh L. Fagot	Robert J. Vicknair
Teddy R. Fambro	Orman J. Walters, Jr.
Bobbie L. Grimsley	Frank J. Weicks, Jr.
Gordon C. Hellmers	Clyde F. Williams, Jr.
Kenneth P. James	Frederick E. Yorsch
Robert G. Jennewine	Robert J. Zeller, Sr.
Howard D. Johnson	Criminalist
Warren J. Keller, Sr,	John F. Palm, Jr.
Jerome L. Long, Jr.	Sgt. Thomas F. Sessum
Fred G. Macdonald III	Harbor Police Department

Award Winners

Frank J. Weicks, Jr.
Police Mutual Benevolent
Association Scholastic
Plaque, Class Ring, Courtesy of Zale's Jewelers, Inc.

Fred G. Macdonald, III
Fraternal Order of Police
Precision Shooting Trophy,
Major Jim Roos Quick
Draw Trophy

Counselors

Rudy A. Melancon
Class Counselor

Fred G. Macdonald, III
Assistant Class Counselor

Class Roster and Award recipients for Class #55

delivered hours of formal classroom presentations that gave us a great foundation for performing our duties on the street. The professionalism and dedication that was common among the Academy Staff and all the Instructors who taught us during the school impacted me greatly for the rest of my career. They, no doubt, were very instrumental in motivating me to become a Law Enforcement Instructor myself in the years that followed.

We also participated in physical training exercises that were very demanding. Hours were spent in the Gym and on the streets of City Park walking and jogging for great distances. During the final weeks of the school, we were required to do "ride alongs" in uniform in various Districts with seasoned Officers to "get the feel" of working in uniform and actually responding to "Dispatched calls". It was an eye opener for us all. We were about to be placed on the street and bridled with great trust and responsibility. We all took that very seriously!

Soon it was graduation day. On Friday October 15, 1971 our graduation ceremony was conducted in the City Council Chambers of City Hall, where just over a year earlier I had begun my application process for the NOPD. We, the graduates, were dressed in our new uniforms adorned with all necessary hardware. As I had watched my

COMMENCEMENT EXERCISES
RECRUIT CLASS 55

NEW ORLEANS POLICE

To Protect & To Serve

"The Beginning Of A Career"

NOPD "Program" for
Commencement Exercises at
the graduation of Recruit Class
#55 on October 15, 1971
(seventeen week academy)

grandfather do many years earlier, I had placed each item, from my badge and nameplate to my whistle and tie clip, meticulously and respectfully onto my uniform. I made sure that each item was cleaned, shined and attached perfectly.

Our new shiny "Sam Brown Belts" were likewise properly adorned with holster, handgun, handcuff case, spare ammunition pouches and the like. We would soon learn that these shiny new belts, holsters, and such would quickly identify each of us to the seasoned Officers with whom we were to begin work the next day. For weeks until we had earned the respect and trust of those seasoned Officers, they would refer to us, among themselves, simply as "New Leather"…

The Director of the Academy, Major Sidney Terrebonne called the event to order and graduation was under way. After an invocation by the Catholic Chaplain, Peter V. Rogers, the Superintendent of Police, Clarence B. Giarrusso welcomed those present. Opening remarks were made by the Mayor of New Orleans, the Honorable Moon Landrieu. A musical selection was performed by the Police Orchestra followed by the guest speaker "Special Agent in Charge" of the FBI New Orleans Division Mr. Rowland C. Halstead. Mr. Halstead gave the key note presentation for the graduation ceremony.

The presentation of awards followed, they were presented by Deputy Chief Sidney Cates III. Frank Weicks received the academic award for the highest scholastic average throughout the seventeen week academy. For his consistently high scores on all exams administered during the academy, the rest of us had respectfully given him the nickname "*Mr. Wizard*". Then it was time for the other two awards which were both for firearms proficiency. One was the Fraternal Order of Police Precision shooting Trophy and the other was the Major Jim Roos Quick Draw Trophy. Throughout the Firearms training portion of the academy, several of us were in stiff competition for the "shooting" trophies. In the end it came down to a

Fred receiving award from Alex Vega, Fraternal Order of Police, "Precision Shooting Award"

contest between Rudy Melancon and me. In the last few scored events, I edged Rudy out by only a few points and won both categories and trophies.

After the ceremony, the Chiefs and other participants in the ceremony shook our hands and wished us all safety and long careers with the NOPD and in Law Enforcement. We were honored to have so many wishing us all well. Both my parents had come to the graduation ceremony and it was indeed an honor to have them there with me. One very special guest had made the trip to my graduation and I cherish his presence at that ceremony still today. My Papa Weston, retired Chief of Police from Picayune, Mississippi was there to watch me receive my diploma and my awards. He was also allowed to be on the stage with me after the ceremony for us to have a highly valued photograph made of the two of us shaking hands as he congratulated me.

Throughout the seventeen week academy, we forged deep friendships, many of which exist still today. Although I have lost contact with many of these men throughout the years, each of them still holds a special place of respect in my memory and in my heart. One of these men was Kenny Solis who was seriously wounded by Mark Essex, the sniper at the Howard Johnson event in early January 1973, just over a year after we graduated from the academy.

Top Row: Patrolmen W. Schultz, K. Solis, C. Southern, W Tamborella, J. Vaccaro, R. Vicknair, O. Walters, Jr., F. Weicks, Jr. C. Williams, Jr., F. Yorsch, R. Zeller, Sr., Criminalist J. Palm, Jr., Sergeant T. Sessum, Harbor Police Department.

Middle Row: Patrolmen B. Grimsley, G. Hellmers, K. James, R. Jennewine, H. Johnson, W. Keller, Sr., J. Long, Jr., F. Macdonald, III D. Mc Cann, R. Melancon, M. Mones, Sr., L. Murillo, D. Piazza, M. Rogers, Jr.

Bottom Row: Patrolmen R. Artigue, A. Asucsion, Y. Benoit, C. Bland, Sr., L. Bourgeois, A. Bowie, W. Brown, Jr., L. Cole, J. Couvillon L. Dixon, J. Dupuis, Jr., H. Fagot, T. Fambro.

Class Photo for Class #55, taken in front of NOPD Headquarters

Kenny and his partner David McCann, another fellow academy student, were responding to the calls for assistance at the Howard Johnson when upon arrival and exiting his vehicle, Kenny was shot in the shoulder by Essex with his .44 magnum carbine. Kenny sat next to me in the academy for those seventeen weeks. Neither he, David, nor I could have imagined the horrors that Kenny would endure just a year later. Kenny was given immediate lifesaving assistance by David, who had been a combat medic in Viet Nam, and survived his serious wounds. He returned to work after more than a year of rehab, and later became a deputy US Marshall. What Heroes!

New Leather in #6

As the academy was coming to an end, we were all made aware of where we would be assigned upon our graduation. Most of us were assigned to various "Districts" in the uniformed patrol division. I was assigned to the "Sixth District". The "#6" as it was lovingly referred to, was one of the highest crime rate areas of the entire city, with high numbers of felony crimes committed against persons and property on a daily basis. It was known for being an area in which Officers were regularly assaulted by suspects and there was never a shortage of "activity" perpetrated by armed and dangerous felons! Sounded like "exactly what I signed up for". Well, it certainly didn't "let me down".

What I experienced over the next nine months while assigned to the #6, was "some of what I expected" and "much more than I could ever have hoped for". There definitely were plenty of those "bad guys" described earlier, but more importantly, there were some of the finest street cops that this ole country boy could ever have hoped to have been placed among. Cops like Harold Richard, Steve Marshall, Lt. Gene Fields, Sgt. Archie Keyser, patrolmen Louie Trudeau, Danny Chunn, Ricky Hart, and many others who

Fred "new leather" Macdonald in uniform and ready for the #6

daily walked and rode the streets of the highest crime rate "car sectors" in the city and "Protected and Served" the civilians in those sectors as though they were family. I learned from seasoned experienced veteran street cops that a real cop must be able to leave the adrenaline saturated scene of an exhausting physical apprehension involving one or more dangerous violent felons, and minutes later arrive at your next "call" and assist a young mother and her small

child who have been involved in a minor car accident and need transportation to their home across town. I learned that an Officer had to be completely capable of going from one extreme to the other and respond as professionally in the physically threatening situation as he did in the peaceful safe environment of a totally non-threatening "call".

These professionals taught me the true meaning of "Objective Investigation". It was no longer just a classroom term. It was a way of life "on the street" with these Heroes. They showed me the importance of having no "pre-conceived" outcome or results in responding to ANY incident. A truly good Cop collects information as objectively as humanly possible and assembles FACTS to work toward a conclusion in any investigation. Anything less yields a potentially false conclusion and a flawed investigation. This ultimately leads to the possibility of apprehending the WRONG person for any given crime. These professionals followed facts and were ONLY interested in arresting the person or persons who *actually committed the crime!* These were among the most professional, honest, brave and dedicated Officers with whom I ever worked.

Shortly after beginning my assignment in the #6, I was placed with my permanent partner Patrolman Harold Richard. Harold was a native of the "Irish Channel" in uptown New Orleans. He grew up living on Annunciation Street just a few blocks from the Mississippi River. I found very quickly that I could not have been assigned to a better Partner! He remains one of my all-time most treasured friends and partners. Harold is the "Real Deal"! I also learned that Harold and I had been assigned to car #602 which was responsible at that time for a section of the #6 that straddled what was then Melpomene Street and included the Calliope Housing Project. This also, as statistics would bear out, was the highest crime rate car sector in the entire City. Did I say that this was "what I signed up for"?

Over the next nine months or so, Harold and I rode car 602 daily and in the process of handling some of the most dangerous calls that I ever responded to, forged a lifelong friendship that we still deeply appreciate and enjoy today. Also working our car sector was Officer Steve Marshall. Steve was assigned to the "one man car" 603, and "shadowed" Harold and me on all of our calls acting as our primary Back-Up. Like Harold, Steve became a highly trusted friend and partner! He too was a dedicated, honest, and courageous Officer who taught me many lessons about being a Cop that I relied upon for the rest of my career. Steve also is the "Real Deal"!

Little Red

Together Harold and I handled calls that included responding to fleeing armed robbers like "Little Red" who, at the ripe old age of fourteen, was responsible for more than twenty armed robberies and multiple aggravated assaults with a gun. Little Red was well known for robbing pedestrians and small businesses near the "Project" and subsequently fleeing into the maze of apartments in one of these housing sections. Then by hopscotching through a number of separate dwellings he would confuse and elude the Officers who pursued him.

The residents of the apartments were petrified of Little Red. They feared him almost as much as, if not more than, his victims did. As Little Red would run into the apartments, he would enter one stairwell, ascend to an upper floor, threaten the first resident with whom he made contact and force them to allow him access to their apartment. Upon entering, he would either hide until the pursuing officers gave up and stopped looking for him, or would exit another area of the apartment, descend using another separate stairwell and repeat the same process until he alluded the Officers chasing him. As a result of Little Red having repeated this escape system successfully for months and injuring numerous residents who would not comply with his demands to allow him access to their apartments, he was feared by almost all who lived in the apartment buildings. He was a dangerous outlaw.

After having been quite successful for some time, his luck finally ran out at the hands of Mr. Richard. Once again we had chased Little Red into the "Calliope" after the latest of his "hold-ups", or as they were referred to on the Police radio a "64-G" or Armed Robbery with a Gun. After we had chased Little Red through several apartments, Harold was smart enough to gain a strategic advantage of "time and space" over Little Red that the young marauder just never saw coming. Harold nabbed him on an upper level of a stairwell where Little Red had nowhere else to go. While enjoying the look of amazement on Little Red's face, Harold took control of the young outlaw, the loot from his last "transaction", as well as the weapon that many had been the victim of. Little Red went to jail at the hands of a Hero, Mr. Harold.

Are you sure you're not dead?

A short time later, Harold and I responded to another call at a bar on the edge of the "Calliope". The street upon which the bar was situated was itself a legend. It was "CLIO" Street. It was the only barrier to separate the bar from the Calliope project. Therefore, it was constantly referred to by victims, witnesses, and even perpetrators as they provided details regarding what they had witnessed pertaining to the most recent felony about which that individual could provide information. The information would invariably start out something like… "Well, Officer… the dude came runnin' cross *CL-10* street and went up in the Calliope, and then…. Well… then he was gone…" So from the local interpretation of and the pronunciation of "CLIO" Street, most of us always referred to the famous street as "CL-10" street. We all knew it well!

The call that we had just received was one that was not uncommon in our sector. Dispatch assigned us to respond to a homicide at the bar. Reportedly a male customer in the bar had been shot in the head by another patron in the bar. The injured man, the *deceased*, had been shot in the head during an argument, had collapsed, and was presumed dead. The shooter had fled the bar but had been identified. Other Officers were in the process of searching for the suspect. Harold and I had been assigned to go to the bar and control and secure the scene until the "Homicide Detectives" arrived and took control of the crime scene.

We drove to the bar and upon arriving near the front door, observed a very large male sitting on the edge of the sidewalk facing the street with his feet and legs in the edge of the street. Now this was not at all unusual… finding a subject sitting on the curb. Also not unusual was the man watching us arrive, get out of 602 and walk over to him while stating "everything here is OK Officers"… What WAS unusual was that the man was offering this assessment of the situation while looking at Harold and me through eyes that had a bullet hole between them. It was even more odd that from that bullet hole was emanating a fair amount of blood that was constantly dripping off the end of his nose.

Well, we continued to be amazed as upon further investigation… objective investigation, we found what appeared to be an "exit wound" of the same approximate caliber as the hole between his eyes. The exit wound was smack in the middle of the back of his head… exactly where Harold and I thought it should be by our estimations of bullet trajectory and all that stuff. It appeared, and we were pretty sure, that the man had been shot between the eyes and the bullet had travelled straight through his head and had exited the back of his head. We saw nothing to conflict with that theory, and if that was accurate, there was absolutely no reason for this man to be sitting on the curb having a conversation with me, Harold, or the man's friend who was also sitting on the curb consoling the "Shot" man.

Harold and I shifted immediately into a familiar "mode" and I got on the radio and explained that the man did not seem to be deceased and that we needed an ambulance at our location immediately. Remember that this is 1972 and medical services were not exactly what they are today. The ambulance that was to be "dispatched" was... let's say, a modified station wagon with a blue light and siren. Oh, and most often they had a stretcher in the rear. A testament to their level of successfully retrieving and transporting the "wounded" was that they were most commonly referred to as the "Meat Wagon". As we waited for the ambulance, we continued to talk to the man and tried to stop his bleeding with a makeshift bandage. Every few minutes during the wait, the man's friend would ask, "Bubba, are you sho you ain't dead?" Each time Bubba would confirm to his friend, "Tony, I told you, I ain't dead!" This went on until the ambulance arrived, and Bubba was placed on the stretcher and hauled away to Charity Hospital.

As was most often the case, Harold and I followed the ambulance to Charity and watched as they rolled Bubba into the Emergency Room. He was immediately placed in an examination room and Harold and I followed. By this time two Detectives from Homicide that we worked with frequently, arrived at Charity and met us in the examination room. After a few X-rays, and a thorough exam, the attending physician told Bubba to sit up on the edge of the examination table. As Bubba sat up, the Doctor was handed a package by a nurse. He pulled out two Band-Aids and with a smile placed one on the hole between Bubba's eyes and one on the hole on the back of his head that by now had been cleanly shaved. Upon adhering the second Band-Aid, The Doctor told Bubba, "OK you are good to go". With a look similar to those that Harold and I must have had when we first met Bubba an hour or so earlier, Bubba looked at the Doctor and said, "You sure I ain't dead?" The Doctor assured Bubba that he would be fine and should be able to go back to the bar by the next day.

The Doctor went on to explain that some unidentified previous injury had left a very large calcium and bone build up in the area of Bubba's forehead. Star Trek being a popular program at the time on TV, the Doctor explained to Bubba that he had a forehead that was a lot like a "Klingon". He said that the bullet had entered Bubba's forehead, struck the lower portion of the "mass" at exactly the right angle, had been diverted, and had skimmed around the inside of the skin on Bubba's head and struck a similar but smaller mass on the rear of his head. The second mass had very effectively caused the bullet to simply exit the back of Bubba's head and continue on safely to some other part of the bar. He told Bubba, "You'll be pretty sore for a few days, but you ain't dead!" Bubba was released to the Homicide Detectives to be taken to Headquarters to make a statement, and Harold and I went back to work. We saw Bubba many times after that night, and each time we saw him on the street or in a bar, he would raise his hand and with a smile say, "Hey guys, I still ain't dead!"

The Broke Gun

In another incident, Harold and I were transporting a "witness" home from an investigative interview, when we were flagged down by an elderly man who resided in the southern edge of our car sector. The gentleman was very emotional and extremely frightened. As I stopped our vehicle in the middle of the street to see what the man wanted, he began to describe the horrific event going on inside his home. This was the "home" that was immediately to the left of where I had stopped our vehicle, 602.

The man was trembling and telling me that his sixteen year old grandson was in his house shooting through the walls with a handgun. He went on to explain that the grandson was shooting at the gentleman's other three grandchildren all of whom were under six years of age. These other grandchildren were in an adjacent room and were screaming and crying for help. The old gentlemen explained that he could not go in and get the small children because the older grandson, the shooter, would see him enter and he had already told the old man that he would kill him if he tried to evacuate the small children. As the old man was telling Harold and me the details, we were exiting 602 and assessing the situation.

Just as I exited the car on the driver's side, several shots rang out and glass from the front windows of the man's house splattered all across the front of 602. From a purely objective point of view, Harold and I both felt that at least most of the old man's story was probably accurate at this point. As the window fragments hit and bounced off 602, I remembered the "witness" in the back seat of 602. I popped the external latch on his door that allowed him to exit, and as he slithered out of 602 and crawled onto the sidewalk, he informed me that he would be more than happy to just walk the rest of the way home.

As the witness gained momentum down the street toward his home, and I realized that he was out of harm's way, Harold and I focused entirely on the old man and his situation. I assessed the outside of the house and asked the man where the young children were. He explained that they were in a bedroom on the "left" side of the house. He further explained the floorplan of the "duplex" style home and stated that the shooter was in his bedroom on the opposite "right" side of the house. He further explained that to reach the shooter, we would have to enter the front left door and move into the right side, where the shooter was, through an interior door.

As Harold covered the front of the house, I made my way around to the left side of the house and was able to quickly and quietly extract the small children through a window in their bedroom. As I was helping the children out of the window, several shots rang out from the shooter's room, and struck the wall by the window. The bullets struck no one, but now I at least knew exactly where the shooter was. After getting the children to a covered position and safely in the arms of their grandfather, I rejoined Harold at the front of the house. Shots were still ringing out from inside the house. Although Harold had informed dispatch as to the circumstances of our situation, we still didn't hear any sirens coming in response to our request for assistance.

Harold and I decided that the shooter had to be apprehended before he injured one of the fifty or so bystanders who had gathered along the street, or fled out the back of the house and became an even bigger threat to the community. Without hesitation, Harold entered the front door of the house, immediately turned right and went through an interior door, crossed what looked like a "living room" and took up cover at the end of a large couch on the opposite wall of the front room. I followed closely behind Harold and as he crossed the room, I took up a position in the area of the interior door, using the door trim as cover from the shooter's gunfire. Immediately on entering and reaching the doorway, several more shots rang out from the room directly behind the room in which Harold and I had stopped. I could tell the exact location from which the shots were emanating by the holes and splinters which were developing in the wall that separated the two rooms each time the shooter fired a shot.

This was the first time that I experienced the "Slow-Motion" phenomenon that occurs with some individuals during extremely high stress situations. It was profound for me in this instance. I could see the holes developing in the wall and could actually see the splinters leaving the wall and flying through the air. I could count the holes as they seemed to slowly appear, and could follow the splinters to where they landed. As I pressed my left shoulder against the *door facing* that I was trying to use as cover, I depressed a "curtain" that was hung in the doorway for privacy. As I watched the splinters flying through the air toward Harold and me, I saw from the corner of my eye, cloth debris flying from the curtain that was compressed by my left shoulder. I later inspected the curtain and found that one of the shooter's bullets had passed just above my shoulder and between my head and the door facing. This was an area approximately three inches by four inches in size.

As the shooter was firing at us through the wall, Harold fired several rounds back at the suspect also through the wall with his shotgun. I also was able to fire my service revolver six times through the wall. After the exchange, the shooter yelled "I'm hit". I told Harold to cover the area of the shooter while I reloaded my revolver. He was already watching the doorway between the rooms and had his shotgun trained on the door. As I started trying to open the cylinder on my revolver, I realized that something was seriously wrong. The cylinder would not open. One of the chambers in the cylinder was expanded and had burst from the rounds that I had fired and had "jammed" my revolver in the closed position. I could not reload my revolver. By now Harold had realized that he had fired all the rounds that were in his shotgun, he had no extras, and had drawn his revolver to cover the doorway. So… there we were. Two cops with one operational weapon between us and an armed active shooter in an adjacent room still out of our sight. So, what do we do?

Well… Standing there with Harold, with one broke gun, and one empty shotgun, I ordered the shooter to come out where we could see him. After just a moment, he appeared in the doorway holding a sheet up in front of his body covering all but his face and head. I ordered him to drop the sheet so we could see him and his hands. I was still covering him with my "broke gun", but with all the confidence in the world that Harold "had him covered" with a real operational gun with real live bullets. After a brief pause and several determined and strong suggestions of compliance from Harold and me, the young man dropped the sheet.

Just as the sheet began to fall, we both saw that he was holding a revolver in his right hand. As he tried to drop the sheet, and employ the gun, he somewhat fumbled the gun and in the brief moment that he lost control of his weapon, I was able to cover the short distance between us and physically engage him. During the struggle that ensued, I was able to remove the weapon from his hand and subdue and restrain him. All the time knowing without a doubt that Harold was only a step or two away and could and would, if necessary, have protected me with whatever level of force had been necessary. What an incredible feeling of confidence in one of my greatest Heroes.

As we exited the house with the suspect handcuffed between us, our "back-up" arrived on the scene. We learned that because the event had occurred exactly at "shift change", there had been no other Officers in the #6 still "on the street". The Officers from our shift had gotten off duty and gone home and the next shift was still in "Roll Call" at the time that we had requested "back-up". Harold and I looked at each other with that "Go figure" look and placed the suspect in the back seat of 602. We transported the suspect to Charity Hospital where he was treated for lacerations and a few contusions about the head which occurred during the scuffle that transpired during the process of subduing him and assisting him in his decision to forfeit his handgun. After being treated, we transported him to Central Lock-Up where he was booked on several felony charges including aggravated assault on Police Officers, and attempted murder on his siblings.

After the incident, we conducted a thorough inspection of my revolver and ammunition. The department issued all of our service ammunition. We were issued *eighteen* rounds (bullets) per year. Up until a couple of months earlier, the department required that we carry a .38 caliber revolver, and for that revolver furnished by the individual Officer, the Department had issued a 158 grain, round nose, solid lead, "Lubaloy" bullet for service. We had just been issued the "New" .38 caliber rounds for our revolvers after much research by the department. The new round was a more efficient soft nose, jacketed, 160 grain .38 caliber round. These rounds were manufactured specifically for the NOPD and were sold only to NOPD. The fact that they were "specialty" rounds manufactured in 1971 for a single group or customer yielded what could be considered now as somewhat poorly managed quality control. The rounds that I fired in my revolver were simply "over-loaded". The excessive powder charge caused the round (bullet) to expand/explode inside my chamber, and "jammed" my revolver in the closed position. This was the first gun fight in the department in which the "new ammo" was utilized. It didn't get my vote!

I still carry several lessons from this incident with me. They have served me very well in many instances since the one described above. One lesson is, always carry plenty of extra ammo that is readily available! Running out of bullets in a gun fight is not acceptable! Another lesson is, always have a backup for everything! This includes your weapon. A "broke gun" or disabled one, is a *club*. Never bring a club to a gun fight! And finally, always... always... always practice with the ammunition that you plan to carry. If you believe that you may find yourself in harm's way and your life will likely depend on a particular weapon and its ammunition... know that when your life does depend upon it, your weapon will function, the ammo will "go bang", and you know without a doubt, from ample experience and training, how to make that occur!

Mardi Gras in #6

While working in #6, I had the opportunity to work the street in uniform during the world famous Mardi Gras. Because of where the #6 is located geographically, with St. Charles Avenue running virtually right through the middle of the District, I quickly learned that many of the biggest Parades that occurred during this season also ran right through the middle of the District. St. Charles was one of the main "Parade Routes" in the City. Having grown up in Picayune which was only an hour or so away now that the Interstate Highway systems were mostly complete, I had been aware of the Mardi Gras events in New Orleans for most of my life. I had, however, no possible way of knowing the true nature of the circumstances that surrounded this "ten day drunken party"! From the "side of the fence" that I now occupied as a Police Officer in the middle of "the party", it took on a whole new significance. What had looked like a lot of fun in younger days, now became a daunting challenge.

The normal population of the City was more than tripled during the Mardi Gras. The number of Police was NOT tripled. The approximate eight hundred sworn Officers of the NOPD at that time, seemed to "shrink" when compared to the temporary population of "party animals" that walked the city streets for about twenty three-of the twenty-four hours of each of the ten days of the "season". The Department's answer to the swell in population and the accompanying swell in numbers of crimes, was to require that all Officers with few exceptions, work in uniform and work extended shifts. These extended shifts resulted in many, many hours of overtime for every Officer throughout the Department. For the ten days of Mardi Gras, it was not uncommon for Officers to consistently work eighteen or more hours per day, with no days off. For many of the Officers, this was the only time of the year that they could expect to work any *paid* overtime. While the extra pay was very pleasing and highly anticipated throughout the rest of the year, it was a tough way to earn it… all in a single two week period.

For many decades, the NOPD had earned and maintained a reputation for its competence in the area of "Crowd Control"! There was no agency in the Nation that was more competent in the skills associated with this task. From the uniformed Officers on the front lines managing crowds during the parades, to the Uniformed Officers who worked along Bourbon Street and physically managed the army of drunks that occupied the streets of the French Quarter throughout the Mardi Gras season, to the Mounted Patrol Officers who were called upon to disperse the worst of angry drunken mobs, the NOPD could control any crowd!

Car "603" after being "broadsided" as Fred was transporting an injured "resistor of arrest" to Charity Hospital on Mardi Gras day 1972

Most of the hours for officers working in #6 were spent first working a regular shift in your normal car sector, and then working the remainder of the "overtime hours" either standing a position along the parade routes, or riding in one man cars to provide extra manpower for the District during and after the parades. It was quite an event to say the least. In addition to the scheduled parades conducted by the various "Krewes" who owned the parades, there were also numerous spontaneous and many planned "parties" that broke out in all corners of the District and the city.

These "parties" may occur as a group of people in a neighborhood who all knew each other, would go into the streets and start a "Throw-Down" with live or recorded music from a forty pound "Boom-Box". Or… they may be a purely unplanned happenstance of a hundred or so likeminded people who had never seen each other before, gathering on a sidewalk, in a street, or in an un-approving local resident's front yard to likewise "Throw-Down". In either case, the propensity for several of the "party animals" to become engaged in one version or another of a "physical altercation" was extremely high.

With large quantities of alcohol and other substances of abuse being plentiful and very accessible, the likelihood that the altercation would require some type of "Official Intervention" was also VERY high. I learned very quickly that I needed to bring several extra uniform shirts and trousers to work each day and have them available in the event the uniform that I wore to work that day got *ripped off* while I worked Mardi Gras in the #6. It was quite a learning experience with a very steep learning curve! One way or another, experience was gained at a very rapid pace! The presence of highly experienced and trustworthy Officers and supervisors insured that the young guys, including me, survived the learning curve of #6.

Some years ago now, the old #6 station house that we all worked in and out of during those days, was torn down so that a new station could be built. A very dear friend, fellow NOPD Officer, and highly regarded NOPD Hero rescued a souvenir from the old station debris. Captain Jeff Winn personally delivered to me a "Brick" from the old station house in honor of my having worked there some forty years earlier. That "Brick" holds a place of honor among other tokens of my history in Law Enforcement that create a tangible link to the hundreds of Heroes that I have met and worked with for many years.

What an experience was the Sixth District! Whether it was riding daily with Harold in 602, responding to violent crimes throughout the district with any of the other Officers that patrolled those streets, or working Mardi Gras as a one man car, it was an honor to have been there and worked with each of the Heroes of #6. They impacted my life and my entire career with priceless experiences and true lasting friendship.

Back to Vice

After about nine months in #6, I was contacted by Paul Melancon from the Vice Squad. Paul asked if I would be interested in returning to work within the Vice Squad. After some consideration, I said yes and within a few days, I was back with the Team with which I had first started my time within the NOPD. While I missed my team in the #6, it was truly good to be back working in plain clothes and working "City wide" again. It didn't take long to be back in full swing with the Vice Squad crew. We worked hundreds of misdemeanor and felony cases involving gamblers, prostitutes, biker gangs, and con men. It was exciting and there was never a dull moment. Most of the suspects that we encountered were relatively docile, however there were many who were just determined to commit crimes and were also determined to use whatever means necessary to avoid going to jail. They would fight, physically resist arrest and often assaulted the Officers trying to arrest them.

It was during this second assignment to the Vice Squad that we all experienced an event that was un-paralleled in the history of NOPD. That event was the "Howard Johnson Sniper Incident". At that point in history, the NOPD had no SWAT unit. That concept was still in its infancy and most of the departments that had these units were on the west coast, Los Angeles in particular. While other larger cities were developing these units, NOPD still had what was called its

"Riot Squad". Most incidents in those times which required a large scale or specialty response were classified as "Civil Disturbances" and demanded a responding group capable of crowd control. But times and incidents were changing. What was being experienced around this time period was more likely to be perpetrated by an individual or by a small group of likeminded criminals. They attacked without warning and targeted innocent civilians, former co-workers, and often Law Enforcement Officers and first responders.

The attacks often came in the form of bombings or sniper attacks. Their most common products were mass casualties, heavy property damage, chaos, and fear. As a result of these attacks and their aftermath, the need for a better method of responding to these situations was recognized. The SWAT concept was born.

The Howard Johnson incident was such an attack. A lone gunman named Mark Essex had begun an assault on Law Enforcement Officers some weeks earlier with the shooting of a young officer at Central Lock-Up and another K-9 Officer who was in the process of searching for Essex after that first shooting. Essex lay low for several days after the second shooting and on Sunday Morning January 7, 1973, Essex entered the downtown Howard Johnson Hotel, set several fires, shot several civilian guests and employees, and upon the Fire department and Police responding to the incident, Essex wounded and killed several Officers, Firemen, and civilians. Obviously there were no cell phones, internet or anything of the kind, so notifications were much slower than if this occurred today. But Officers and civilians began to respond as news media began to transmit images and video from the scene. Almost immediately every radio and TV station for miles around started live coverage of the incident and as more and more Officers and civilians continued to respond to the scene, more of the responders were wounded and killed.

One Officer who was killed early in the attack was Deputy Chief Louis Sirgo. The Chief had been at home when the attack began and responded to the Hotel when he learned of the event. Upon arriving at the scene, The Chief met several other Officers who were already there. They discussed the situation and after gathering what information was available, decided to go into the hotel after Essex. They entered a stairwell that gave access to each floor of the hotel and started ascending through each level or floor of the building. As they reached each floor, they would enter that level and travel down the corridor searching for Essex as they made their way through the building.

After repeating this process on several floors, the group was ascending a flight of stairs to search the hallway at the next level. As the men began making their way up the flight of stairs, Essex stepped out onto the stairwell above the group. Essex fired one shot striking Chief Sirgo in the middle of the back. The .44 magnum round traveled through the Chief's body inflicting a catastrophic injury. The wound was not survivable and a short time later the Chief was dead.

Essex simply stepped back into a hallway, the door closed behind him and he vanished from the group's view. By this time there were numerous casualties in and around the hotel from Essex's gunfire. Other Officers and Firemen as well as civilians had been wounded or killed. It was during this initial portion of the attack that Kenny Solis, by whom I had sat throughout our academy, had been seriously wounded. As reports of the wounded and dead victims spread, the scene digressed to one of total chaos.

I was off-duty and in my hometown with one of my partners from the Vice Squad, Tommy Casey. We were at my dad's store installing carpet in Tommy's van and had our favorite radio station blaring out our favorite current hit songs that now are referred to as "Golden Oldies". Suddenly, we realized… the music had stopped and the oldies had been replaced with what sounded like a script from one of our favorite "Cop Movies". We immediately realized, however, that this was not make believe… it was a real deal, and it didn't sound good at all. From what we were hearing, the "Good Guys", OUR good guys were taking a serious licking on the "Home Turf"! We immediately stored our tools and materials that we were using on the "van job", and after a quick trip to my Dad's house to inform everyone there of our intentions, we made a high speed return trip back to New Orleans. This was normally about an hour trip. It was shorter this time!

As we arrived back in New Orleans East, we stopped at my apartment for me to pick up my vehicle and all my "gear". We had heard on the van radio that a Marine Helicopter was flying recon over the Hotel and was staging in an area of the city with which we were familiar. Our plan was to get my vehicle and gear and go to the Helo staging area and get on the chopper and see if we could "intervene" in the situation that by now we knew had cost several of our fellow Officers' lives. As I entered my apartment with Tommy on my heels, I heard my phone ringing.

That was the phone in my apartment with a wire that connected it to the wall… my only phone. I reluctantly walked over and answered the phone. It was Jay Moore, who was also assigned to and standing in the Vice Squad. I said, Jay I can't talk, I'm heading to try to get on the helicopter. I heard a fumbling of the phone and then heard the voice of our unit commander, Dave Kent. The Boss! The Boss said very calmly, "Fred, come straight to the office and I'll inform everyone where to go and what we are going to do to respond to this situation." My heart sank… in my mind, I was minutes away from getting in the air and "doing something" to end the attack. I said "Yes Sir" and hung up the phone. I turned to see Tommy looking at me with the "Tommy Look" and simply asked… "Did you tell him I was here?"... As I told him "No"... he was pulling out of my driveway... I didn't see Tommy again until several days later after the incident was over.

I grabbed my gear and drove to the Vice Squad Office. I was met by almost all of the members of the unit except Tommy. By now, Sgt. Kent had been in communication with the Narcotics Division and the Tactical Patrol Division. These units along with the Vice Squad were the three elements of the "NOPD Riot Squad" as mentioned earlier. In these discussions, Kent had arranged for the members of the Vice Squad to travel to and occupy positions within and around Charity Hospital. The Emergency Room at Charity was where the injured Officers and civilians were being transported to for treatment.

The problem, or one of the problems, was that the sniper had a clear line of sight from the hotel straight to the "Emergency Entrance" at the back of Charity. While the distance was some several hundred yards, this had not prevented Essex from "Lobbing" .44 Magnum rounds into the walls and parked vehicles in the area of the entrance. Some of these rounds barely missed Officers and civilians in and around this entrance. Our mission at Charity was to prevent any intrusion or assaults into or around Charity by Essex or anyone else who might have similar intent.

We positioned ourselves throughout the ground level of the hospital to insure that we could accomplish this assignment. Some of our members, including me, were armed with rifles, and while positioned near the emergency entrance received fire from Essex's .44 magnum carbine. Some of our members were actually successful in returning fire into the area of the hotel from which the incoming .44 magnum rounds had originated. The problem was that after Essex would fire a round or volley of rounds from one position, he would quickly move to another vantage point. From his new position, he could determine locations from which Officers' return fire was originating.

He was lighting fires, and creating other diversions by which he generated great confusion that lasted many hours. He would place a string of "firecrackers" at one edge of a curtain on the sliding glass doors that led to the small balcony outside each room. He would then set fire to the other corner of the curtain using phone books. Once the curtain was burning, he would exit that room and go to another room some distance from

Burned Phone Book at base of curtain on upper floor of the Howard Johnson (Photo Provided by Charlie Faught)

the original room with the "Fireworks". As the curtain eventually burned to the area of the "fireworks" they would become ignited, explode, and blow ashes and soot out of the sliding glass door onto the balcony. As this occurred, the Officers on the ground would fire at the open door and what appeared to be and sounded like gunfire from Essex. As they fired, Essex would determine the Officers' positions and fire on these Officers from his remote and new location that gave Essex the advantage. Essex would then repeat the process. Essex's position in the hotel constantly changed until much later when he made his way onto the roof and into a cubicle there.

Over the next thirty plus hours, there was the constant sound of gunfire from all areas around and from within the hotel. Individuals including Officers from distant jurisdictions had responded to the scene to offer "assistance". In a totally

Fires bellowing from open balcony doors on upper floor of Howard Johnson Hotel as result of burning phone book

uncoordinated effort they had taken up positions in and on top of various buildings around the hotel. From these positions they had fired hundreds if not thousands of rounds of ammunition into the building and into the cubicle on the roof in which Essex was believed to be hiding. The gunfire never seemed to cease. The Marine helicopter would periodically make passes over the roof of the hotel and shots could be heard and seen coming from the chopper in response to what seemed to be shots emanating from the area of the hotel roof.

Then after more than thirty-six hours of chaos, the Marine helicopter made what would be a critical "pass" over the roof of the hotel. As the helo approached the area over the roof of the hotel,

Essex ran out of his hiding spot in the cubicle on the roof. As he ran out onto the roof, he again fired several shots at the Marine helicopter from his .44 magnum, with what was later learned to be the last of his ammunition. He struck the helicopter several times with his well-aimed shots. Ignoring the rounds penetrating the helicopter around him, an Officer in the helicopter fired several shots back which struck and killed Mark Essex. That Officer was none other than Tommy Casey! As Essex ran toward the helicopter on the roof of the Howard Johnson, a barrage of gunfire erupted from the weapons of Officers all around the Hotel. While many of these rounds struck the murderous assassin, and many Officers have claimed that they *eliminated the threat* posed by Essex...

Firemen and Officers crouch behind vehicle to avoid gunfire from Mark Essex

My money was and still is on Casey!!!

Upon learning of Tommy's Heroic actions in and from the

Marine Helicopter makes a pass over the roof while passengers Detective Tommy Casey, and other Officers, attempt to locate Essex

helicopter, I was extremely proud of him and for him. I was also struck with the thought that but for one phone call answered at my apartment, I too might have had a hand in ending the attack, just as Tommy and I had discussed and hoped for on our ride back from Picayune. Then and for many years since, I have also thought that but for one phone call, I may have actually been in that helicopter and might just have been sitting where one of those .44 Magnum rounds, in my absence, had harmlessly passed through the *body of only the aircraft*. I have thanked Heaven many times for the courage and brilliant leadership of Dave Kent who was experienced enough and mature enough to take control of an eager, testosterone and adrenaline charged group of young men and protect us from ourselves on so many occasions while we all learned to be the "Real Police".

What Heroes I rode with!!!

Those NOPD Officers wounded or killed by Essex included

David McCann renders first aid to partner Kenny Solis after Kenny was wounded by gunfire from Mark Essex

Police Cadet *Alfred Harrell*, shot at Central Lock-Up or CLU, on New Years' Eve 1972. Harrell died at the scene. *Eddie Hosli Sr.*, was the K-9 Officer, who was shot shortly after Cadet Harrell. Hosli died on March 3, 1973 as a result of his wounds inflicted by

Essex. A third Officer *Lt. Horace Perez* was also wounded at CLU by Essex on New Years' Eve. At the Howard Johnson, Officers *Philip Coleman, Paul Persigo,* and *Deputy Chief Louis Sirgo* were killed by Essex. Officers *Charles Arnold, Kenny Solis, Lawrence Arthur,* and *Sgt. Emanuel Palmisano* were all seriously wounded by Essex at the Howard Johnson. Also at the Howard Johnson and at the hands of Mark Essex, *three civilians were killed* and *four others were wounded.* Along with Officers and civilians, New Orleans Fire Department *Lt. Tim Ursin* and Fire Prevention Officer *Joe Anderson* were seriously wounded at the Howard Johnson by Mark Essex.

The NOPD *Police Memorial Monument* and the *Louis J. Sirgo Plaza* in front of the NOPD Headquarters Building on South Broad Street were both dedicated on Tuesday, March 25, 1975. The Monument and the Plaza were created as a result of the Howard Johnson tragedy. The names of all the Officers who lost their lives in the Line of Duty while working on the NOPD are inscribed upon the monument. The NOPD Heroes murdered by Essex are among the names on the Monument. A memorial service is conducted at the Monument each year on January 7, the anniversary of the deadliest day in the history of the NOPD.

During the week after the Howard Johnson Incident there were funerals which honored the Heroes who fell at the Howard Johnson. Among the sadness and anguish of that week, I was given one of the greatest honors of my young career. Along with my close friend and fellow Officer Jay Moore, I was asked to provide security for Chief Sirgo's home and family, before, during and after his funeral. I recall wishing then, as I have too many sad times since that day upon loosing other Heroes, that I could have done more…

After the Howard Johnson incident, many things changed in and for NOPD. A need for a better response mechanism was recognized by the administration. Almost immediately it was decided that the department needed a SWAT team or similar division to handle critical incidents in a more efficient manner. From this process the NOPD SWAT unit was born.

With the Mardi Gras season only a month or so away, and among fears by the Department's administration that there might be another event similar to the Howard Johnson Incident perpetrated by some like-minded individual, the race was on to speedily create a SWAT Team. This worthy task being acted upon, with an actual expectation of success, demonstrates the infancy of the SWAT concept and philosophy in our country. Building a competent, capable, properly trained and equipped SWAT unit is MUCH MORE than a few week endeavor. The desire was to establish a "Team" that would be able to "protect" the numerous parades that would be making their way through miles of tourist packed streets in the city during the ten days of Mardi Gras. The task was assigned to members of the Tactical Patrol Division. The body of the "Team" would still be comprised of members of the "Tac" unit as it was known, along with the Officers from the Narcotics and Vice units. This provided ample manpower to establish a "Team", and we immediately began training.

Remember that this is 1973, and, as stated, the SWAT concept is to say the least, still a "new-born". The Supervisors overseeing the "training" were some of the finest field commanders that I have ever met. They were individually and collectively revered by almost every Officer in the department for their bravery, experience, and for their achievements within the department. However, they, like all of us, could only draw from the experience and training that we had had up to that point. None of us had "SWAT" experience. I learned over many years that followed that the majority of "experts" in the SWAT community at that time were "Ex-Military" and most if not all of the tactics, the training, and mindset that created the SWAT philosophy at that time, WERE from the military. There simply was nowhere else from which to acquire these skills, other than the experiences of seasoned Officers who had previously been in deadly situations in Law Enforcement. We had plenty of those who had that type of experience. By that time, almost all of us had. The result was that those with the most Military experience set the training agenda, managed the "preparations" for our Mardi Gras assignments, and were "in charge".

Our training over the next few weeks was much different than SWAT training is today, but in fairness to the "bosses", they were doing what they knew to do in 1973. We ran through abandoned buildings at an abandoned amusement park on the beaches of Lake Pontchartrain, did calisthenics, ran through sand on the same beaches, did more exercises… until it was time for Mardi Gras to start. After what must have been much discussion and deliberation by the bosses, it was decided that our "Team" would be divided into several groups. These groups would be assigned to protect each Parade during Mardi Gras by riding on parallel streets along the parade route while each parade made its way through thousands of tourists and spectators on the streets of the city. If there were to be an "Incident", the closest Team would respond and "handle" the situation with our newest "SWAT skills".

Many of us on the "Team", had also taken it upon ourselves to "prepare" for what we considered to be our potential "requirements" during what was to be our Mardi Gras assignments. Most of us had more than a little street experience by now and had been in serious life threatening situations in which we individually had recognized

Dave Henly test-fires the S&W model 76, sub-gun prior to Mardi Gras SWAT assignments in 1973

particular "Needs" that were absent during those previous critical events. In other words, we had had our butts hanging out and didn't have the hardware we needed to get our butt home that night! After getting home from such an event, one ponders not only what has just occurred, but how it happened, why it happened, how to prevent it from happening again, and most importantly... if it DOES happen again how can I be better prepared to survive the event next time!!!

Fred test-fires and practices with a S&W model 76, 9mm sub-machine gun prior to Mardi Gras SWAT assignments in 1973 shortly after the Howard Johnson Incident

This concept became the foundation for a training point that I have shared with thousands of Officers that I have trained since that time. It goes like this..."It's Ok to make mistakes... Everyone makes mistakes... Just don't keep making the SAME mistake over and over, *knowing it's a mistake*, until someone gets hurt or killed because of the same mistake."

So, in preparation, we all made sure that all our weapons were in good condition, that we had plenty of ammo, and other "supplies" and that all of our "necessities" were in containers that could be easily transported and stored within the vehicles to which we were assigned during the parades. In short we tried to be as prepared as possible for whatever might have happened. Thank Heaven once again, no such incident occurred!

Throughout the Mardi Gras season of 1973, the members of the Vice squad also fulfilled their other responsibilities regarding our normal assignments for the season. The normal duties for Officers assigned to the Vice Squad during Mardi Gras involved donning a regulation, or near regulation uniform and patrolling the streets of the French Quarter on foot. Our primary assignment was to stand

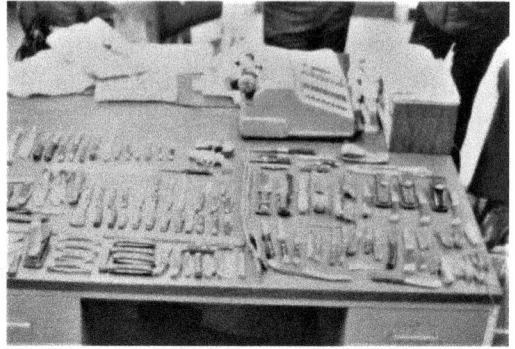

Knives and other weapons seized by members of the "Vice Squad" during Mardi Gras (1973)

positions along a several block section of Bourbon Street and "enforce the law"… or at least as many laws as possible. Most people cannot imagine the constant state of affairs created by thousands of drunken humans crowded into an area that could not normally sustain the presence of a few dozen such humans without creating serious crisis. This is at best, an understatement of the chaos experienced for at least twenty hours of each of the ten days of the Mardi Gras season along the world famous Bourbon Street of New Orleans. It is a sight to behold!

Imagine now that the reader is inserted into that environment and instructed that if anyone commits a serious crime, the reader is to stop the illegal activity, subdue the suspect if necessary, apprehend and restrain the suspect, extract the suspect from the area through the thousands of individuals present who sympathize with the suspect including some who undoubtedly are "involved" with the suspect and transport that suspect through that crowd for several blocks of sympathizers to the nearest "Paddy Wagon" for transport to Central Lock-Up. This was the continuous chain of events that describe a day on the street during Mardi Gras for the officers of the Vice Squad, as well as other plain clothes units.

We constantly broke up fights, disarmed suspects in the process of assaulting Officers and other individuals, and intervened in hundreds of assorted crimes in progress for hours on end each day of Mardi Gras. We became so proficient at identifying various weapons in the pockets of the individuals walking on Bourbon Street that we could tell with almost certainty what "brand" of knife or gun the person had in their pants pocket before we approached them. We arrested armed suspects by the dozens and seized deadly weapons by the hundreds throughout Mardi Gras. We fought and wrestled suspects who resisted arrest and made numerous trips to Charity Hospital with injured Officers and suspects who refused to comply during arrests for violent crimes witnessed by our Officers.

By the time Mardi Gras ended and we had ridden for ten days along parades for hours anticipating an attack around every corner, and worked for hours on end in uniform on Bourbon Street, we had each accumulated more than two hundred hours of "On Duty" time for the Mardi Gras season. While the overtime pay was great, we knew and felt like we had certainly earned it!

While preparing for and riding in those parade assignments, we all realized how important it was to develop a specialty unit for such assignments. However crude these beginnings of the NOPD SWAT Unit may have been, I was and am extremely proud of having been a small part of that Team's beginnings! The men with whom I rode along those parades were and are some of the bravest souls with whom I have ever had the opportunity and honor to serve.

That beginning gave birth to what is now one of the finest most capable SWAT or Tactical Units in our Nation. I have known many of the Unit's personnel and command staff since those early days and the accomplishments and traditions throughout the Team's history are unsurpassed in our Nation. Leaders like Captain Jeff Winn, highlight the Unit's proud history. Captain Winn, as Unit Commander, led the men and women of that Unit for many years. He not only trained the Unit's members, but led them through hundreds of critical and extremely dangerous incidents throughout the city. Safely and successfully concluding these operations, Jeff and his Team always got the job done.

Even through the horrors of a post Katrina New Orleans, Captain Winn led his Unit on hundreds of rescue missions throughout the city rescuing hundreds of endangered civilians from the worst imaginable situations. Through many years Captain Winn has been a close friend and highly honored Officer, SWAT operator, and Commander. Together we have travelled and trained thousands of Officers all across our Nation. Much of that training and the information that we have shared with those Officers originated from our experiences with the New Orleans SWAT Unit for over forty years. In 2007 I had the opportunity to go back to New Orleans and conduct three training programs for the NOPD SWAT Unit. The classes that my training group and I delivered to the NOPD SWAT Unit were three iterations of my High Risk Event Planning System. In this program, we teach Officers how to assess, plan for and manage High Risk Events. Many of the concepts that are taught in that program were conceived and later developed into this planning system based upon lessons that I learned while I was an Officer on the NOPD and a member of that original SWAT Team. The men and women that I served with on the NOPD stand out as some of my greatest role models and some of the greatest Heroes of my life.

It should also be noted that shortly after being reassigned to the Vice Squad in late 1972, another major event in my life occurred. On Friday November 17, 1972, while I was deer hunting and camping at a State Game Management Area near Alexandria, Louisiana, my

Papa Mac died from a massive heart attack. The local Sheriff's Office was asked by my family to locate me and my hunting group after he died, but they were unable to find our campsite in the densely wooded areas of the Louisiana countryside. Unaware of his death until I returned several days later, I missed the funeral of one of my all-time greatest and most loved Heroes. After returning to Picayune late Sunday night, I went to the cemetery and sat by his grave most of the night. My Papa Mac was gone!

The Detective Bureau

For a short time after the Mardi Gras season ended, I remained within the Vice Squad. Then one day I was contacted by a close friend from the old #6. Detective Steve Marshall asked during our conversation if I might be interested in coming to work in the armed robbery division of the Detective Bureau. He further stated that another friend, Lt. Gene Fields, who was then the supervisor of the robbery unit, had asked Steve to see if I might be willing to "transfer". I told Steve that I was very interested and he said they would work it out. After a conversation with Dave Kent who was still commanding the Vice Squad and several other Vice guys with whom I had become very close, they each wished me well and I was off to the "Third Floor". While each division within the department held its own special position of significance, the Third Floor... The Detective Bureau... was a Kingdom of its own! Over the several years that I had been a part of the NOPD, I had come to learn that when an event occurred and a crime was committed anywhere within the city, and a "Detective" showed up on the scene... that Detective was immediately "in charge" of the scene and most things pertaining thereto. That was a logical condition because the detective was responsible for managing the "follow-up" investigation that would be conducted in an attempt to solve whatever crime had been committed.

However logical it may have been, it placed the Detectives in a position of great respect by most of the Officers of the department. It was a position to which I had, for some years, aspired. And now, all of a sudden, I was about to be a Detective. Little could I have known then how challenging it would be to fill the shoes of the amazingly talented and unbelievably courageous Detectives behind whom I was about to follow.

So for the next year or so, I would learn investigative skills including crime scene management, interview and interrogation techniques, evidence handling procedures, report writing, stake-out techniques, and dozens of other skills that I was to use almost every day for the rest of my career. And I was to learn these skills from some of the best Detectives ever in the business. Men like Major Henry Morris, Captain Tony Pallito, Lt. Gene Fields, Lt. Richie Hunter, Detectives Charlie Faught, Rhett Magnon, Billy Roth, Tim Walker, Jerry DeRose, Pat King, and many others who were professional and patient enough to share their many years of combined experience with a well-intended but greatly "out-classed" country boy! These guys were the "Real Deal"!

Bullet holes in armed robbery suspect's windshield as a result of a "shoot-out" with Police. Suspect was wanted for more than twenty five armed robberies and assaults from New Orleans to Pascagoula, Mississippi

We worked throughout the city responding to the scenes of armed robberies on individuals, businesses, and banks. We rolled up on armed robberies in progress, engaged in high speed car chases, and on too many occasions responded to Officer involved shootings in which Officers had been injured or killed. We conducted stake outs and apprehended dangerous felons during the commission of armed robberies. We worked with Officers from out of state including the Texas Rangers, and assisted with the extradition of suspects who had committed violent crimes in those other jurisdictions. I worked alongside highly experienced detectives who not only helped me "learn the trade", but taught me how to survive highly dangerous and life threatening events and to WIN in those situations! They taught me how to "get home at night"!

The Doctor

During one investigation, my then partner Rhett Magnon and I received an assignment regarding a Doctor who lived in "Uptown" New Orleans in the "Garden District". We learned that the doctor was receiving threatening phone calls from an unknown individual. The caller had contacted the Doctor several times and stated that if the Doctor didn't pay a very large amount of money to the caller, he would kill the Doctor and his family. At first the Doctor dismissed the calls as simple prank calls, but after the caller described members of the Doctor's family and described the Doctor's home and where it was, the Doctor became extremely frightened and contacted the Police Department.

Rhett and I were assigned the case. From the detective Bureau, Rhett and I called the Doctor to gain more information. We informed him that we were working on a plan that we felt would work. We went to the Doctor's home and met the Doctor and his family. We conducted surveillance in and around the Doctor's residence until the caller again contacted the Doctor to make further demands. After listening in on the caller as he threatened the Doctor, we also were convinced that the caller was serious about following through on his threats if his demands were not met. The caller had also given a time frame for his next call to the Doctor and by which time his demands must be met. His threats were specific, emphatic and very aggressive! We believed the caller would do harm to the Doctor and his family if his demands were not met, or we did not intervene!

Knowing that we had some time before our "outlaw" was to call the Doctor back, Rhett and I contacted the telephone company and quickly arranged for a "trap and trace" to be placed upon the Doctor's phone at his residence. Remember now, this is December 1973 and all the phones were either in a "phone booth" or were wired to the wall.

The phone company agreed to our request after the required verification of our identity, and an explanation of the circumstances. The "trap and trace" was initiated. For explanation, a "trap and trace" was a method used by the phone company to electronically "trap" or lock an incoming call to a specific phone number, and while not "releasing" the incoming caller's phone from the connection, trace the incoming caller's phone to the location at which it was "installed". Trap... and Trace... We gave the phone company all the necessary information to contact us through the department upon the "trap and trace" being activated so that they could tell us the address from which the suspect had called. After notifying our dispatcher of the probability of the notification from the phone company, we were all set.

Once the system was in place, we drove back to the Doctor's home to wait for the suspect to call with further instructions. After only a short while, the suspect called the Doctor. Almost immediately we received a call from the dispatcher with the suspect's address.

Having the suspect's name and address, the Detective Bureau had also pulled the suspect's arrest records. They gave us all the information about the suspect as we sped toward his home. We now had his name, and full description. Luckily, it was a short drive from the Doctor's house and we were there within only a few minutes. Rhett and I approached the door of the house just as the suspect was exiting the door.

After a brief "interview", he admitted to having made the calls, and gave us permission to search his home. While Rhett watched the suspect, who was by now sitting handcuffed in the back seat of our vehicle, I entered the house and found the Suspect's telephone. It was back "on the hook". When I picked up the handset, it was still connected to the Doctor's home with the Doctor still holding his phone's handset to his ear. I said "Hello, is someone on the line?" The Doctor immediately said "Yes, It's me Detective Macdonald…. Did you get him…?" I told the Doctor that we had the suspect in custody and handcuffed in our car. The Doctor very emotionally expressed his relief and we hung up the phones.

We took the suspect to the Detective Bureau where he was processed and then transported to Central Lock-Up. After the suspect was in jail, we again returned to the home of the Doctor and his family to insure that they were all safe and well. They were still quite shaken but were extremely relieved that the suspect had been apprehended. We completed all of our investigative paperwork, and soon departed the Doctor's home.

As we were about to leave his home, the Doctor became quite emotional. He was overcome with gratitude and in expressing how sincerely he and his family appreciated our efforts, he commented, as we had heard a hundred times before from many other victims of serious crimes… "If I can ever do anything for you, please call upon me!" We thanked him and departed the home.

It would be several years before I would speak with the Doctor, but on a cold winter morning in 1977, I needed to speak with him again. It was after a duck hunt along the Pearl River about nine miles west of Picayune with a good friend and fellow Law Enforcement Officer with the Mississippi Highway Patrol, that I needed the Doctor's help.

Trooper J.L. Johnson, his young son Joseph, and I were on an early morning hunt and had arrived at one of our favorite hunting spots. We had spread out along an old country logging trail that was parallel to a bayou that ran off of the Pearl River on the Mississippi side of the river. As it began to get daylight, the ducks, as always, began to fly over in large groups. J.L. shot first and knocked down a mallard, I shot and likewise had one on the ground. Then I heard a different sounding shot which came from the area where J.L.'s son was standing.

When I looked in his direction, I could see him bending over in an awkward position. At the same time I heard him yell for his dad and I could tell the boy was in great pain by the sound of his voice. His dad and I immediately ran to him and saw that his shotgun had exploded out the side and had almost blown his hand off. Immediately J.L. began consoling his son and I tore off part of my shirt and made a makeshift bandage to try to stop the bleeding. We started back to J.L.'s old truck and once inside, J.L. drove and I held the boy and kept pressure on the bandage. That nine mile drive back to town seemed like a two day trip! By the time we got to the emergency room at the hospital in Picayune, the boy was starting to go into shock.

We got him inside and the doctors started to work on him immediately. After a short time, J.L. came out of the room where they were treating his son. He looked as if he was about to pass out and was extremely emotional. I got him to sit down on a chair in the waiting room and he told me that the local Doctor had told them that he was going to have to amputate part of or all of the boy's hand. Now I became emotional! And in a blink... I thought of a Doctor friend that I had in New Orleans. A Doctor who was a specialist and had once told me if I ever needed anything I could call upon him. As I was explaining to J.L. that I "had a friend", the local Doctor came out to where we were seated and told J.L. that he needed to give the Doctor the approval for the surgery and the sooner the better...

I gave J.L. a negative shake of my head and after a look or two back and forth, J.L. said "I'm gonna have to think about this some"... I went to a phone and called information and got the Doctor's number in New Orleans. The Doctor answered his phone on the second ring. I told him who was calling and he immediately asked, "What's going on Fred?" I explained what had happened and what the local Doctor had told J.L. Without hesitation he told me not to allow anyone to do anything until he looked at the boy's hand himself.

The Doctor told me that he had another Doctor friend who specialized in reconstructive surgery specifically of "Hands". He said he would contact that Doctor and they would both meet J.L and his son at a designated hospital in New Orleans. After several other arrangements were made, J.L. and his wife took their son to New Orleans and were meeting with the Doctors within a couple of hours. After an examination, the Doctor with his team took the boy to surgery and after a lengthy surgery, the Doctor came out and informed J.L. that he and his team had successfully saved the boy's hand and that with some "Rehab", he should regain full use of the hand and be near normal after his recovery.

By the time they received that news, I was back at my home in Picayune, and almost back to a normal heart rate. J.L. and I remain friends still today and worked closely for many years. And by the way, his son Joseph recovered completely and grew up to be a fine young man. Following in his dad's footsteps, in December 1987 Joseph graduated from MHSP Recruit School #45 and became a "Trooper". Recently, as his dad had done years before, Joseph retired from the Mississippi Highway Safety Patrol!!!

Having once been a hero to a humble and thankful Doctor in New Orleans, that same Doctor later became one of my heroes who I'll never forget! He also became a hero to two Troopers by whom he would have never otherwise been known had it not been for a random assignment of one of hundreds of investigations within the NOPD Detective Bureau several winters earlier.

During my time in the Detective Bureau, I was fortunate enough to have experienced dozens of incidents in which the bravery, professionalism and often the humor of the Detectives around me created memories that impacted me throughout the course of my entire career. I worked among men who could, and frequently did, walk with total confidence into the most dangerous of circumstances responding to an ongoing violent crime in progress. Then upon dealing with the threat posed by these dangerous felons, would, within moments, be comfortably, competently, and calmly consoling victims and assembling witnesses to find and document reliable facts that would help successfully conclude the investigation and prosecute the perpetrators.

The Bathroom

On one cold, rainy, and windy evening in the city, my partner Jerry DeRose and I were working the evening shift. As we rode away from the small restaurant at which we had just enjoyed a late supper, we received a call from dispatch of an armed robbery in progress in a bar just off Esplanade Avenue near the French Quarter. As we responded and arrived at the bar, numerous uniformed Officers were likewise arriving on the scene. We quickly determined that the armed robber had departed the bar but not before successfully robbing the establishment of all of its cash which had been in the register at the end of the bar. It seemed that the robber had also expressed his intent to likewise rob all of the patrons of their individual wealth, but upon hearing the sirens of the "Uniformed Officers" approaching, he had decided to depart and forego the robbing of the customers so as to insure his escape prior to any intervention by the NOPD.

He had "cut and run"!

After having secured the scene, it was time to start the process of trying to identify the perpetrator and determine exactly what had happened during the course of the robbery. In initially inquiring of the first of the customers in the bar, exactly what each patron had observed, it quickly became obvious that the prevailing attitude and unanimous response of each of the customers was "I didn't see anything... I was in the bathroom". Obvious that the customers didn't want to be witnesses and further incentivized by the fact that none of them "had lost anything" in the robbery, my immediate thought was... "Well, this is going to be like dozens of previous robberies we have investigated.... they were ALL *in the bathroom!*" This was a rather common response by would be witnesses in many similar investigations. Many witnesses simply did not want to get involved in spite of the fact that their refusal to provide the vital information that they possessed to the investigating Officers, allowed a dangerous criminal to continue committing violent crimes and endangering other citizens in their community.

As I was standing there watching Jerry ask over and over... "OK what did you see... or were you in the bathroom too?" Suddenly, I saw a light come on in Jerry's eyes. He stopped interviewing customers and walked to the bathroom. There was only one bathroom for the entire bar and it was simply identified by a plaque on the door as the "Bathroom". Upon getting to the bathroom Jerry opened the door to what was a very small, maybe five foot by five foot bathroom with one toilet, a sink and a very "full" trash can. He looked at me and then at the closest customers and said "alright you, you, you…. Get in the bathroom". After several minutes of summoning Patrons and placing them into the bathroom, the ole "one-holer" had filled to what I comfortably considered to be well over maximum capacity.

The patrons stuffed into the bathroom were holding arms in the air and assuming some quite unusual positions and postures to allow the last of Jerry's designees to be crammed into the bathroom. As Jerry too realized that the bathroom was "packed", he shoved the door closed as he pushed arms and legs into the small cubical barely allowing the door to close. Once the door was successfully forced closed, we could hear the voices of the patrons inside the bathroom yelling… "Come on…. OK…. Let us out of here…open this *#@*# door…"

Jerry turned around and looked out over the remaining twenty five or so customers still in the bar and said, "OK the rest of you folks obviously weren't in the bathroom, so all you guys must have been witnesses. Y'all can give your statements here or we'll have you all transported to the Detective Bureau for your interviews. Who wants to be the first to tell us what happened and what the robber looked like?" Well…. You couldn't have sandpapered the smile off my face right about then!!! Ole Jerry had absolutely "outdone himself"!

The patrons lined up and Jerry and I began taking information from them. As a result of the information we gathered, we were able to help identify an armed robber who had been committing robberies throughout that area of the city for months. A short time later the robber was apprehended and with evidence collected by several other investigators and what we had learned at the bar, the robber was convicted and sentenced to serve a long term in Angola Penitentiary for his crimes.

After the trial, Jerry and I were discussing, with some humor attached, the investigation at the bar that night. As we talked and quipped about the "process" of soliciting "witnesses", Jerry said with his subdued but almost ever present grin… "Just think what we might have learned from all those other guys, if they hadn't all been *in the Bathroom*"!!!

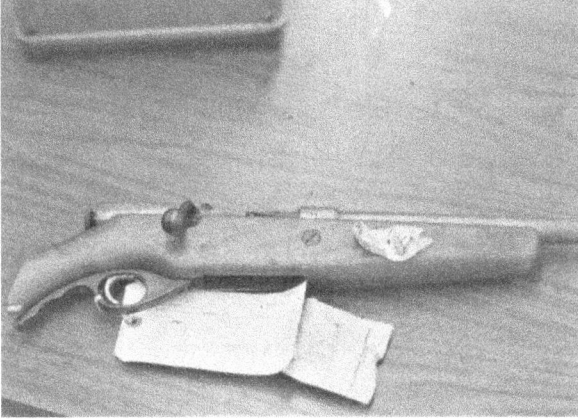

Sawed-off shotgun seized from armed robbery/murder suspect by NOPD "Robbery Unit" Detectives in 1974

Top Ten Wanted

While still in the Detective Bureau in mid-1973, I had the opportunity to assist other detectives in an investigation being conducted regarding a group of highly dangerous suspects operating in the New Orleans area. The group consisted of numerous individuals who had been involved in crimes throughout the nation. They were known for perpetrating vicious attacks upon Law Enforcement Officers and Police Stations around the country and were suspected of killing Police Officers from New York to San Francisco.

Our Detectives had received information that some of the suspects being pursued in New Orleans were on the FBI's "Top 10 Most Wanted" list at the time. NOPD Detectives had developed information that these men were in our area and that they were using

New Orleans as a "safe house" to organize their group and gather resources with which to assist in perpetrating future crimes around the nation. After several weeks of following the group and hours of surveillance on them and their residences, the Detectives had identified these individuals and determined that there were numerous warrants for many of the group's members from various areas of the country.

The Detectives continued to follow the suspects during their daily movements and after determining as much as possible about the suspects activities and realizing how dangerous these individuals were to Officers and citizens in the area, a decision was made to apprehend the suspects for whom the warrants existed. Commanders and members of the Detective Bureau created a plan for the suspects' arrests and briefed those of us who would participate in the arrests regarding the plan and what our parts would be in supporting the plan.

The plan called for the monitoring of the suspects and insuring that at the time and place that the arrests were to be made, the Detectives would have every advantage to insure that the suspects were successfully arrested with the least likelihood for injury to any of the Detectives, innocent citizens in the area, and also the least likelihood for injury to the suspects. The concept of "Safety and Success" was obviously paramount in the planning of the arrest of these highly dangerous wanted felons!!!

In watching how meticulously the plan was developed and executed, I learned lessons from these men that guided me in the planning and execution of hundreds of high risk operations that I managed for many years to follow. These men were trail blazers in planning such events!

As the surveillances were being conducted, the suspects moved about in what had been determined to be their normal routines. Because of the preparations by the other detectives and the amount of knowledge gained by having surveilled the suspects so well for many days, the predictions of the suspects' actions and activities upon which the plan was based were almost like watching a movie for the second time... We all knew what was about to happen next...! Because of the exceptional plan and the experience and expertise of the Detectives and the Commanders of the NOPD Detective Bureau, the plan was executed flawlessly. The suspects were all arrested without incident. The bad guys were in jail and no one was hurt.

A search warrant was served on the house where most of the suspects were staying. During the search, a large cache of weapons, ammunition, and explosives were found in the attic of the residence. The suspects were charged with offenses related to the weapons and explosives and were booked awaiting extradition back to the jurisdictions from which warrants were issued for their arrest. One of the "Top 10" suspects was extradited back to New York State where he was incarcerated, tried and convicted for his part in the murder of two New York Police Officers several years earlier. He served almost forty-five years in a New York penitentiary and was just released in April of 2018 after a parole board approved his release and *Governor Andrew Cuomo signed his pardon.*

Other Detective Bureau Lessons

While in the Detective Bureau, I had the opportunity to work with many Detectives and supervisors who influenced my career in many ways. Charlie Faught was one of the Detectives from the Homicide Unit who were assigned to manage the post incident investigation regarding the Howard Johnson sniper attacks. While many Officers and Detectives assisted Charlie in that investigation, he was the lead investigator and "wrote the report" of the incident. That investigative report became NOPD's official position regarding the events during that horrible attack on those Officers, firemen, and

Charlie Faught "in uniform"... Charlie led the investigative team which conducted the follow-up investigation regarding the Howard Johnson Incident. Charlie was and is a remarkable Hero.

civilians who were injured and killed during the event. Charlie's professionalism in conducting the investigation and compiling the reams of paper which became the official report were ample indicators as to why Charlie was assigned this unbelievably challenging task. He was and still is a stellar example of a true investigator of the highest caliber! He remains unequaled in my experience of working with hundreds of the best investigators in our Nation!

Many experiences from my time in the Detective Bureau guided my decisions and actions in almost every aspect of my career for all the years that followed. Even now in conversations with old partners and friends from those days, I refer to events that we shared "on the job". Inevitably we recall either how closely we came to meeting our demise or how funny a memory still is of some unforgettable event that we shared "back in the day".

A call from Larkin... MBN

In early 1973 just after being assigned to the Detective Bureau, I had a call from my old friend and partner, Larkin Smith. He was by this time, the "Chief Investigator" for the Harrison County Sheriff's Department on the Gulf Coast of Mississippi, and we talked frequently. Often on my "days off" from NOPD, I would go to the Coast and work with Larkin in an unofficial "Undercover" capacity gathering intelligence information for him in the bars and other businesses along the coast that were owned and frequented by individuals known to be involved in criminal endeavors.

Many of these criminals were part of what was known as the "Dixie Mafia". They were career criminals who regularly travelled throughout the southeastern United States committing a variety of felonies. After receiving my "intel updates", Larkin would then send in his own investigators armed with accurate actionable information and conduct their own investigations regarding the criminal activity which I had reported to him. The efforts yielded a great deal of knowledge, successful arrests, and prosecutions. Unknown to me at the time, the knowledge and experience that I gained in these investigations would become an invaluable resource in the years that followed when I would work on the Gulf Coast in another capacity.

But this phone call was different and never could I have imagined where it would lead me within my chosen profession. Larkin told me that he had a friend in Jackson, Mississippi who he had known for many years. The friend had also been involved in Law Enforcement for years and had recently been appointed to a position that Larkin thought might interest me. He went on to state that a little over a year earlier, The Mississippi Legislature had separated the "Drug Enforcement" responsibility away from the Mississippi Highway Patrol and created a new Agency. The Agency was now known as the Mississippi Bureau of Narcotics, or the MBN. Larkin's friend had been appointed as the first Director of the MBN and was searching for and recruiting Agents for his new Agency. Larkin said that he had mentioned my name to the Director in a conversation they recently had, and the Director told Larkin that he would like to meet with me and discuss the possibility of hiring me as an Agent with the MBN. Larkin asked if that was something that I might be interested in. I told him that while I was absolutely satisfied with my current position, I would very much like to at least talk with the new Director.

A couple of weeks later, I made the hour and a half trip to the coast and met Larkin. We visited briefly and then he drove the three hours to Jackson in his vehicle. We drove to a small office complex in Jackson just off Lakeland Drive and went inside. The offices were totally unmarked and simply appeared to be a part of other commercial businesses in the same buildings. Once inside, we were met by a young radio operator and a receptionist just inside the front door and after the normal swapping of several joking comments for which Larkin was well known, we were escorted upstairs to the Directors office area.

Just outside the Director's office door we were again met by a receptionist and the Director's secretary, Marty Olsen. After an exchange of pleasantries with the Secretary, she escorted us into a large office with a huge desk on one end and an even larger conference table at the other end. There were a number of chairs positioned about the room and several smaller tables upon which were stacked large piles of what appeared to be documents of various types. Marty spoke to the Director as we entered and said, "Mr. Fairly, Larkin is here".

That would be Mr. Kenneth W. Fairly!!!

Unimaginably to me in that otherwise unknown office in Jackson, I met a man who would unquestionably become one of my most significant Heroes. Mr. Fairly became a true Icon in my career and set an example of professionalism and leadership equaled by very few in my life! And there I sat… unknowing… and talked and joked with him and Larkin as if we had all known each other all our lives. Mr. Fairly was immediately recognized as one of those rare individuals with whom one establishes an immediate bond of friendship and mutual respect! We really hit it off!!!

We discussed experiences that we both had had in Law Enforcement and while growing up. We had numerous experiences in common. We discussed what I had done in various assignments in Law Enforcement and he told me of the different assignments and jobs that he had previously held. All during the three hour conversation, Larkin would also inject some humorous experience that he had "lived through" with one of us. He would, of course, elaborate on stories with which he could make either Mr. Fairly or me the "butt" of a "war story" with one of us becoming the "punch line". It was only fair that we did the same to him. It was a great visit and experience.

After several hours, Mr. Fairly paused, and with a stern stoic look over the top of his "reading glasses" assumed a persona that only he could ever project... the "Fairly look". At that point, He simply asked...

"Well boy, you gonna come to work for me, or what?"

I felt like I had felt several years earlier standing in Chief Morris' office. And once again... I had to do some deep soul searching about his offer, and make a decision that I didn't expect to have to make in this first visit. I absolutely did not expect the Director to offer me a job "on the spot" when I told Larkin that I would ride with him to meet the Director of the newly formed MBN. But here I was, and there he was, looking over those "half lens" glasses. He was looking at me with the look that I would see directed at me and dozens of other Agents and civilians for many years into the future..... A look that, as "Captain America" of the old "Hill Street Blues" TV series would say, could...

"Make good men tremble, and bad men wet their pants"
That was the look!!!

But as the hair began to lay back down on the back of my neck, I realized that the rest of those looks were still in my future. I looked at Larkin, and could read his mind... he was thinking "well Fred's going to need a moving van..." And then I turned back to Mr. Fairly and said, "Mr. Fairly, I just got transferred to the NOPD Detective Bureau, and that is a position that I have wanted since I was a kid. I would really like to work there for a while longer and then talk to you about possibly coming to work for you with the MBN." He didn't say a word for what seemed like about two days.

Then his eyes warmed, he smiled a "Ken Fairly smile" and said " you go be a Detective down there in the big city son, and when you're ready to leave all that excitement, give me a call and come on back up here… I'll keep you a spot open". I was as humbled as I was honored! I didn't know it then, but in those few hours, we had established a friendship that would last a lifetime!!!

What a Man!!!   What a Hero!!!

So, Larkin and I drove back to the coast, I drove back to New Orleans and went back to work with the Detective Bureau. And for the next year or so, I gained experience and learned skills and techniques that I would never have even been exposed to had it not been for my time in the NOPD Detective Bureau. The Officers and Detectives that I have already mentioned and countless others on the NOPD contributed to my Law Enforcement fabric in ways that most of them never had any way to imagine. I hope that through some of these stories and those that follow, each of them will understand how much I appreciate and cherish the time that I spent with them in these early years of my career and how they impacted my safety and success in the years that followed. Each of them hold very special positions in my life and in my heart!

Well, after some time, I still had Mr. Fairly and the MBN on my mind, and as the months passed, the lure of going back "undercover" began to tug pretty strongly at my ole "Narc psyche". So, after more than a little deliberation, in the early fall of 1974, I called Mr. Fairly. I told him that I was ready to come back to Mississippi and work for him and the MBN if he had that "spot" still open. He immediately said yes and over the next several weeks, we talked and met again. Soon all the details and paperwork were worked out for me to move to Jackson and go to work for the MBN.

When the arrangements were made, I went to work and informed my supervisor, Lt. Richie Hunter, in the Robbery Unit that I had been offered another job and had accepted it. He asked if there was some problem that was causing me to leave NOPD and I assured him that there was not. After explaining to him my reasoning for leaving the NOPD and going to work with the MBN, he was very supportive and told me that he would work out the details through the NOPD personnel office. After only a few minutes, a supervisor from the Homicide Unit came to me and said, "The Chief wants to see you". I followed him back to Chief Morris' office, entered the office, and the supervisor closed the door and left me alone with the Chief.

In the most cordial of conversations, Chief Morris asked why I was leaving and was there anything he could do to talk me into staying with NOPD. He complimented me on my work while with the Detective Bureau and we visited for some time. We talked about investigations that had been conducted while I was there and where he thought the detective Bureau was "going" in the future. He told me several old "war stories" of his time as a Detective "back in the day", and we laughed about how times had changed. He honored me with what he and I both knew was a farewell visit, and I appreciate his efforts with and for me still today.

He was a man who could dispense strong decisive power when needed and could extend a gentle helping hand in the toughest of situations just as comfortably and effectively! His trade mark gruff, barking, short bursts of "conversation" while easily understood, sometimes needed a moment of interpretation to insure that the recipient was doing *exactly* what the "Chief" wanted done.

Whether it was when he showed up on the scene of an armed robbery with injured victims, a homicide with multiple fatalities, or a shooting in which an Officer or Officers were the victims, when the "Chief" came onto the scene, his presence instilled confidence in the other Detectives and Officers present and a simple word or two from him always let us know.... "He had our Back"!!! They just don't make many like the "Chief" anymore!!! I am extremely honored to have known and worked for Chief Henry Morris!!!

After our visit, and after making all the necessary arrangements within the NOPD, I soon arrived at my final day with the department. After a cordial farewell with my fellow Detectives, I was off and on my way to the MBN.

Throughout my tenure with the NOPD, I was constantly surrounded by some of the most capable, honest, and courageous Officers ever to wear a badge. Whether in uniform riding the streets of the sixth district, in street clothes working the far corners of the city with the Vice Squad, or working in a coat and tie in the city wide Detective Bureau, I was constantly in awe of the vast experience, bravery, and comradery of the men and women of the NOPD.

I left with mixed emotions regarding my departure from NOPD and more than a little uncertainty and anxiousness regarding my new job opportunity. It was while I was driving away from the NOPD Headquarters building for the last time that I was struck with a sobering lump in my throat, and I realized that...

"I Rode with Heroes"!!!

Section IV
Working for the MBN

Arriving in Jackson, Mississippi, I met with Mr. Fairly at the MBN Headquarters. As we had discussed during my hiring process, I would be required to attend an MBN academy which was about to start. Upon successful completion of the eight week academy, I would be assigned to a section of the state yet undetermined and would probably be working undercover assignments for some time. At this point in the history of the MBN, the agency was "centralized" and all Agents lived in the Jackson area and travelled out to their assignments to conduct investigations as dictated by the Agents' individual supervisors.

Going to the academy required that I be a resident of Mississippi. After making the two hundred mile move into a rental house in north Jackson, I arrived at the Mississippi Law Enforcement Officers' Training Academy, or MLEOTA, on Sunday October 20, 1974. For the next eight weeks I would attend a very demanding and challenging academy program. While some thirty-six recruits started the class, only thirteen would graduate. Like the NOPD Academy, the classroom training was outstanding with lecturers from MBN Agents and supervisors, a variety of members of other Law Enforcement Agencies, and various Institutions, as well as Professors from several Universities. Also like NOPD, the physical training was more than a little demanding. Our "Class Counselor" was an MBN Agent named Joe Madison. Joe was a former Airborne Ranger, if that offers any insight into our challenge in meeting his standards of physical fitness. Drill Instructor Joe or "DI-Joe" as we lovingly referred to him, could and did run "backwards" farther, faster, longer, and more easily than any of us could run the distance like a normal human! Other calisthenics, obstacle courses, and whatever physical challenge ole DI-Joe could dream up daily, yielded more than enough of a challenge for most of the recruits, including myself! He was a machine. Battling old knee injuries from a very limited high school football career, I was quite challenged to perform at DI-Joe's level of acceptance throughout the school. However, during the eight weeks of the academy, I went from a *comfortable* 248 pound "Post Detective" structure to a streamlined 215 pound "road ready narc". Thanks Brother Joe, for all you did! It is certainly more fun to laugh and joke about those experiences now than it was to live through them then.

Finally having survived DI-Joe's many challenges, and successfully concluding all other academic requirements, the thirteen remaining recruits arrived at graduation day for the MBN academy on Friday December 13, 1974. One may note that we had thirteen (13) recruits graduating on Friday the 13th. Now, I am not a superstitious person, in fact the consecutive digits "1 and 3" have occurred frequently and have always associated themselves with good fortune for me throughout my life. BUT... there were some of the recruits who were more than a little troubled by this coincidence. Nonetheless, on Friday December 13, 1974, Director Kenneth Fairly graduated and appointed 13 new Agents to the Mississippi Bureau of Narcotics. I was and am very proud to have been one of those new Agents. From the time that we had been informed that we were accepted to the MBN academy, we had all been instructed that we could admit to no one for whom we worked nor by whom we were employed. This would remain our admonishment for some time into the future. We were to remain anonymous, until instructed or otherwise advised by the Boss, to all those with whom we came in contact. We were given or had created fictitious identities and "cover stories" as to our employment and backgrounds. We were

"Undercover", and we knew that we had better stay that way, or our new employment opportunity would be promptly terminated by a very unhappy Mr. Fairly!

MBN Class, (Fred's), 12-13-74 Standing L-R: Hal Martin, J.C. Denham, Charles Spillers, Eddie Dickey, Fred Macdonald, Chris McCurley, Robert Lee Donley, Jr. Kneeling L-R: Jim Kinslow, Dwight Ingram, Randy Corban, Earl Pierce, Barry Newsome, Ben White

While attending the MBN Academy, I had an experience which changed my life forever! On October 30, 1974, I was summoned from class by DI Joe and told that I needed to contact my dad immediately. Joe led me to the Academy Director's office and I was told I could use his private phone to call home. After the Director and Joe left the office and closed the door, I reluctantly called my Dad at his home in Picayune. His words scorched my ears and broke my heart! Less than two years after losing my Hero Papa Mac, my Mama Nina had also passed from this earth.

The loss was monumental!

Never again would I be able to visit with two of my greatest childhood Heroes. Those mornings spent drinking coffee and watching the sunrise with Mama Nina were gone forever. Sitting in Papa Mac's den and hearing about hunting adventures while holding guns with which he had hunted trophy animals, were now only memories. The "living human nexus" for those memories were now both gone.

From then until now, my most vivid memories of these incredible mentors are reignited through the presence of several tangible items which we shared mutual interests in, and memories through, and which were passed down to me through the years. I still occasionally drink coffee from the *"old faded green mug"* shared by Mama Nina and me over sixty years ago. I likewise often sit in my Den on a couch similar to the one owned by Papa Mac's many decades ago. Admiring a few remaining relics which we both held and discussed in our conversations in HIS Den on the banks of the Pearl River more than half a century earlier, I still can recall the love and patience demonstrated through his endless stories.

As I attended the graveside service a few days later for Mama Nina, and listened to the loving words spoken about her as she was being laid to rest, I was comforted knowing without a doubt that she was in Heaven and...

Mama Nina and Papa Mac were back together!

Columbus

After graduation, we all enjoyed about one full "day off" and on Sunday December 15, we all travelled to the corners of the state that would be our areas of assignment for the foreseeable future. Fellow classmate and now fellow Agent James Kinslow and I were assigned to the Columbus area. Our immediate supervisor was a highly respected Agent named Jim Walker. Jim was also to become highly respected as my supervisor and would remain a valued and trusted friend for many years into the future. He always had my back and provided much needed advice and support the entire time that I worked under his supervision.

On Sunday December 15, Kinslow and I left Jackson in our shiny new undercover car headed for Columbus to meet our local Law Enforcement contact who was approved by Mr. Fairly to know our identity. Arriving in Columbus at about 10:00 pm, we met with Columbus PD Narcotics Officer Billy Pickens. We drove to a small motel in West Point, Mississippi, and entered a rented room to meet with Billy and create a plan for attacking the drug problem in Columbus and surrounding area. After only minutes with Billy, I could tell that he was the "real deal". His demeanor, manner of speaking, knowledge of offenders in the area, and types of drugs readily available all depicted him as a very knowledgeable and professional Officer. Since that day in 1974, Billy has proven my first evaluation of him hundreds of times! He became and remains one of my dearest lifelong friends and most trusted confidants and fellow law Enforcement Officers! He has been a true Partner of the highest caliber, for over forty-five years, in our every endeavor!

After meeting with Billy we travelled the twenty or so miles back to the Columbus area. Jim and I checked into the Ramada Inn and moved our few belongings into our room. The Ramada was to be our residence for several months while we worked in the Columbus area. Over the next weeks and months, we infiltrated many of the drug dealers and their networks in Columbus. We arranged dozens of drug deals with dozens of dealers and purchased virtually every type drug that was available in the area. Some of the deals involved relatively small quantities of common drugs while other purchases involved record amounts of drugs that were very rare in our state at that time. We frequented the bars and other "hangouts" of local dealers and were successful in convincing many of them, for a variety of reasons, that we needed varying quantities of assorted drugs. We arranged purchases of these drugs, and completed numerous transactions using Official State Funds or OSF, to pay for the drugs. All the currency was "marked" meaning that each serial number had been recorded by Jim and me prior to each transaction. While writing our "Reports of Investigation" each bill spent during the transaction was documented by serial number in the corresponding report. Each piece of evidence that we purchased was properly sealed and marked for transportation to the state crime lab for analysis. Each such transaction yielded a prosecutable felony against the seller of the controlled substance which was safely secured within the crime lab until time for court.

We repeated the process time after time, night after night, and day after day for almost six months. Upon completion of our investigations in Columbus, we had made prosecutable cases on every major suspect that was known by Billy and the Columbus Police Department at the time of our arrival in the area. We had also purchased drugs from several dealers who had previously been unknown to Billy and the department.

"Narcs Die Young" painted on overpass in Mississippi as a threat to MBN undercover Agents in mid 1970's

The Significant Alias

During our work in Columbus, I had met a young man and subsequently purchased drugs from him on several occasions. He had identified himself to me giving me a first and last name and a phone number. I followed up on his story as I had numerous times before in an effort to positively identify him so that we could insure his correct identity for arrest and prosecution. Also because I was making multiple purchases from him I wanted to be able to justify the continued and increasing volume of OSF spent to accomplish the transactions. It was getting somewhat expensive. In determining his true identity, we found that he had lied about his name. While that was no surprise, in fact it was quite common, what I learned from the MBN records division regarding his true identity would soon run tremors through our Headquarters, all the way to the boss's large mahogany desk! Upon positively identifying the young man from whom I had now purchased substantial quantities of controlled substances, we (MBN and I) had learned that he was none other than the son of a prominent state Senator. Not just any old prominent State Senator, he was the son of THE prominent State Senator who had been instrumental in creating the law in the state legislature that established the Mississippi Bureau of Narcotics back in 1971. The same Senator who was one of Mr. Fairly's strongest allies in the Senate and one of his closest friends.

Learning that I had made several felony cases on the son of THE Senator, I felt it necessary and appropriate that I contact Mr. Fairly myself and inform him of the cases and the circumstances surrounding the purchases of drugs that I had made from THE Senator's son. Honestly, I had no idea how the entire situation would be taken by Mr. Fairly or how he would respond. While I trusted Mr. Fairly completely, it seemed to me at the time that it would certainly have at least the potential of causing more than a little heartburn for him in dealing with the Senator in the future. This also, I thought, could affect MBN directly regarding our budget and overall support depending upon how the Senator responded. So, I called Mr. Fairly... on the black phone behind his desk. He had one too. When Mr. Fairly answered his phone, I responded to his usual questions about how my assignment in Columbus was progressing and upon a brief lull in the conversation I said, "Mr. Fairly, there's something I need to tell you about." With the voice, inflection and ever-present air that only Mr. Fairly could project, he stated, "Son…. I don't have a clue what it is, but I have a feelin' it's gonna deserve eva ounce of my attention... so go ahead...... What?"

After a detailed and full description of each of the cases that I had made on the young man, and having identified him in each instance by the name that the young man had used as an alias, I finally said... "And we just found out that this was an alias... the young man is actually THE Senators son." Without a moment hesitation Mr. Fairly simply said ..."So...?... Son, if he sold you dope, put his ass in jail...!" So, I did. He later pled guilty and received a stiff sentence for multiple counts of sale of controlled substance. And Mr. Fairly never backed up one inch. He was then and in every other instance that I ever observed him in action... A Rock! After the Senator's son was arrested, Mr. Fairly contacted the Senator and explained that his son had sold drugs to an undercover MBN Agent in the Columbus area. The Senator's response was almost identical to Mr. Fairly's response to me. The Senator never intervened in any way, in any part of the process, at any point. He, like Mr. Fairly earned an even larger place of honor in my heart forever.

The Oklahoma Connection

After several months of working in the Columbus area, Kinslow was reassigned to another part of the state and I continued to work in Columbus. During the next several months, I continued to make undercover buys from dealers who I either met in the bars around town or from dealers to whom I had been introduced by various informants provided by Billy and the Columbus PD. The process was the same for most of the undercover purchases... Buy the drugs with OSF, process the evidence, write the reports, and take the evidence to the crime lab. Toward the end of the assignment, I had the occasion to meet a man from Oklahoma. We met in a local bar and soon were engaged in a conversation similar to those with dozens of other dealers which had led to numerous U/C buys in which I spent the OSF and "Let it walk". The quantities were within the price range that allowed me to spend the money to purchase the evidence knowing that we would never recover the OSF... The money would "walk".

This guy was different. He was talking about selling me quantities of various drugs that were large enough and expensive enough that I knew my supervisor would not approve letting the funds walk. We were talking hundreds of thousands of dollars. The drugs included Quaaludes, LSD, amphetamines, opioids, and large quantities of marijuana. When we first met, the man discussed only smaller quantities of some of these drugs, but as we talked and discussed our mutual desires to become major dealers in different geographical areas of the country, he continued to better explain what his resources for drugs actually were. He began to perceive me not as a competitor but a business partner. We were finally moving in the direction that I wanted him to go. More discussions followed until finally I convinced him that he should bring me several large samples of some of the drugs to which he had access in Oklahoma. He agreed and we discussed the quantities of various drugs that he was to return to Oklahoma for. After several discussions over several days during which he would call his various sources out west, we finally agreed on "Samples" that he had immediate access to and could simply go back, acquire and return with to Columbus.

The quantities of drugs and the cost associated with the drugs required that I call my supervisor and arrange for a larger supply of OSF than I routinely had on hand. The purchase price for the drugs would be over $30,000.00. While this is still no small amount of good ole U.S. currency, in 1975 one could have purchased a small farm for the cost of these drugs. Therefore, some amount of pre-planning was in order to insure those important factors of "Safety and Success".

After getting approval for the funds I met with Billy and discussed the planning for the meeting and purchase from the "Oklahoma Connection", my "source".

With the source on his way to Oklahoma to acquire the drugs, Billy and I began making our preparations. We arranged for a room at a local hotel that was literally at the bottom of the hill from what was then Billy's home in the city of Columbus. We arranged for surveillance during the transaction by other plain clothes Officers from Billy's Unit. These Officers would monitor the transaction but would also provide back-up and physical security for me during the purchase. Since there was so much money involved, we fully expected that the source would bring back his own "back-up" in case I planned to rob him for the drugs.

It was quite common for dealers to have their own back-up during deals of this type. It was also not uncommon for dealers to "fake" a sale of drugs for large quantities of money and during the fake sale, rob the buyer for the money. A "Rip" as they were called, was probably one of the greatest concerns of Agents doing undercover work because the Agent was most often alone or at best outnumbered by the dealers or "bad guys". Most of these bad guys were also most often heavily armed. They were all very paranoid by nature and hypersensitive to every molecule of activity around them... especially while they were selling quantities of drugs that would either get THEM ripped off, killed, or placed in prison for many years. Simply put, the greater the quantity of drugs and money involved in a deal, the greater the danger to everyone present! This deal fit that formula perfectly.

Therefore, we were taking every precaution to insure that whatever happened, we would maintain the control of the environment and the situation. Having notified Jim Walker that I needed the large amount of OSF to make the deal, he had arranged for the funds and arrived in Columbus on the day of the undercover purchase from the source. After all arrangements had been made we waited for the source to return from Oklahoma with the drugs. I had given the source my room number at the local hotel so that he could contact me on his return to Columbus. I had told him that I had buyers waiting for the drugs that he was bringing to me and that I needed to do the transaction and leave town as soon as possible. All of our resources were in place for the deal and the money was in Jim's hotel room a few doors down from my room.

We had arranged the rooms so that the money was readily available for the deal, but the source and his possible back-up had no way of knowing where the money was. In the event the bad guys intended to rip me off, the money would not be present in my room until the last moments before the transaction. If they "showed up early", there would be no money in my room. With my surveillance in place at Billy's house and all around the hotel, we waited for the call from the source telling me that he was in town and ready to do the deal.

Late in the afternoon, after we had been prepared for the meeting for several hours, the source called my room. He said he had just gotten to town and wanted to get the deal done as soon as possible. I asked him how far he was from my hotel and he said about twenty minutes. I told him that was perfect, and told him to come straight to my room. He agreed. I notified Billy and Walker that he was on his way. They said they were ready and would monitor the hotel area for any activity that would indicate that the source had his own back-up. I stepped next door to Jim's room and acquired the OSF and returned to my room with the money.

Just as I was entering my room, the phone rang and it was Billy. He told me that his team had watched the source arrive at the hotel in the same pickup truck that he had left town in. Billy also said that while there were several other people in the area when our source arrived at the hotel, he appeared to be alone. Billy also told me that the source had exited his truck carrying a small bag of some kind. I turned on the audio transmitter that I had earlier installed in my undercover room so that Billy and Jim could hear and record the conversations between me and the source. It was show time.

After several minutes the source knocked on my door. Still anticipating a possible rip, I had placed the money behind the chest of drawers and Television in my room. I opened the door and the source was holding a small brown duffle bag. As he nervously looked into the room and up and down the walkway outside my room, I told him to come in. He entered and sat the duffle on the table in the room. As he sat it down, he turned rather quickly toward the door and looked at me as though he had seen a ghost. His right hand was behind him and I couldn't tell if it was now occupied by an uninvited handgun. Watching him closely with my already well placed hand on my S&W .357 magnum snub-nose revolver that I had under my sweater, I asked… "You OK pard?" Still looking a bit out of sorts, he said …"Dammit…. I forgot something in my truck that I brought for you as a surprise." Concerned that he may be using some trick to get me to open my door and unable to get any updates from my surveillance as to possible comrades that the source may have waiting outside my door, I said "Well… let's get the deal done and I'll walk back to the truck with you… I have a surprise for you too…!"

With that, he calmed down to near normal, and opened his duffle and began withdrawing bags of assorted drugs and placing them on the bed for my inspection. As he was unloading the drugs, he asked if he could see the money. I walked to the area that I had hidden my part of the deal, the cash, still watching him carefully for any signs of evil doings. He kept pulling out drugs. I carried the money bag to the bed and before opening it, I inspected the drugs.

Each type of drug and associated quantity was present and correct. The drugs included 7,000 amphetamine tablets in seven 1,000 pill baggies, 1,000 LSD tablets in two 500 tab baggies, 100 barbiturate capsules in a large baggie, and 3 pounds of marijuana in three separate bags.

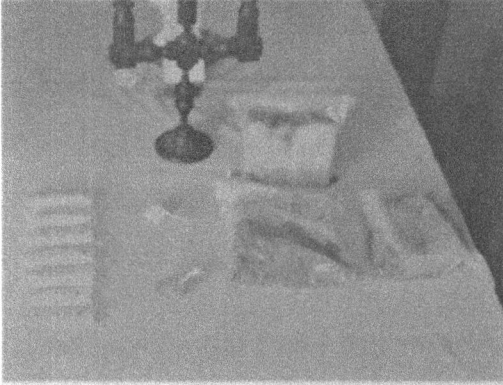

"Oklahoma Connection" drugs purchased by Fred in Columbus in 1975. 7,000 amphetamines, 1,000 tablets of "LSD", 100 barbiturates, and 3 pounds of marijuana...

Once I had verified that he had delivered the drugs that we had agreed to, I opened my bag and dumped the money on the bed. His eyes swelled and began to gloss over a bit. As he was inspecting the OSF on the bed, I asked if he was satisfied and if we could consider the deal complete. As he was smiling and saying yes, I told him that it was time for his surprise. For a moment, his smile grew even bigger. Then I told him that I had brought him a bonus for making the trip so quickly. With those smiling eyes, he asked me what... I said "I brought you some *Gold*". I thought he was going to break his cheeks with those pearly whites beaming until I threw my Gold MBN Agent's badge onto the bed.

As I said "surprise", he fixed his eyes on the badge that must have looked like it was the size of a wagon wheel. I simultaneously also produced that S&W .357 to consummate the deal and

MBN Badge and S&W Mod. 19 revolver
carried by MBN Agent Macdonald

demonstrate my sincerity! I told him he was under arrest for sale of controlled substances to a State Narcotics Agent and advised him of his Maranda rights. He offered no resistance. As I helped him to the floor and into a posture that would insure compliance, I reached over and opened the door to the awaiting Officers that I knew would want to join the party.

Billy, Jim and other CPD Officers entered my room. The CPD Officers searched and handcuffed the suspect and again advised him of his rights. After the suspect was secured, the Officers escorted him to the awaiting patrol car to transport him to the local jail for processing.   Jim and I secured the OSF and evidence for transportation back to Jackson. The deal was done.

As we searched the suspect's truck in the parking lot of the hotel, we found several large caliber handguns and a rifle among his belongings. Also found on the front seat of the truck was a nicely wrapped package with a card that was inscribed…

" To: Frank (me), From: *Your Oklahoma Connection*"…
It was a *large* bottle of Jack Daniels, Old #7.

The Round-Up and Beyond

By now our investigations were winding down in the Columbus area and it was time to arrest those from whom we had been buying drugs for almost six months. Through our Headquarters and through the resources of the Columbus PD and most especially with the assistance and guiding hand of my now close friend Billy Pickens, we had positively identified all of our dozens of defendants in the area. We had likewise determined where each defendant, with only a very few exceptions, resided. After a lengthy series of presentations of each of our cases to the Grand Jury, we finally had a Capias or *Grand Jury Arrest Warrants*, for each of our defendants. They had all been indicted by the Grand Jury. We prepared for and planned the "Round-Up" by which several dozen Officers, Deputies, and MBN Agents would, as near simultaneously as possible, arrest all the defendants. They would be arrested, transported to the local jail, advised of their charges and await the process of having their individual bonds set.

After all plans had been made and all logistics were in place, on May 13, 1975 (yep… 13) the "Round-Up" began. Teams of Officers, Deputies, and Agents all went to predetermined locations and began arresting the suspects. The plan and most of the arrests went smoothly. All the defendants were caught off guard and most were arrested without incident. Billy, another Agent, a deputy and I made up one of the arrest teams. Since I had made almost all of the undercover buys, my team was assigned the defendants who were least known by local Officers so that I could positively identify them during their arrests. We had arrested and transported several of the defendants and decided to go after one on our list who was felt to be most likely to resist or flee if given the opportunity.

We travelled to his mobile home in the outskirts of town accompanied by a uniform Patrol car to insure that the suspects knew that the "real police" were knocking on their door. Upon arriving at the residence, Billy and the others went to the front door and I started making my way around the house to cover the rear. As I heard Billy knocking on the front door and announcing himself as the "Police"… I was rounding the back corner of the trailer. Just as I got to a point where I could see the back of the trailer, the back door flew open and banged hard against the back wall.

Just as the door began moving, I saw a young male jump over the back door steps and land on the ground. He never broke stride and immediately fled into a dense wooded area behind the trailer. I also began running and followed the suspect into the woods. It was dark and as I entered the woods, I realized that I could not see well at all. The only light that was available was the dim glow of a back porch light on a neighboring house some distance away. As I processed all this in the three to four seconds of entering the woods, I started to slow down my pace… it was too late.

The suspect was slightly off to my left and just as I detected his movement from the corner of my left eye, he stood up and helped me "alter my path" directly into a protrusion that I assumed emanated from a pine tree. The protrusion struck me… or I should say I struck it just below my rib cage. Once again, I lost my breath! This time it would last a bit longer… I was able, however, to "grab him back" and in a very brief struggle that ensued, I adequately subdued him, handcuffed him and began escorting him back to the front of the trailer. Meeting my team mates along the way, they eagerly took control of my suspect and helped him and me back to the awaiting vehicles in the front yard. By the time I got back to the front of the trailer, I realized that I had a noticeable laceration on my abdomen, my shirt had been partially shredded, and I was just barely catching my breath!

As it turned out, we had arrived at the trailer just as my suspect and his crew had begun preparing their most recently acquired drug cache for resale. They were all sitting around the kitchen table "cutting" their dope and when Billy came calling at the front door, the most logical response in their minds was to "cut and run" through the back door. Billy and the rest of the team were able to subdue the other members of the group before they could exit the back door but my new friend had made his escape... he thought. All the suspects were arrested for possession of controlled substances, and transported to jail after being processed at Billy's Office. My new friend was also charged with aggravated assault on an Officer.

I still carry a scar from the encounter with the protrusion. My buddies said they were tempted to charge me with "assault on a pine tree". I argued that they had no credible witnesses, and all the physical evidence, that being my bobo, was in my favor! What I have carried all these years in addition to the bobo, is a lesson.

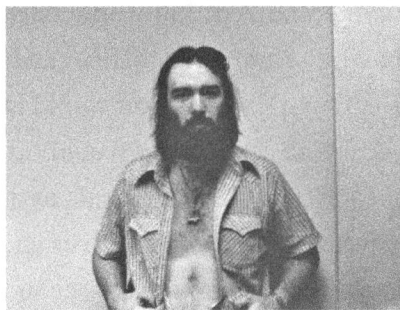

Fred after "encounter" with tree limb during "round-up" in Columbus, MS in 1975

Never run blindly into a dark unknown place chasing a suspect at full speed... always slow down *before* you hit the woods line!

With the round up complete, and all suspects in jail, my first assignment in an undercover capacity with MBN was complete... except for the court cases that would follow for the next couple of years. All the defendants either pled guilty or were convicted. For a while at least, the streets of Columbus had a few less drug dealers.

These investigations would never have been conducted, the drugs never bought or seized, the arrests never made, nor would the citizens of Columbus been made safer, had it not been for the hard work, honesty, and dedication of my friend and hero Billy Pickens.

Billy and his remarkable wife Sandy supported me in every moment of my work in Columbus, and without their unrelenting and unwavering love and support, I would never have been successful in Columbus. They are both among my greatest heroes!!!

Going Home

After Columbus, I worked in several other areas of north Mississippi for several months. Earlier, in February of 1975, I had received word from Headquarters that all Agents were to come to a meeting in Jackson. Upon attending the meeting a few days later, we all learned that the MBN had been reorganized. It would no longer be "centralized" but would be divided into Regions with each Region having a separate office and Agents directly assigned to these Regions. Each Region would have a Supervisory Agent and all other Agents in the Region would operate under his or her authority. This meant also that the Agents assigned to these Regions would have to physically move themselves and their families to an approved area of each Region. So for the second time in less than a year, I was going to have a new mailing address. In March, I travelled to Picayune with my wife and looked for a house to move into. In April, we purchased a home and began making plans and preparations to move. I was to be assigned to the Gulfport Regional Office. I would be primarily responsible for all investigations by the MBN in Pearl River County (the county in which Picayune resides), but would report to the Gulfport Office each day for duty assignments. I would be back home… right where I had started almost seven years earlier.

While waiting to actually make the move to Picayune, I continued to work in north Mississippi for several months. I established an undercover apartment in Oxford and worked out of this location until May. I was still under the supervision of my good friend and trusted partner, Jim Walker during this time. Jim along with other

Agents, made numerous trips to various locations in the northern portion of our state providing back-up, surveillance and much needed liaison between other Law Enforcement Agencies and me. Together we purchased and or seized large quantities of LSD, Amphetamines, Barbiturates, Cocaine, and marijuana.

While working in the northern portions of our state, I met and worked with many brave, honest, and capable Agents of the MBN. Men like Jim Wallace who ran the "Technical Services" unit, Kent McDaniel who was another supervisor within the state, Ricky Peterson, and Mickey Robbins, to name only a few, were constantly eager to provide support and advice to a new man on the job. They, along with many other Agents, spent long hours on the phone with this young Agent providing priceless insight and invaluable technical information that enabled me to perform safely and successfully in a very hostile environment for the months that I worked in my first assignments within the MBN. Once more, as I departed one assignment and headed to another, I was humbled and honored. I knew without question, once again, that…

"I rode with Heroes"!

Section V
The Gulfport Office

O n May 28, 1975, we moved into our new home in Picayune which was within the "Region" controlled by the MBN Gulfport Region Office and was my newly assigned "Post of Duty". After settling in and completing all necessary logistics associated with a move like utility deposits, unpacking, setting up the coffee pot, and so forth, it was time to get back to work. I immediately started making contact with all of my Law Enforcement friends and associates in the area including Officers, Deputies, Chiefs, and Sheriffs. I also met other Agents assigned to the Gulfport Region Five or "R-5" as it was most often referenced.

These Agents included Supervisor John Souder, Agents Louis Guirolla, Dean Shepard, and Agent Steven Preston Ford. While these men would constitute the core of Agents with whom I would most frequently work over the next few years, Steve Ford would quickly become one of my closest and most trusted partners and friends and would remain so for the rest of my career and life. He remains and always will be, one of the first to whom I would turn if I needed back-up for myself or my family.

There is a saying among western Lawmen and other respected Cowboys out west. If, for example, a Ranger or a Cowboy comes to sufficiently respect one of his peers, he will honor that peer by telling him,

"I'd be proud to Ride the River with you"!

This compliment connotes a level of trust and respect that requires a special understanding of the extreme dangers associated with "riding the river". It also conveys the fact that an offeror of such a high compliment would, along that dangerous river, be willing to place his life in the hands of that Cowboy who is the recipient of the compliment. Along all the rivers that we have ridden or ever will ride, Steve Ford is one of those rare Cowboys with whom I feel completely comfortable "Riding the River". *We've been down a lot of rivers!*

As I got to know Ford and the other Agents in R-5, I also met and worked with many other Officers, Deputies, and Agents who were employed by dozens of Local, State, and Federal Agencies throughout south Mississippi. I worked undercover assignments with other Agents and Officers, ran surveillances during various investigations, and provided support as needed throughout the Region. We made undercover purchases of various drugs, ran search warrants, and assisted in arrests in MBN investigations and those conducted by other Agencies. I was fortunate enough to re-establish contacts with old partners on the NOPD and assisted them with joint investigations on both sides of the State line. We developed contacts and relationships with members of the Louisiana State Police and particularly their Narcotics Units. Members of the Alabama Bureau of Investigation soon became members of our Coastal network. As our network grew and strengthened with all the Agencies along the coast, we were able to exchange investigative information regularly and began to make substantial cases on major violators. Most of the Agents lived relatively close to Gulfport. Dean Sheppard and I lived some distance from the R-5 offices. We both lived about an hour's drive from the R-5. Living in Picayune, I was the "local" or "Resident" Agent for the Picayune area and Dean was the Resident Agent for the Pascagoula area. This usually meant that we would conduct whatever business we might have in our respective primary areas of responsibility, and then make our way to the R-5 offices to assist with whatever investigative functions needed our support in other areas of the Region. There was always something going on in the Region and we all stayed busy.

Jumping a Robbery

On September 12, 1975, I was working in the Picayune area and had gone to lunch with Chief Kenny Bounds and other local Officers including Don Frierson and Junior Penton. After lunch, I was going to drive back by my home and pick up some equipment and then make one of my regular trips to the R-5 office. As I drove north on Highway 11 through the middle of town, I approached a small four door Chevy car occupied, and being driven by, a single male. As I came closer to the car, which was stopped in the middle of the highway, I could see the driver almost standing up behind the steering wheel apparently trying to see into the front windows of the "Gulf Finance Company". Drawing from my experiences with the "Robbery Unit" of the NOPD, it immediately appeared to me that the driver must have some "special interest" in the finance company or someone/something inside the business. Call me over-suspicious, but guess what.... I was right!

As I approached even closer, the driver saw me in his rear view mirror, but did not become overly suspicious because I was in a completely unmarked car, as in "undercover" car. Seeing me stopped behind him, he adjusted himself back behind the wheel and began driving his car north on Highway 11. As he moved, I began to follow but employed some of those old, hard learned surveillance techniques that I had been taught by all those experts with whom I had previously worked, and for a while he never suspected anything. He continued driving, paying little attention to me as he circled the block in which the finance company was located. However, after he had made one complete trip around the block and again stopped directly in front of the finance company and I was, once again, stopped right behind him... He *noticed* that I was there. I too, though, had done some deductive reasoning. I had concluded that either he, and a yet unidentified partner in crime, were robbing the finance company and he was the getaway car driver, or there wasn't a cow chip in Texas…

While I was still piecing together more clues, I also called the Picayune PD on my covertly installed but readily available VHF High Band Police Radio. I told the PPD Dispatcher what I was observing and that I needed "Uniformed" back up immediately. The driver became too impatient to wait any longer for the "inside guy" and looked at me over his shoulder and with a wave to his partner inside that seemed to relay that the inside guy was "on his own", the driver bolted and drove hastily north on Highway 11. After only about half of a city block, he "ran" the main red light in town and continued north. Well… that was about the most significant clue thus far that at least most of what I suspected was accurate. But the most valuable clue was still to be collected. After making my way through the light without causing any major accidents, I was able to tell Dispatch that I was in fact, in pursuit of the vehicle and its driver. Just as I had given our location to Dispatch, he turned east on Fifth Street and accelerated. By now I had turned on my also well disguised blue lights and siren and was right on his bumper at a speed that was somewhat above the posted speed limit.

After he bounced through a couple of intersections running the stop signs, with me still in tow, I saw him make what is known "on the job" as a *furtive movement*. He lifted a blue steel, long barreled revolver over the top of his seat with his right hand as he continued to speed down Fifth Street steering his car with his left hand. After a quick glance down the street to make sure he was still between the ditches, he again turned, looked at me, now some twenty feet behind his car, and pointed the revolver at me through his rear window. As he did so in a very threatening manner, his vehicle swerved and he once again turned to direct the car back into the middle of the street to avoid crashing.

I was convinced that his intention was to fire his revolver at me in an attempt to do me great bodily harm. In my mind his overt actions with an obviously deadly weapon, constituted a real, timely, and pending threat to me and my wellbeing. That being considered a deadly threat, I fired several shots toward the suspect and his car from MY blue steel, long barreled revolver. My shots had no effect on his car, but I could tell that they concerned him.

Well... one may have noticed that by this point in the still unfolding episode, there was a whole lot happening in a pretty brief amount of time. I was however able to also notify Dispatch that shots had been fired and that the suspect that I was chasing was armed and dangerous. With our chase still continuing and every Law Enforcement Officer within a three county radius trying to find the chase and assist with the suspect's capture, there was a lot of noisy activity on the streets of Picayune.

While the suspect continued down the street, he again tried to turn and fire his revolver at me and my vehicle. Unfortunate for him, and quite acceptable to me, while looking back at me, he missed a very important street sign indicating that the road we were on was about to make a 90° right turn. As the road turned, he didn't. He and his car continued straight for another hundred feet or so through the yard of the home owner located at the east end of Fifth Street... the "Dead-End". His car became entangled with several species of Oak trees common to our area and stopped abruptly in a very awkward position. Before the car came to a complete stop, the suspect jumped from the front seat carrying the revolver, fired several rounds in my direction, and fled away from his car into the neighborhood.

Being highly "occupied" with the process of stopping my vehicle without assuming a posture similar to that of the suspect's car, I was unable to "return fire" toward the suspect. However, neither my car nor I were struck by any of the rounds that the suspect fired at me. By the time I got my vehicle, safely stopped, and radioed Dispatch where we were and what had happened, the suspect had vanished into the community. After exiting my car and visually inspecting the inside of the suspect's car for other possible suspects, numerous Officers began to arrive on the scene. While Officers maintained control of the suspect's car, the other Officers and I began a search of the neighborhood. With the area now surrounded, we searched for the suspect for almost an hour.

Then we received word from dispatch that a citizen in the area had just seen an armed male force his way into an occupied residence near where we were searching. Upon getting the address of the residence, Officers quickly surrounded the house. After several minutes of shouted threats from the armed suspect from inside the residence, he jumped from a side window of the house and landed on the ground just outside the house. Still armed, the suspect pointed the same blue steel, long barreled revolver at an Officer near where he had landed. The Officer, being in fear for his life, fired one shot from his twelve gauge shotgun and struck the suspect in his leg. The shot broke the suspect's leg, but he still managed to flee for some distance before being captured and arrested by several Picayune Police Department Officers.

The suspect was taken to the local hospital for treatment of his injuries. After he was treated, the suspect was questioned by Officers. He readily admitted to being the driver of the "getaway car" in the armed robbery of the Finance Company. He also identified his partner in the robbery, the "inside man".

Over the next eighteen or so hours, I assisted Chief Kenny Bounds, along with Detectives and Officers of the Picayune PD with the investigation concerning the robbery of the Finance Company. After hours of going through records, and determining the address of the suspect identified by the now arrested "driver", we determined the residence of the "inside man".

Search and arrest warrants were issued by a local Judge, and just after lunch on September 13, 1975 (yep…13), a search was conducted upon the suspects' residence. As Officers and Detectives entered the suspect's house, he was found sleeping and was arrested without incident. Evidence was also found that indicated that the suspects had both been involved in numerous armed robberies in south Mississippi over the months that preceded the chase. We also recovered the guns used in the robbery of the Finance Company along with wigs worn by the suspects as disguises during their robberies. All the money from the Finance Company was likewise recovered. The suspect was processed and booked into the PPD Jail and along with his accomplice awaited preliminary hearings.

As I gave my statement regarding the events surrounding the robbery and chase to the PPD Detectives, we discussed how the suspect had fired those several shots at me and disappeared into the neighborhood. The Detectives expressed amazement that the driver could so quickly and comfortably escape into a residential area and just "vanish". We talked about how the suspect had forced his way into the local residence and had hidden from us as we searched the neighborhood for him. I couldn't resist telling them a story about a young man called "Little Red" that I had encountered several years earlier while working for the NOPD and riding in the #6 with Harold Richard. Like Harold back in #6, I told these Detectives that they too had outsmarted the bad guy at his own game and on his own turf. Because of these Detectives' skills and hard work, the two outlaws were now behind bars and would be for a long time. And like "Little Red", these marauders "never saw it coming" before it was too late!

A Hero is Born

As a quite important "side-note" to the above story, I'll mention that during this time my first wife Beverly, was pregnant. Later in the evening on the day that the robbers were arrested, we travelled to a hospital in New Orleans and Beverly was admitted to a room. She had gone into labor and at 11:27 am the next morning, September 14, our son Chad Gray Macdonald was born. Chad was a "preemie" and proved himself to be a fighter from his first breath. After several days in the hospital, he was released to go home. Since his birth and still today, Chad has always been one of the biggest motivators and inspirations of my life. He is in every way a "Hero" to me and to our entire family.

Chad and Dad showing-off their "catch" after an afternoon of fishing in May of 1980

The Cigarette

For the next several months, activity in R-5 was pretty normal. Then on December 4, 1975, we became involved in an investigation that would change MBN for years to come. I was very much asleep at about 5:00 am when the phone rang at my residence. That was still the phone with a wire that hooked it to the wall. My supervisor, John Souder, was on the other end of the call. It was not at all common for John to call at such an early hour so I immediately expected to hear news about something of significance. John simply instructed me to come to the Biloxi Small Craft Harbor as soon as I could get there, and meet him at the Harbor Master's Office. Then the phone went dead. Knowing that John was not a big advocate of drama, I knew that whatever it was that prompted him to call me before daylight must be at the least, very important!

Once dressed, I grabbed my *"possibles"* and left my house. Possibles are those work related items without which any self-respecting Narc simply cannot function. We all had, *constantly at the ready*, all of our possibles in what we referred to as our "Go Bag". It was never far from our reach. It still isn't! Upon entering my MBN vehicle, I immediately started to hear some chatter on the MBN radio/repeater system. The radio traffic was limited but was sufficient to indicate that I was not the only Agent that had been summoned to the Harbor.

It was about an hour and a half drive to the Harbor and when I got there, several other Agents had already arrived. I parked and walked up several flights of stairs to the Harbor Master's Office where I was met by Souder, the Harbor Master, and several Agents from R-5. John began to brief us on the situation. It seemed that the Harbor Master had observed a boat coming and going from the Harbor for several nights at extremely unusual hours. The boat was being operated by the same individuals each night. It was leaving the

Harbor in the late evening and returning just before daylight each night. The demeanor of the boat's crew and their actions had made the Harbor Master very suspicious that they might be involved in some illegal activity. With this limited information, we began a surveillance of the boat and its operators and ultimately a larger group of individuals associated with them.

After establishing stationary surveillance positions around the Harbor and mobile surveillance teams in the surrounding area, we waited for the operators to return to the boat. Having visually inspected the boat, we had determined that it was an off shore racing type boat, and the first one of its type. It was known by the relatively few racing aficionados who were

Open water "Cigarette" racing boat

familiar with such craft as a "Cigarette" racing boat. It was designed and manufactured in south Florida and as far as we could determine, this was the prototype. Long, narrow, and low to the water, the vessel could achieve speeds that would exceed most watercraft's speedometer capacities. It quickly became the consensus of all Agents present that whatever the crew of the Cigarette was involved in… they didn't want to get caught!

Soon we began to see activity around the boat and identified several people and vehicles associated with the Cigarette. By the end of the first day watching the boat, we had expanded the surveillance to areas throughout the Gulf Coast area and into Louisiana. Souder had called Headquarters and requested additional Agents from other Regions and had been promised every available Agent from across the State. Within a few hours Agents were arriving from all corners of the State to assist with what was growing into a massive surveillance effort.

In watching the suspects and weighing their actions against those of previous suspects and what we had all learned in earlier investigations, we collectively believed that these folks were involved in some type of smuggling operation. Believing that was what we were on to, we were diligent in our efforts to surveil the group without being detected. For almost a week we followed the group twenty-four hours a day. We divided into teams and were assigned to specific suspects. Following our designated suspects for hours at a time, we would swap suspects when we felt that we had been seen enough by our target that he or she might recognize us and become suspicious of being followed. We constantly "rotated" between suspects following them from hotels, to remote "load sites" to restaurants, to unknown associates and locations.

Slowly over several days, a pattern was beginning to develop and important "players" within the group started to emerge. Other vehicles were identified and activity at the boat was observed that indicated that something important was about to occur. One of the vehicles identified after almost a week of watching the suspects was a "U-Haul" truck. Having checked the registrations on the vehicles and boat, we had determined that several of the owner/operators were in fact suspected smugglers in the Florida area. Having never worked a smuggling case before we were all working pretty hard at the "Learning Curve" thing. But once again, having the good fortune to be working with outstanding investigators and amazing fellow Agents, things started to fall into place.

We followed the members of the group to remote sites near inland waterways where the roads were so narrow and traffic was so limited, we had to be extremely cautious not to be detected. We had no air support at the time so we were limited to our ground resources and the Agents' expertise in conducting close in surveillances. We also had no water resources, so when the boat left the Harbor and literally got "out of site" we had no way to know where the vessel went or with whom it met. We had concluded among ourselves that the inland waterways to which the vehicles were travelling were probably "load sites" but we were limited in our ability to monitor the vehicles and their drivers while they were at any of these locations. So we continued to watch and surveil the group for hours and for days as they moved about the coast and to and from Louisiana.

Then on December 11, 1975 the U-Haul, after having travelled to one of the "load sites", was stopped on a remote highway about seventy miles north of Pascagoula by a team of MBN surveilling Agents. The truck was occupied by three of the individuals that we had been surveilling for almost a week. Inside the truck was fifteen thousand pounds of marijuana. The suspects were all arrested and transported to a local jail where they were processed by

"Bales" of marijuana... samples of those seized during Cigarette Investigation

Agents and locked up. They were later interviewed and provided much insight into the activities of their group.

The marijuana seized from the U-Haul was packaged in fifty pound "bales" and wrapped in heavy plastic. They were then placed in burlap bags. We would learn that the plastic was to protect the bales from water during transit across the open waters of the Gulf of Mexico and the burlap was to protect the plastic from being torn. While the packaging was somewhat crude, it got the job done. It would also improve greatly over the next several years and become more compact, more consistently shaped, and better protected from the elements.

We all learned a great deal from this investigation and much more from those arrested during the seizure. For example, those trips out of the Harbor at night were all practice runs from the Harbor to the designated meeting location where the *Cigarette* would meet the "load vessel". The load vessel was to later arrive at a designated location after travelling from South America. After making a practice run to the "meeting" location, the *Cigarette* crew would then travel to several different predesignated "Load-Sites" along the coast and simulate offloading the cargo of marijuana. These were the sites near the inland waterways to which we had followed various vehicles associated with the group including the U-Haul. Then they would return to the Harbor and dock the boat until the next practice run or until the actual load. They practiced the entire process until they were comfortable with their plan to bring the load from open water to the load truck. They developed their plan and they rehearsed their plan until they were ready to execute their plan.

Part of the group's plan also included the placement of the

The Cigarette, shortly after seizure by MBN Agents in Biloxi. Dempsey Newman (standing left), Louis Guirola (seated in boat), Fred (standing in boat with cowboy hat), and others

boat, individuals, and vehicles that would be involved in their smuggling operation. They had placed the boat some thirty miles from where the marijuana would be off-loaded into the U-Haul load truck. With the range and speed of the boat, they could avoid, elude, or escape any Law Enforcement efforts on the water. With the boat's extremely low profile, it was virtually invisible to radar along the Coast... if there had been any.

The suspects were staying in several different motels which were some distance from each other. This would make them harder to identify as a "group" if stumbled upon by Law Enforcement. Therefore if one of their group became compromised, the others could continue with their operation. Their travels each day along the coast to meet and make preparations were also efforts to identify any possible surveillance by Law Enforcement. If surveillance had been detected, they felt that they could adjust and keep enough of their group unidentified so that again, they could complete their operation. For this group's day and time, they were quite sophisticated.

Thankfully, our Agents were equally sophisticated and with their experience as Investigators, and as street cops, they were able to flatten that "learning curve" and apply previously developed skills to what was then a very unique environment for us all. The Agents of the MBN constantly set the water mark for competence, integrity, and professionalism in the Law Enforcement community across the nation. The capacity to run this complex of an investigation particularly with the demanding nature of the surveillances involved, is a tribute to the caliber of individuals that collectively comprised the MBN at that time. I remain in awe of these men, their dedication, and their skills at a time when resources were limited. They most often had to work by the "seat of their pants" to get the job done and they never failed! They continuously and consistently took on investigations like "Operation Cigarette" and literally travelled into the dark, found the light switch, and got the job done! *Heroes!!!!*

This was the first smuggling load seized by MBN. It was to be one of many over the next several years along the Gulf Coast and throughout the State. A mixture of Marine smuggling and Air smuggling investigations would challenge the Agents of the MBN throughout the state. While most of the Smuggling cases would be made along the coastal counties, several Air smuggling cases were successfully conducted inland. Tons and tons of marijuana would be seized from various types of vessels and aircraft in a variety of circumstances and conditions by MBN Agents assisted by Local, State, and Federal Law Enforcement Officers. While each of these operations provided its own unique investigative challenges, each also provided a level of excitement and potential danger that kept us all actively engaged and cautiously aware of our environment at all times! We all knew and accepted that you could get hurt doing this stuff! Working with that caliber of Officers in those types of environments developed bonds of friendship, respect, and mutual trust that were deeply honored by those accepted into the group. The confidence and competence developed by this environment are rare commodities... They are two of the required commodities that make winners and winning teams!

How It Is On The Street

In late December of 1975, I was contacted by my former supervisor, good friend and current "Director of Training" for MBN, Agent Jim Walker. Jim had been running training since the "re-organization" in mid-1975 and worked out of Headquarters. He was currently organizing the MBN Recruit Class that was about to begin in Jackson and was soliciting Instructors for the program. He told me that he wanted me to teach a class in the school but he "didn't know what to call it". Knowing Jim well by now, I was more than comfortable in "jesting" him about his statement. I said, "Well Walker, if you don't know what the Hell to call it, how am I supposed to know what to teach"? After we both laughed at ourselves for a minute, he said, "No, really... I just want you to come up and talk to the students for a couple of hours, and tell them how it really is on the street and how to cover their ass and get home every night"!

Well... I was kinda set-back a bit. Ole Walker had just dumped the wagon on ole Fred. I was immediately struck with a sense of appreciation that overwhelmed me. To think that Walker, this Agent that I respected as much as any other, would trust me with such an unbelievable responsibility was more than humbling. To me it was epic! I had taught a few brief classes to small groups of Officers in very informal settings before but nothing like what Walker wanted me to do. The thought of teaching a class of this importance at the MBN Academy was more than a little bit sobering! I spontaneously repeated what he had just said and then asked, "Are you sure"?

He went on to elaborate and said that he wanted me to tell them some stories about events "on the street" and explain what happened during bad situations and how an Officer must deal with what's going on and... "go home at night". Well after a long conversation with Walker and several more in the days that followed, I taught what would become my first "Officer Safety" class to the recruits of the MBN cadet class in Jackson on January 9, 1976. This class would create the foundation from which I would teach thousands of Officers from across the nation and abroad for more than forty-five years. There was no possible way to have imagined how Walker's request would impact the rest of my career and life. And it all started because one of my biggest Heroes trusted me to teach those cadets in Jackson in 1976.

Technical Services

During those early years with MBN, with the leadership and unwavering support of our Director, Mr. Fairly, we possessed some of the finest surveillance equipment in the nation. Even Federal Agencies often called upon our Agents to assist with a variety of investigations and to support them with such technical equipment as "Bird-Dog" tracking devices, high tech cameras and video recording systems, body transmitters, and the like. Mr. Fairly had, at one time, been the head of that era's version of the federal "Grant" system within the State.

He had managed the dissemination of millions of dollars' worth of equipment purchased by the federal Department of Justice and issued to Local and State Law Enforcement Agencies. This equipment was literally the best on the market at the time, and for most Agencies, would never have been possible to possess had it not

Agent Steve Ford standing by MBN surveillance van in late 1970's

been for the federal *Law Enforcement Assistance Administration* or "LEAA" program. When Mr. Fairly became the Director of our Agency, he not only knew the best equipment available, but he also knew how to get it! As a result, we had the best of everything, and plenty of it.

A category of equipment that enhanced narcotics investigations particularly was "Technical Surveillance Equipment". Having obtained a large inventory of this category of equipment, and understanding its usefulness and importance in the field, Mr. Fairly had established a "Technical Services Unit" within the MBN. He had

Inside an MBN surveillance van of the 1970's

appointed Agent Jim Wallace to manage the high tech equipment, keep it serviced, and deploy it in the field in support of Investigations being conducted by our Agents. When MBN was decentralized in

1975, Mr. Fairly and Wallace established a network of Agents in each Region to be trained in the use of our High Tech equipment. This allowed "local" Tech-Services Agents to support investigations in their respective Regions with the technical equipment owned by the MBN. This system multiplied the number of Tech Support Agents throughout the State and greatly enhanced the quality of the cases being made in the Regions. Armed with technical corroboration such as audio and video recordings of undercover purchases, the Agents were able to successfully prosecute virtually every case that they presented in court. For 1976 this was no small deal! Before this technical network and equipment were available, most Agents went into court armed only with their testimony regarding any given investigation. Most often, the Agent's word was sufficient, but more and more, Juries wanted to "hear" or "see" the actual "deal". That required a determined effort, a lot of ingenious imagination, and the best available hardware to capture "recordings" of actual undercover operations where they occurred and present them in court. The MBN "Tech Guys" almost always made it happen.

The Banker's Wife

In early January of 1976 The MBN R-5 Agents, and other Law Enforcement Officers in the area, were requested by the FBI to assist with an investigation that was developing in the Gulfport area. The FBI revealed to our Agents that an individual had kidnapped the wife of a local Bank manager and was demanding a large ransom for her return. The FBI, knowing that MBN owned a covert surveillance vehicle, requested that we place our vehicle near the Banker's home and conduct continuous surveillance on the home and all activity around the home throughout the investigation. Steve Ford was our Region's Tech-Support Agent and had control of our surveillance vehicle which was known to all the R-5 Agents by its official MBN vehicle number "74". Steve also managed all other R-5 specialty surveillance equipment in the Region. Working together with Steve on a daily basis, he often requested my assistance with special surveillances. I had always had an interest in technical equipment and had, like Steve, employed this equipment in many investigations.

We met at the location where #74 was stored and made some hasty preparations to be in the vehicle in a stationary position for what we knew might be many hours. After readying ourselves and #74, we drove to the area of the Banker's home and established a stationary observation post or "OP". For the next several hours, we monitored traffic around the house and neighborhood. While we were "set-up" on the residence, other Agents assisted the FBI with other aspects of their investigation concerning the kidnapping. Throughout the hours that Steve and I managed the OP, we received constant updates from the FBI Agents involved in the investigation. We learned that the suspect/kidnapper had made several calls to the Banker and had given specific information regarding when and how the ransom was to be paid. He was emphatic that no Law Enforcement was to be involved in any way and he threatened that he would kill the banker's wife if he thought Police were present.

The FBI had immediately arranged for a "tap" on the banker's phones so that they could listen in on the calls from the kidnapper. They hoped to not only listen directly to what the kidnapper said when calling the banker, but also hoped to identify the caller by the number from which he was calling. They quickly learned that the kidnapper was calling from what seemed to be random "pay phones". Each time he called, it was from a different pay phone in a different area of town. As the calls continued, arrangements were made for the money demanded by the kidnapper. Because of how he was moving randomly about, it was impossible to "locate" the kidnapper and establish moving surveillance on him and his vehicle. With few viable options, at the time and location designated by the kidnapper to deliver the money, the ransom was delivered.

The meeting location was in an area of the adjoining county (Hancock County) just off Interstate 10 and near State Highway 603. The site was approximately thirty miles from the banker's residence. During the Ransom meeting, the suspect became suspicious of vehicular movement near the site. Knowing now that this was in fact the kidnapper, and convinced that he was acting alone, the FBI made the decision to apprehend the suspect at the payment site.

As arresting Agents moved closer to the payment site to apprehend the kidnapper who was still in his vehicle, he quickly accelerated and fled from the meeting site. Driving south on Highway 603 and then east onto I-10, the suspect fled the area with numerous FBI Agents, MBN Agents and a host of local Officers in pursuit. A high speed chase involving speeds in excess of one hundred miles per hour ensued. The chase continued across the Hancock County line back into Harrison County. With numerous Blue Lights and sirens blaring, the suspect was chased for another twenty miles into Gulfport where he exited I-10 onto US Highway 49 and travelled north from the Interstate. Turning off of Highway 49, the kidnapper was finally cornered and captured in the area of Norwood Village, a small sub-division just off the highway.

Once in custody, the kidnapper immediately admitted to the kidnapping. He agreed to fully cooperate and told the FBI Agents and other Officers that he would lead the Officers to the banker's wife. He did. In a densely wooded area several more miles north on Highway 49, along the Big Biloxi River, the kidnapper led Officers and Agents to the body of the Banker's wife. He openly explained that he had gone to the banker's residence and abducted his wife when she answered the door. He explained in a calm, unemotional and calculating voice that he had put the lady in his car, drove her to the spot near the river and shot her dead. He went on to explain that *after she was dead*, he started making the ransom demands of the Banker. By then there was no chance for the Banker to have ever seen his wife alive again. The purely evil nature of many of the "bad guys" who surround us all daily as we go about our lives in our towns and communities, can never be underestimated! Most of our population cannot imagine, much less understand the dangerous individuals with whom they brush shoulders each day, ...*until one knocks on their door!*

The unbelievably brave individuals who make up the barrier between these bad guys and the rest of our society, are the men and women who risk their lives daily to stand between the good and the bad and keep the good guys safe. Men and women who, like the Agents and Officers in this investigation, will go into the dark, willingly confront dangerous violent felons, and chase and apprehend these individuals, when necessary, at great peril to themselves. They perform these acts daily to insure that the rest of our society can remain safe with their families and in their communities. Most often, the protected go about their daily routines and are never even aware of the actions of the protectors. These protectors are the men and women of our nation's Law Enforcement Community. They are among our nation's greatest Heroes!

Gulf Stream Shrimp Boat

The Gulf Stream

Throughout the early months of 1976, the Agents of R-5 participated in a variety of investigations. Most were somewhat routine by now with undercover purchases by Agents being conducted daily. These required surveillances by the "non-undercover" Agents in order to protect the "undercover" Agents as well as corroborate the purchases and act as witnesses for the prosecution of those selling the drugs. Some of the purchases were for relatively small quantities of various drugs, while some of the purchases involved larger quantities of drugs and therefore larger amounts of OSF with which to purchase the drugs from the dealers. Remember the rule... it's always the same... "The more money involved... the more dangerous the transaction..." There were plenty of opportunities for us all to sharpen our investigative and Officer Safety Skills... We got plenty of practice. There were also numerous requests for our Agents to assist other Agencies with their Investigations, and we almost never refused to assist them. They, likewise, very frequently assisted us when we needed extra manpower, special resources or special expertise.

On May 10, 1976 we became involved in an investigation that would require much manpower, many resources, and all the skills that everyone involved could muster. Once again I received an early morning call from John Souder. John told me of another possible smuggling operation that was believed to be ongoing in the Hancock County area. He told me to go to the R-5 Offices and retrieve all the necessary surveillance equipment and meet him at the Holiday Inn hotel in Slidell, Louisiana. He also told me to contact Steve Ford and for us both to insure that we had adequate resources to maintain a stationary surveillance post in a rural area for about a day or so.

He further instructed that we should keep our radio traffic to a minimum due to the fact that it was believed that the smugglers had scanners and other counter-surveillance equipment. We had encountered several well organized criminal groups recently that were extremely well equipped with various types of technology used to detect Law Enforcement presence within the areas that the groups were operating. I told John that I would be on my way shortly and would see him and the other Agents and Officers in Slidell by about 2:00 pm. After I hung up my home phone, I gathered my "possibles" and headed to the Gulfport office.

I arrived at the R-5 Office about two hours after talking to John. I was met by Steve Ford who by now had retrieved our surveillance vehicle, #74. Steve had fueled the vehicle and checked to insure all necessary surveillance equipment and supplies were properly stocked in #74. He also had placed adequate ice in the "on-board" cooler and we had plenty of ready to eat snacks to hold us over for many hours if needed. While at the office, we were also met by another Agent, Charlie Spillers. Charlie told us that he also had been contacted by Souder and instructed to meet Ford and me at the Office. Charlie went on to say that Souder told him to come to Slidell with us to be briefed on the investigation. At about 1:00 pm, after insuring that we were all properly equipped and supplied, we drove to Slidell and met with Souder and the other Agents involved in the investigation.

Arriving at the Holiday Inn at about 2:00 pm, we met with Souder and several other Federal and State Agents. We learned that members of the U.S. Customs Enforcement Unit had begun a surveillance on a group of suspects believed to be involved in smuggling a very large quantity of marijuana into the Hancock County, Mississippi area later that night. The Customs Agents had been watching the group for several days in the Slidell area and had followed members of the group into Mississippi the night before. The Smugglers had travelled to a marine industrial complex in Hancock County known as "Port Bienville". During their surveillance, the Customs Agents were able to determine that the group had driven to what the Agents believed to be a "load site" on Mulatto Bayou within the Port Bienville complex. The Agents were certain that the smugglers were conducting a "dry-run" to the load site in order to prepare for the arrival of their load and also to check for surveillance that might possibly be ongoing by Law Enforcement regarding their group. The Agents were not detected and the smugglers returned to Slidell after doing their run to Port Bienville.

During their investigation over the previous days, Customs had been able to identify several of the members of the smuggling group and had determined through records checks that at least two of the group were documented smugglers within the U.S. Customs computer system. They had also surveilled members of the smuggling group to a motel in Waveland, Mississippi and had located what they believed to be the "load vehicle" that would haul the Marijuana away from the load site at Port Bienville to a yet unknown location for distribution. The load vehicle was an eighteen wheeler, tractor trailer truck colored red, white, and blue.

With this knowledge and other activities of the group over the previous several days, The Agents were certain that the group was preparing to meet a load vessel in Port Bienville within a day or so. Because the load was expected to actually arrive in Hancock County, the Customs Agents had contacted Souder and requested the assistance of MBN and the R-5 Agents. While in Slidell, the R-5 Agents received our initial assignments from Souder regarding our support in the investigation. While the bulk of the involved MBN and Customs Agents would be assigned to watch and surveil the eighteen wheeler, Steve Ford, Charlie Spillers and I would go to Port Bienville and establish a fixed surveillance post at one of the businesses located at the Port. We would also be assisted by a young detective named Kenny Smith of the Jefferson Parish Sheriff's Office. The JPSO had become involved in the investigation early on when the Customs Agents believed that the load would be brought in to a port in the Metairie, Louisiana area, which is within Jefferson Parish. Now that the load seemed more likely to arrive in Hancock County, the JPSO had requested to remain involved so that if the actual load site were to switch back to Jefferson Parish, the JPSO detective would be up to date on the investigation and could effectively support the Customs Agents.

After receiving our assignments, Ford, Spillers, Smith and I travelled back to Mississippi and into the Port Bienville Complex. Once there, we drove to the business with which Souder had made arrangements for us to use as our surveillance post. We had been given a hand drawn map of the area and knew that the presumed load site was a short distance from our Post. We also knew that the eighteen wheeler would have to pass by our position to enter into the area of the load site. As we drove to our post, we observed the entrance to the load site and the surrounding area and terrain. Other than a few scattered trees, the entire complex was covered with tall grass and thick brush. The cover was very dense and tall enough that it prevented visual observation for more than about fifty yards in any direction once you left the main road. We could not see the actual load site from the main road on which we were travelling.

Once we arrived at the business that would become our surveillance post, we were met by the manager of the company. He introduced himself and escorted us to a parking spot inside the main building so that we could place our vehicles out of site from the waterway and from the main road. After we parked, he then led us to his office area which was upstairs and provided a perfect view of the main road into the complex and what we now knew was the entrance into the load site. We moved all of our surveillance equipment into the office, pulled up four chairs and we settled back for what we all knew might be a long night. By now, Souder, the other MBN Agents, and the Customs Agents had travelled to the area of the hotel where the eighteen wheeler was parked. They had checked into several rooms at the hotel and were set up to monitor the truck and wait for it to move.

Because we were extremely concerned about "counter electronic surveillance" by the smugglers, we had limited our radio communications and were using coded language that we often used that was designed to mislead anyone who might be monitoring our radio conversations. Also after getting settled into his motel room, Souder had called us at our post on the "land line" telephone… the one with a wire connected to the wall… and told us his room and telephone number at the motel. Now we could talk with no possibility of being monitored. For the next several hours there was not much to talk about.

Then, at about 11:00 pm. Souder called and told us that there was movement around the eighteen wheeler. Several male subjects were going back and forth between two rooms and the truck and appeared to be preparing to leave the motel. Shortly after the call from Souder, we observed a large vessel moving very slowly up Mulatto Bayou past our surveillance post. The vessel was completely *blacked out* with no visible lights anywhere on the boat… inside or out. This was very unsafe and very unusual in the marine complex. We were certain that this large boat was bringing the load to the load site.

With our new information from Souder and what we had just seen, I would be less than honest if I said that we were anything less than plum excited! I called Souder back in his motel room and told him what we had just observed and in turn, he told me that the eighteen wheeler had just pulled out of the motel parking lot. He told me that the mobile surveillance Agents that had been positioned in their vehicles all around the motel, were following the truck and as soon as the truck was a safe distance from the motel, the rest of the MBN and Customs agents would join the mobile surveillance. It was "show time". I also knew that when Souder and the others left the motel room, we would be limited to our radio communications… we would have to be brief and guarded in what we "put on the air"!

After what seemed like hours, but was only about thirty minutes, we saw vehicle lights enter the Port Bienville complex onto what had, up to now, been a totally unoccupied main road for over three hours. Within moments we could tell that it was the eighteen wheeler. As if on "auto-pilot", the truck drove to the entrance to the load site, turned onto the narrow dirt road and disappeared into the dense brush. Because we did not know where the eighteen wheeler was delivering the load of marijuana, we did not want to seize the load at the load site. We wanted to follow it to its destination and arrest others who were suspected to be involved in the management and funding of the smuggling operation.

So, our plan was to wait until the truck came back out of the load site and departed the complex before our team would go to the load site and attempt to apprehend the crew operating the load vessel. With the help of a U.S. Customs boat and a U.S. Coast Guard boat which had both been positioned close by at the mouth of the Pearl River, we would also seize the load vessel. The mobile surveillance teams would follow the truck to its destination and seize the load and arrest all the suspects involved in the operation at that location.

After about forty minutes, the eighteen wheeler, old "red-white-and-blue" came lumbering out of the load site and back onto the main road and departed the complex. Knowing that the mobile teams now had surveillance of the truck, we put our plan into action. Ford and I were already in #74 and ready to move, Spillers and Smith had already started toward the load site through the brush along the bayou. I was driving #74 and with no headlights on, we left our hidden parking spot, drove onto the main road then onto the small dirt road that was the entrance to the load site.

Having never been to the actual load site, I drove very cautiously around the curves in the narrow road to prevent driving up too closely to the load vessel and potential threats posed by the load crew. After several curves, we drove onto an open area about fifty yards square that bordered the bayou. As we entered the open area, we immediately saw the load vessel. It was a huge shrimp boat and had its bow against the bank of the bayou on the edge of the open area that we had just driven onto. We were about fifty yards from the boat and could see from the limited star and moon light, that there was activity around the bow of the boat.

I drove #74 about twenty yards closer and told Ford "I'm gonna light it up". He said OK, and I activated the truck's headlights and two Aircraft landing lights mounted on the front bumper of ole #74. All of a sudden... It was daylight... Those landing lights were *retina scorchers* and would ignite tender vegetation at about fifty feet. With them on and now pointing at the load vessel, the whole eighty-five foot open water shrimp boat was "lit-up". As the lights came on we could tell that part of the crew appeared to be trying to lift the last remaining crew member from the ground near the bow onto the shrimper using a large piece of bow line.

Now that the smugglers knew that they "had company", the "on board" portion of the crew abandoned the "off board" member

and let him drop from the bow into the edge of the bayou. As he scampered into the weeds at the edge of the clearing, Ford said "I'll get him", and left me and #74 and headed straight toward the spot where the abandoned member hit the bushes. I had exited #74

Ariel view of "Load Site" where the shoot-out occurred between Fred and members of the Gulf Stream Crew

and was standing just outside the driver's door still well behind the lights emitted from the front of our truck. I yelled to the crew on the boat and instructed them to turn off the boat's engines and for the entire crew to come onto the deck at the bow of the shrimper.

By now, Ford was in the edge of the brush near where the abandoned crew member vanished and he was partially obstructed by the same brush. He was also barely inside the illuminated area created by the lights on #74. As I was trying to watch and listen for Ford, I realized that none of the crew of the shrimp boat were complying with my instructions. Just as I was about to yell at the crew again and glancing toward Ford to check on him, I saw movement on the boat. In the door of the wheel house on our side of the boat, a male subject stepped out onto the deck with what appeared to be a sawed-off double barrel shotgun being held across his chest with both hands.

I immediately yelled "GUN" to Ford and as I did, the subject stepped backwards through the same door and into the wheel house of the boat. Just as he stepped into the darkness of the interior of the wheel house and became only a silhouette, I saw and heard two muzzle blasts from the sawed-off shotgun that appeared to be fired in the direction of me and #74. Being no stranger to muzzle blasts, I immediately

"Ole #74" surveillance truck at the load site still parked where shoot-out occurred. US Customs truck on right, arrived later. Deputy Kenny Smith standing outside door of #74 with unknown officer

concluded that the subject with the shotgun had just shot at me. I also knew that those shots placed me in imminent danger of great bodily harm or death and that the same subject also posed the same imminent threat to Ford who was even more exposed to the danger than I. Still seeing shadowy movement in the wheelhouse from where the shots originated, I fired a series of shots from my handgun into the wheelhouse in an attempt to eliminate the threat and to provide cover for Ford as he escorted the now arrested crew member who had been abandoned from the bow of the boat.

As I fired into the boat, I heard the boat engines' RPM's increase and saw the boat slowly move backwards away from the edge of the bayou. I fired several more rounds at the boat after reloading and the boat continued straight backwards across the hundred yard wide bayou. By now Ford had the arrested crew member under control and safely back by #74. As I watched for movement on the boat, I saw movement off to my left in the direction

Bullet holes from Fred's revolver in cabin door of Gulf Stream

of our surveillance post. It was Spillers and Smith making their way out of the dense brush and into the open area of the load site. Looking back toward the boat, I heard a loud crunching sound and saw it rock sharply to the port side and come to a very abrupt stop. It had run aground stern first on the opposite side of the bayou.

By now with the sound of gunfire ringing across the marsh, both the Customs boat and the Coast Guard boat arrived at the load site in an effort to "back us up". After giving the customary instructions to *"heave two and prepare to be boarded"* the Coast

Gulf Stream and US Customs boat, after shoot-out

Guard crew boarded the shrimp boat and found it to be completely abandoned. At some point after the gunfire erupted, the crew had departed the shrimp boat on the opposite side from Ford and me and had "swum", crawled, slithered, and run away from their boat. Because the bayou was a parallel waterway to the Pearl River with several miles of marsh and swamp surrounding both, the crew had no idea into what danger they fled.

As the Coast Guard and Customs Agents searched the shrimp boat, they found that during the attempted escape by the boat's captain and the subsequent "running aground", the boat had hit its stern so hard on the bank of Mulatto bayou, that it had split its bottom along the keel and had started to sink. The propeller and rudder assembly were also heavily damaged which left the boat inoperable. The Coast Guard placed a portable water

Fred (left), Steve Ford (right), and Charlie Spillers (behind ropes) on the bow of the Gulf Stream shortly after shoot-out

pump in the boat and was able to keep up with the flow of water into the vessel. They kept it afloat long enough to tow the eighty-five foot long "Gulf Stream" shrimp boat approximately thirty miles to the R-5 office near the harbor in Gulfport. It was anchored there in front of R-5 for almost a week waiting to be towed to a dry storage facility in Alabama.

As the Coast Guard and Customs worked aboard the Gulf

The 18 wheeler containing 20,000 pounds of marijuana from the Gulf Stream. The truck was seized at the smugglers' farm in northern Hancock County, MS, near "Catahoula". (from right...) Dean Shepard and John Souder (MBN), others unknown

Stream, Ford and I met with Spillers and Smith and explained the details of what had just occurred at the load site. We also contacted Souder and updated him regarding the events. In talking to Souder we learned that the mobile surveillance teams had followed the eighteen wheeler to a remote farm site in northern Hancock County. The Truck had been seized by the Agents at the farm and found to contain what would later be determined to be almost twenty thousand pounds of marijuana. The farm was occupied by several individuals and they were arrested with the occupants of the eighteen wheeler. Also found at the farm were several other vehicles owned by the smugglers. Inside each vehicle and inside the farm house were found technical devices used to detect radio frequency activity. They also all possessed a variety of Police scanners capable of monitoring Law Enforcement radio communications. The group had in fact, been conducting electronic counter surveillance against our Agents and Officers throughout the operation.

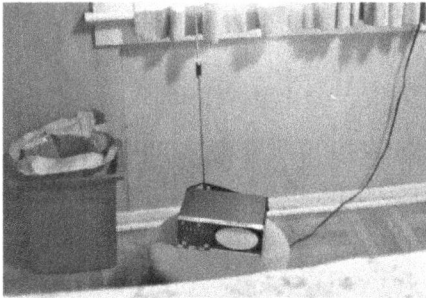

Police band scanner found at smugglers' cabin in northern Hancock County during Gulf Stream Investigation

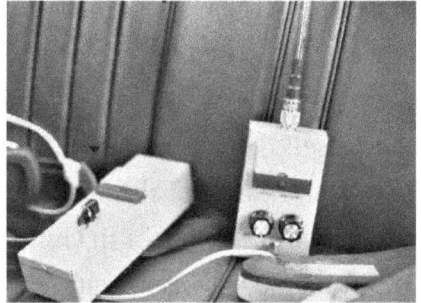

Counter surveillance equipment used by suspects to detect Officers' communications during Gulf Stream Investigation

Upon examining the scanners, we found that the smugglers had the radio frequencies of the Jefferson Parish Sheriff's Office and numerous other local, state, and federal agencies programmed into their scanners. It was later determined that the smugglers had in fact intended to bring the load into the load site near Metairie, Louisiana but during their practice runs into that area had heard radio traffic indicating that they were being followed. At that point they had switched their load site to the Port Bienville complex.

Over the next few days all Agencies involved in the investigation stayed highly engaged in the follow-up activities surrounding the smuggling investigation. A court order was obtained for the destruction of the bulk of the marijuana. After being taken to the Department of Transportation scales and weighed, the eighteen wheeler was driven to a remote land fill in north western Hancock County to be burned. Random samples of the entire load were taken on site by the Mississippi Crime Lab personnel who had been summoned to the land fill. The random samples along with several actual bales of marijuana were retained by the Crime Lab to be used as evidence in the prosecution of the smugglers. A bulk fuel distributor was hired to deliver diesel to the burn site to insure that all the drugs were consumed in fire and totally destroyed. After the samples had been taken and the truck was completely unloaded into a burn pit created in the land fill especially for the occasion, the fuel delivery truck poured several hundred gallons of diesel onto every inch of the mounds of marijuana from the Gulf Stream.

After insuring that all personnel had moved a safe distance away from the pit, the load was *ignited*.... And that is known as a

Over 400 bales of marijuana from the Gulf Stream about to be burned at a landfill in northern Hancock County.

"gross understatement"! When the diesel began to burn, the fire, smoke and heat from the pit were literally breath taking! The fire bellowed from the pit to more than one hundred feet into the air. The smoke was so dense that it darkened the sky, and the heat.... Well, suffice it to say that the *safe distance* calculated for bystanders and observers was likewise "grossly underestimated"! It was quite an event.

Having burned very few loads of marijuana by this time, we were all   somewhat inexperienced in the skills associated with these investigative duties. We simply had no way of calculating, at the time, how long it would take to burn twenty thousand pounds of marijuana in a landfill. As we were to learn, it is not a speedy process. After three days and nights of monitoring and guarding the burn site, while waiting for the last of the load to be consumed in fire, we realized that burning a boat load of dope was a lot like manual labor!

By now the packaging *improvements* that I explained regarding the load from "Operation Cigarette" had begun to occur. The bales from the Gulf Stream were more compressed and well wrapped in several layers of plastic and burlap. Because the bales were better compressed and wrapped, they didn't absorb diesel like the earlier bales had. The result was that the diesel would burn off the bales after penetrating only a few inches and the other forty or so pounds of marijuana would simply sit and smolder for hours before burning up. Each bale had to be manually broken up with rakes and other tools and re-saturated with more diesel. This process continued for days and nights until finally the load was destroyed. After the fire was out, the pit and the ashes from the load were covered with dirt by county bulldozers and we left the land fill.

Also during the hours and days following the shootout and seizure of the Gulf Stream, members of the boat's crew were arrested at various locations in and around the communities that bordered the marshy areas that surrounded Port Bienville. Because the complex was situated near the Pearl

Fred standing in front of the 20,000 pounds of burning marijuana from the Gulf Stream

River, which is the state line between Mississippi and Louisiana in this area, some of the crew swam and crawled onto dry land in Mississippi and some in Louisiana. Early on the morning of May 12, 1976 we received a call from the Sheriff's Office in St. Tammany Parish. This is the Parish that borders Hancock County on the Louisiana side of Pearl River and in which Slidell is located. The SO indicated that they believed that they had two of the suspects from the Gulf Stream in custody and requested that Ford and I come to the SO to identify the two crew members.

Ford and I immediately drove to the SO in Slidell and upon entering the front door of the SO were immediately spotted by the two suspects who were seated at the far end of the hallway that we had just entered. As Ford and I entered, both suspects immediately pointed at us and began telling the Deputies and Officers present "That's them…. That's the ones who sank our boat and shot holes all in it". Well… in spite of the fact that they omitted some important information like they had just unloaded twenty thousand pounds of marijuana and had fired a shotgun at us first, they pretty much eliminated the necessity for US to identify THEM! They had unquestionably and spontaneously informed us all that they were in fact part of the crew, had in fact been involved in the smuggling operation, and were involved in everything associated therewith.

The two suspects had been observed by a Louisiana State Trooper as they walked down old Highway 90 just inside the Louisiana line. As the Trooper cautiously stopped and approached the two crew members, they were so filthy, exhausted, and mosquito eaten from their experience with the marsh and swamps along the river that they immediately admitted to being the Captain and First Mate of the Gulf Stream and surrendered to the Trooper. He then transported them to the SO and had asked the dispatcher to call MBN. The Trooper was and is a good friend of mine and has always been highly respected by both the citizens of Louisiana and by Law Enforcement throughout the area. He later ran for and was elected Sheriff of St. Tammany Parish and had a long successful career as Sheriff. His name... Pat Canulette. Pat participated in many other notable events throughout his career and remains one of my great Heroes.

After identifying the Captain and First Mate of the Gulf Stream, Ford and I traveled back to the Hancock County Jail. Another suspect had been transported to the jail after being arrested in a small subdivision called "Oak Harbor" located on the Mississippi side of the Pearl River while trying to break into an unoccupied home there. The suspect was immediately recognized by Ford and me as one of the crew members who was trying to lift the last crew member onto the bow of the Gulf Stream as we drove onto the open area of the load site. The last of the suspects to be arrested was another crew member from the bow of the boat who was apprehended in Hancock County on May 15 by Deputies patrolling the area near Pearlington, Mississippi. As the Deputies drove down a rural dirt road, the last suspect simply walked out of the woods near the road, flagged down the Deputies, told them that he was part of the Gulf Stream crew and surrendered. At that point, arrest seemed like a very pleasant option for the last crew member of the Gulf Stream. He was transported to the County jail where Ford and I later identified him as being part of the crew.

In all, counting the Gulf Stream crew, the driver and crew of the eighteen wheeler, and the crew at the farm, over ten suspects were arrested in "Operation Gulf Stream". More than twenty thousand pounds of marijuana, an eighteen wheel tractor trailer truck, several passenger cars and one pickup truck, a farm and a large stash of electronic counter surveillance equipment were seized during the operation... Oh... and one *85 foot long shrimp boat...* The Gulf Stream!

As a side note, shortly after the arrests, a preliminary hearing was conducted for all suspects. Agents, Deputies, and Officers testified as to our roles and observations during the operation. All suspects were "bound over" to the subsequent actions of a Hancock County Grand Jury, and bond was set for all suspects. The suspects slowly began to post their respective bonds and were released from the County jail. Over the weeks that followed, we began to receive word that members of the Gulf Stream crew were being found dead at various locations throughout the United States. First, the First Mate was found shot to death in a northern city, then the Captain, then the suspect that Ford had apprehended after being dropped from the front of the boat. Within a couple of months, we had learned that every member of the crew of the Gulf Stream was dead as a result of unnatural causes. Other suspects involved in the driving of the eighteen wheeler and from the farm likewise had met their untimely demise.

MBN Director Ken Fairly (center with tie), Assistant District Attorney Dickey Smith (right with tie), and others, monitor the destruction of marijuana seized in the Gulf Stream investigation

It would be some time before we were to learn from a Federal Agency that an arrest had been made in one of the murders of a crew member from the Gulf Stream. The murder suspect admitted that he and others had been contracted to kill all the members of the operation by those who had financed the multi thousand pound venture. It seemed, according to the murder for hire suspect, that the financiers believed that one of the members of the operation had *informed* Law Enforcement regarding the operation and had "set-up" the load for their own financial gain. The financiers, not being sure who had set them up, decided to have them all killed to insure that they eliminated the guilty member. This way they would insure no more of their loads would be compromised and lost, and they would set an example to their other crews on future loads that they were not to be "double crossed". So much, I suppose, for the "It's a victimless crime" theory. Who says "marijuana never killed anyone"?

Throughout "Operation Gulf Stream" the Agents, Officers, Troopers, and Deputies who participated in the investigation honored themselves and their Departments and Agencies by their heroic actions. Telling the story simply does not adequately convey the true caliber of individuals who went into harm's way in so many phases of the operation, to make arrests and to take dangerous felons and contraband off the streets of our States and Nation. Although I am most often the person who is recognized for firing back at the "shooter" on the boat and "jested" for sinking an eighty-five foot shrimper with my handgun, there were many other heroic actions during the operation.

Remarkable actions, like Steve Ford running from the safety of #74 into the dark underbrush along Mulatto Bayou to arrest a suspect who he knew nothing about, set Steve apart as a true hero. He had no way of knowing whether the suspect was armed or not. The bravery of Charlie Spillers and Kenny Smith that they demonstrated by running through dense brush, in the dark, *toward the gunfire* at the load site to provide back up for Ford and me elevated these men to hero status. They had no way to know what they were actually running into, but they came to our assistance anyway.

The Bravery demonstrated by the U.S. Customs Agents and the Coast Guard personnel as they approached a darkened Gulf Stream in the middle of the night just after a heated gun battle, to board and search the vessel and protect the Agents still on shore, was legendary. Seeing our Nation's protectors in action from only a few yards away was like seeing the Cavalry come over the hill in an old western movie. It was humbling! America never looked better to this ole country boy. We all knew that our "Team" was "On Deck"!

And finally, the heroic actions performed by Trooper Pat Canulette and the Deputies of the Hancock County and St. Tammany Parish Sheriff's Offices were, to them, just part of their daily routines. To me and many others involved in "Operation Gulf Stream", however, these men also went into harm's way to support us and to take dangerous felons off the streets of our Counties and States. Their courage and dedication to our citizens and to our profession is still remembered and deeply appreciated!

As "Operation Gulf Stream" came to an end, all Agents, Officers, Deputies, and Troopers went back to their respective normal assignments. We had all learned a great deal during the investigation. We had gained valuable experience that would contribute greatly to our individual and collective successes in future investigations involving well organized and well-funded smuggling groups. In the years that would follow, we all would draw from experience gained here to better plan for and manage complex smuggling investigations throughout our state.

Looking back now, I know without question that the "Gulf Stream" gave us the foundation from which we launched dozens of smuggling investigations that resulted in the seizure of hundreds of tons of marijuana, hundreds of thousands of Quaaludes and other depressants and stimulants, hundreds of kilos of cocaine, millions of US dollars, and countless numbers of vehicles and other personal and real property that was either placed into service by our Agency or sold for funds that in turn helped run our Agency.

For over ten years MBN, in cooperation with dozens of other local, state, and federal Agencies, made history in the numbers of seizures, arrests, and convictions achieved against dozens of the most significant international smuggling groups of that era. Our Agents were second to none in their expertise regarding these highly complex, physically exhausting, and very dangerous investigations. ***They were among the best of the best and the bravest of the brave!*** **These guys always won!**

20,000 pounds of "Columbia Red" going "up in smoke" pursuant to a Hancock County Circuit Court Order

The Denham House

Exactly one Month after the last arrest in the Gulf Stream Investigation, Agents of the MBN were once again about to be hurled into an investigation unlike anything that our Agency had ever dealt with before. On June 15, 1976, at about 9:00 pm, I received a call at my residence. This call was from MBN Headquarters and was somewhat unusual. Normally when I received a call that required some immediate action, I would receive at least some indication of what generated the need for immediate action. This time I was simply told that there was an emergency in the Meridian area which was about one hundred fifty miles north of R-5 and directly east of Jackson. I was further instructed that I was to meet Mr. Fairly and other Agents at the Holiday Inn ASAP and I was given a room number at which to meet the others. I asked if anyone else from R-5 was summoned to Meridian and the dispatcher answered "just you and Ford". I hung up and called Ford who was just about to leave his apartment in Gulfport. He said he would swing by my home in Picayune and we would convoy to Meridian in our separate MBN vehicles. I told him I would be ready to depart for Meridian when he arrived.

About fifty minutes later, Steve arrived at my home. I was already in my state vehicle and we immediately departed for Meridian on I-59. The trip was normally about a two hour and fifteen minute drive. This was not a normal trip. We arrived in Meridian somewhat quicker than normal. Upon arriving, we drove straight to the Holiday Inn and to the designated room. As we drove through the parking lot, we recognized several familiar MBN vehicles and by now had a general idea of at least some of the other Agents who had been summoned to Meridian. On entering the motel room, we were met by Agents from all over the state. These were Agents who we all recognized as those who were summoned when "something bad" had happened and Mr. Fairly wanted his "team" present to handle the special situation. Mr. Fairly was seated in the only chair in the motel room and everyone else was standing or seated on the floor or one of the two beds in the room. A couple more Agents arrived after Ford and me, and then Mr. Fairly, not too calmly, stated "Boys... earlier this evening, a car load of thugs drove by Denham's house and fired three shots from a shotgun through his front window. They drove off, and got away. We have no idea who was in the car, or even what kind of car it was."

J.C. Denham was an MBN Agent that I attended our basic MBN Academy with in 1974, and at this time was assigned to the Meridian Region. Mr. Fairly went on to explain that J.C was not at home at the time of the shooting but his wife was. His wife had been seated in a chair in the room where the targeted window was located. Just moments before the shots, she had left her chair and walked through a door near the chair and into the kitchen of their house to put her empty bowl in the sink having just finished a bowl of ice cream. As she entered the kitchen, the three shotgun blasts rang out and shattered the front window in the room where she had just been seated. It was determined by Meridian PD Officers who responded to calls regarding the shots, that a total of six '00' buckshot pellets from the shotgun blasts had struck the chair from which J.C.'s wife had just risen. Had she not left the chair exactly when she did, she would undoubtedly have been seriously injured or killed by the shotgun blasts.

Mr. Fairly, in his own not so subtle manner, expressed his feelings to our group and in essence stated that this event was "not acceptable"! After explaining that he would provide any and all resources necessary for our team to investigate and solve this attack on one of his Agents, Mr. Fairly looked around the room and expressed his confidence in us individually and collectively. He told us that he would personally support whatever it took to solve this attack and bring the perpetrators to justice. We completely understood his sincerity and determination!

After Mr. Fairly's "briefing" we had a group meeting and quickly divided into two man teams to conduct the investigative activities necessary to solve this unprecedented attack on a State Law Enforcement Agent and his family. Our group consisted of about twelve Agents and we all knew each other well. There was no formal rank structure within the group. We all understood that in this situation, our two man teams would be directed by Mr. Fairly who would be manning a makeshift command post in the motel room where we had gathered. We were told by Mr. Fairly that he would have a team of secretaries and support staff in Meridian by morning and he would have a temporary office established in the motel room to support us with report typing, warrant preparation and any other administrative support that we needed.

I partnered with a good friend and highly trusted and respected fellow Agent Dempsey Newman. Dempsey was from the McComb Regional Office and we had worked together on many investigations including "Operation Cigarette" and other "special assignments". He, like Steve Ford, was one with whom I had "rode the river"! After discussing many of the investigative actions that needed to be accomplished, Dempsey and I left the motel room to begin what was to be a long tedious process of developing and chasing down leads regarding the shooting at J.C.'s home. We interviewed residents in the area of J.C.'s home and followed leads generated by those interviews. We followed up on other information developed by the Meridian PD, and other Agencies in the area which were trying to assist with the investigation.

On June 18, Dempsey and I were called to the County Court House to meet Mr. Fairly. When we arrived inside, we were met by the Boss and a Circuit Judge who were standing in the large hallway outside the District Attorney's offices. Mr. Fairly spoke to us and introduced us to the Judge. Then the Boss told us he had an assignment for us. He instructed us to drive to the state penitentiary at Parchman, Mississippi, and to "check out" an inmate there who he identified as someone who had made threats on Agent Denham's life after being placed in Parchman for selling drugs to Agent Denham. I asked the Boss if the Parchman officials would just "release" the inmate to us on our request or demand.

The Judge then handed me a Court order signed by "his truly" that instructed the Parchman personnel in no uncertain terms to present the inmate and release him into our custody *forthwith*! The Boss instructed Dempsey and me to bring the inmate back to Meridian to be questioned by our group to determine if he had any knowledge as to the perpetrators of the attack on J.C.'s home. Parchman was about three hundred miles from our current latitude and longitude...

Over the next *several* hours, Dempsey and I drove to Parchman, retrieved the inmate and drove back to Meridian. After a lengthy and in-depth interview that began upon leaving Parchman and concluded some time after returning to Meridian, we determined that while the inmate unquestionably did threaten Agent Denham, we believed that he had nothing to do with the attack on J.C.'s home. The Inmate was subsequently placed in the County Jail in Meridian where he served the rest of his sentence for the sale charges for which he had been convicted.

During the interviews with the inmate, he did however mention several individuals who he knew to be very angry with Agent Denham for his enforcement efforts in the Meridian area. After eliminating most of these suspects for various reasons, one seemed to be a strong possibility. After a quite extensive effort over a couple of days to locate the person named by our inmate, the subject that he identified was located. He was in the Navy and stationed just outside Meridian at the Naval Air Station or NAS. Once again, Mr. Fairly sent me and Dempsey to interview this individual.

On June 22 in the early afternoon, Dempsey and I arrived at the front gate of the NAS. We identified ourselves to the guards at the gate and told them that we needed to interview one of their personnel assigned to the NAS. The guards were very quick and blunt in their response and explained that we would not be allowed to interview *anyone* on the NAS. Well... I knew that this was not at all what the Boss would want to have us come back to the motel and report, so I asked one of the guards if I could borrow a telephone. He pointed to the building immediately to the right of the guard shack and said, "You can walk in the office and ask the desk clerk to use his phone"

So I walked in, asked the clerk for the phone, dialed the motel and asked for Mr. Fairly's room. The Boss answered the phone. I explained that we had been told rather bluntly by the guards at the gate that we couldn't interview anyone at NAS. There was a brief "Fairly pause" and then the Boss said, "What is the number that you are calling from"? After confirming with the clerk that the number on the phone was correct and that it would receive an incoming call, I gave the number to the Boss. He instructed me to stay by the phone and someone would be calling this number shortly that could "clear this thing up". He then instructed me to ask for whoever was in charge at the "Gate" and to instruct that person to contact his Commanding Officer or "C.O." and ask him to come to this phone immediately.

After hanging up with the Boss, I asked the clerk for his boss and almost immediately another person appeared behind the desk and asked what I wanted. I introduced myself and explained that the Director of the MBN had requested that the "C.O." come to this phone immediately and that it was of the utmost importance. That was all I could think of on such short notice. To my amazement, he picked up another phone behind the desk and dialed a number. I could see in my mind's eye, a black rotary phone ringing on a small table behind the "C.O.'s" desk. After a brief, very brief conversation, the "uniform" behind the clerk's desk hung up the phone. He slowly looked up and said "The "C.O." will be here in a minute". His look of amazement was only exceeded by mine!

Within three minutes, we were joined by a curious and not too happy Commander and adequate "Staff" to solve most worldly problems. The "C.O." walked into the area where we were waiting and walked up to me and asked "are you the Director of MBN or whatever that agency was?" I smiled and said "No sir" he will be calling in just a moment on that phone" and I pointed to the phone on the clerk's desk. The "C.O." looked at me and through reddening eyes said "you mean you got me over here to wait on a phone call…?" As I was about to answer, the phone rang. I answered the phone expecting it to be Mr. Fairly and was greeted by someone of a somewhat higher "rank".

The caller asked politely "Is this Agent Macdonald? I replied "yes" and he then introduced himself by saying "this is Senator Stennis, Agent Macdonald, is the Commanding Officer there?" *Point of explanation…* this was U.S. Senator John Stennis, *then head of the U.S. Senate Armed Services Committee*, on the phone talking to Agent Macdonald and asking *me* if he can talk to the Commanding Officer. Well… by now, I was getting pretty good at recovering from losing my breath, so after only a brief pause, I said "Yes Sir, hold one moment". Without introduction, I just handed the phone to an obviously annoyed "C.O.". He snatched the phone from my hand and as he was trying to say "hello", he suddenly snapped briskly to attention. Well, I couldn't hear anything else on the Senator's end, but every response after "hello" on the "C.O.'s" end was a crisp "Yes Sir"!

Before the "C.O." hung up the phone, his whole personality had been reprogrammed. I think… no, I'm sure he lost HIS breath a couple of times during his visit with Senator Stennis. When he finished talking to the Senator, he *couldn't wait* for us to interview anyone on the base that we requested. By now the "C.O." was recommending personnel to interview. They had the individual who we had originally come to the base to interview, brought to a private office in the building where we waited and we were told to use the office for as long as we wished. Dempsey and I talked to the individual for over an hour and obtained information that corroborated other pieces of information gained earlier in the investigation. We were slowly beginning to piece together facts about the shooting at J.C.'s house that could lead to our solving the case.

After leaving the NAS, Dempsey and I returned to the Motel to brief the Boss on what we had learned. When we walked into his motel room, the Boss looked at us and with a *Fairly grin* asked "Yall talked to anybody exciting today?" I said "not really, just some old guy in Washington with a check book." I thought the Boss was going to hyper-ventilate! We sat down in his room and explained what we had learned and what we thought we needed to do, to try and conclude the investigation. The Boss told us that other Agents had developed another *source* that might possibly help solve the case and add to what we had already learned. He instructed me to meet the source and other Agents in an adjoining room and interview the source regarding the shooting.

After a long tedious interview with the source, and combining information gained during the investigation by the other Agents, we had narrowed our persons of interest to a very small group. We felt that there was one person in particular who we had interviewed that actually knew who the suspects were. We decided to interview him again. During our second interview with this person, he broke down and told us that he "couldn't cover for them any longer". He went on to name the individuals who committed the attack on Agent Denham's home and wife. He stated that the "shooter" had confided in him and had told him exactly what they had done. What the source told us matched and confirmed everything that we had pieced together during our investigation.

Armed with this new reliable and verified information, we were certain that we had the right suspects. We immediately put together affidavits for search warrants and arrest warrants for the suspects and their home. After getting our warrants signed by a local judge, we finished preparations to execute the warrant on the suspects' house. There were three suspects and they all lived in the same rental house in Meridian. At about 5:30 am on June 26, 1976 MBN Agents assisted by members of the Meridian PD executed a search warrant on the suspects' house. All three suspects were still asleep and were arrested without incident. As the three were being helped from their beds and handcuffed, the main suspect, the shooter, spontaneously admitted shooting into Agent Denham's home. He said "I'm just glad this is finally over... we've been expecting y'all every day." During the search of the suspects' house, we found and seized the shotgun used in the attack, additional '00' buckshot rounds similar to those fired into Agent Denham's house, and the car that was used in the shooting.

While we felt that all the evidence compiled during the investigation along with the evidence found at the house and the admission of the shooter would collectively be ample proof of guilt in court, we would be surprised at the outcome of the court proceedings regarding the shooting. Within one month from their arrest, all three suspects had obtained legal representation. The three suspects, through their attorneys, immediately waived preliminary hearings, waived Grand Jury indictment and pled guilty to the aggravated assault on Agent Denham's wife, as well as several other felonies. Upon acceptance of their guilty pleas, *all three subjects requested the maximum sentence for their crimes.* The judge granted them their request and sentenced them accordingly.

Throughout the investigation, the Agents assembled by Mr. Fairly performed with the highest level of character and professionalism. Starting with almost no information or evidence regarding the attack, these Agents were able to piece together clue after clue and within less than two weeks, the crimes were solved and the suspects were in jail. From where the Agents started, knowing only that someone had fired into the residence with what was believed to be a shotgun and then sped away in the dark in an unknown automobile, solving this crime was a remarkable accomplishment on the part of the MBN Agents who were summoned to Meridian after the shooting.

Upon our arrival at the motel in Meridian on June 15, Mr. Fairly told us in his briefing that if necessary we would remain in Meridian "till it was time to eat turkey dinner for Thanksgiving"! Thanks to the skills and expertise of the Agents, we all ate turkey at home that year!

The DEA National Academy

In late June of 1976, I received a call from Souder which was a bit different than usual. He told me that he needed me to come to the R-5 offices for him to meet with me. A few hours later, I was sitting in his office in Gulfport. He handed me a folder that I could tell had several documents in it. As I opened the folder to inspect the documents, I quickly realized that it was a "Training Order". As I read further, I quickly realized that the order instructed me to travel to Washington, DC and attend the National Academy of the Drug Enforcement Administration or DEA, which was to begin about a month later. The DEA academy, at that time, was a ten week long school and all MBN Agents were required by our policy and by state statute to attend the program within two years of our hiring date.

Since my official "hire date" was December 13, 1974, my compliance window was closing pretty rapidly at that point in time. I also knew, after doing a bit of mental math, that attending the next academy which, according to the training order, would begin on July 19, and would not end until September 24. Continuing to "cypher", I determined that I would miss my son's first birthday. I was not at all pleased with that fact and immediately asked Souder if I could perhaps attend a later academy. He told me that I could call and talk to the Deputy Director, Larry Burris, and request to postpone my attendance, but Souder said that he felt that Burris was pretty set on my going to this class. I called Burris and after a brief discussion, that I believe he anticipated, he told me that I must attend the scheduled class beginning in July.

So… after taking about two weeks of vacation time, I departed for Washington on July 17, 1976. I first drove to Jackson and picked up a very close friend and fellow Agent, Steve Mallory. Steve *"Booger"* Mallory was also to attend the upcoming Academy. After getting Steve and his luggage loaded into my MBN vehicle, we departed Jackson. We spent the night in Atlanta and arrived in Washington at almost midnight on Sunday, July 18. We had reservations at the "Burlington Hotel" which was a mere stone's throw from the White House. After checking into our rooms, we moved in and began to get settled for the ten weeks ahead. We had both been issued "advanced, out of state travel funds" from Headquarters and were instructed to pay all of our expenses during the academy from these funds. Each month we filled out an expense voucher for our expenditures and were reimbursed funds to repeat the process throughout the school. One example of the "high finances" involved is that the cost of a hotel room at the Burlington, in downtown DC in 1976 was a whopping $21.06 per day.

After getting a good night's rest, Steve and I set out the next morning and located the DEA Headquarters Building in which the Academy was located. After completing an adequate amount of required paperwork, and being issued the necessary ID tags that would allow us access to the secure building during the course of the academy, we began DEA Academy Class #13 at about 2:00 pm that afternoon. Yep... Class #13...

Fred's DEA ten week National Academy
"Graduate Plaque"

The next ten weeks were to be filled with some of the most valuable and well-presented training that I received during my years with the MBN. That's quite a compliment considering the volume of training that I was fortunate enough to attend during those twenty five/plus years. Out of some fifty or so specialized schools that I attended, including four actual "Academies", this was among the best. We were taught classes regarding every aspect of "Drug Enforcement" including Drug ID, Pharmacology, Federal Drug Law, Undercover Techniques, Surveillance, Informant Management, Firearms, and dozens of other topics. The instructors were "world class" and not only had the education to present their topics of instruction, but had the experience to back it up. They had all "been there and done that". The training that these professionals delivered, affected me for the rest of my career.

One of the highlights of the academy was the "scenario" based training and the "practical exercises" conducted by the Staff. The resources available to the academy including a fleet of vehicles used by the Staff and students, rented houses and apartments, and a private radio system dedicated for academy use only, created an environment of realism in all of the "hands-on" training that was second to none at that time. Using these and other training resources, the academy Staff was constantly able to construct exercises that placed the students in extremely realistic situations. These exercises gave each student a level of experience that would benefit us all for many years to come in our "real world" investigations. Learning not only investigative skills during the training, but also how to develop and manage realistic scenario based training exercises, was to benefit me for many years into the future as I developed and conducted hundreds of Law Enforcement training programs.

Another highlight of the academy was the firearms training program. The Instructors were top notch. They presented the curriculum very effectively and brought all students to a level of proficiency much higher than when we arrived at the academy. We first started the shooting portion of the academy in a basement, indoor shooting range in a government building next door to the DEA Headquarters, but after a short while, we were moved to special ranges located at the FBI Academy at Quantico, VA. For several weeks, we would be bussed to and from the ranges at Quantico where we participated in various exercises, drills, and proficiency training with handguns and shotguns. We each fired many hundreds of rounds of ammunition during the course of the training program, and each round was well spent in a variety of constructive courses of fire. Each day after completing our live fire training, we would travel back to the basement armory at Headquarters and clean our weapons. Our handguns would each be inspected by a DEA armorer/Instructor and returned to the respective student. Remember, this was 1976... we were encouraged to carry our handguns at all times while on the streets of Washington. We complied.

On the morning of September 1, 1976 at 10:10 am, our class was interrupted by a young female DEA secretary named Gwen who worked at the National Academy. Gwen opened the classroom door and walked in during a legal presentation by a law professor from Georgetown University. Her entering the room during class, in itself, was completely out of the ordinary. But even more unusual was that when she walked in she looked visibly "upset". In her hand I could see that she was holding a yellow note that I recognized as a "phone message" memorandum. As she paused just inside the door, she first looked at the professor and then... straight at me. My heart sank! I had no idea what this interruption was about, but my "Police mind" immediately told me...

"This ain't gonna be good"! I was right!!!

Gwen motioned for me to join her and I exited my seat and walked to where she was standing. Having seen all the same "indicators", my trusted friend Mallory also jumped up from his seat and followed me to the door and stood by me as I met Gwen. She told me to come with her and we, all three, stepped outside the classroom door. She said "Fred I hate to be the one to tell you this but...". She hesitated, became somewhat emotional, and handed me the yellow phone memo. She said, "If you need to use a phone, you can have mine".

As I read the note, my heart sank even deeper. It conveyed to me that Deputy Kenny Smith, who had run with Charlie Spillers "toward the gunfire" to back up me and Ford at the "Gulf Stream" load site just four months earlier, had been killed the night before while serving a search warrant in Jefferson Parish, Louisiana. Ford had called and given the message to Gwen and asked that she get it to me as soon as possible. I immediately went to Gwen's desk and called Ford at the R-5 office. He was, understandably, just as upset as I was. He said that details were somewhat sketchy still, but he knew that Kenny had been shot in the back in front of a house that he and his fellow JPSO narcotics officers were searching late in the evening of August 31.

In the weeks that followed, we would learn that as Kenny and his team had secured the residence they were about to search, Kenny walked to his JPSO vehicle parked in front of the suspects house. With other Deputies still responding to the scene to support the deputies in securing the residence and suspects, he called his dispatcher on the radio in his car and advised that the scene was secure and that he would need no more Deputies to respond. In "Police radio talk", he called a "Code-4" on the scene.

Fred, Charlie Spillers, and Deputy Kenny Smith at 0300 hours on May 12, 1976, onboard the Gulf Stream Shrimper shortly after the shoot-out in which Charlie and Kenny rushed to support Fred and Steve Ford upon hearing the gunfire. The last time I saw Kenny!

As the deputies on the scene, who had been providing perimeter protection for the team which was securing the house, heard Kenny call a "Code-4" on the radio, they began departing from their assigned perimeter positions. As the perimeters began to collapse, the brother of the suspect walked onto his front porch directly across the street from the suspect's house and fired one shot from a rifle. The well-aimed shot struck Kenny in the middle of his back and severed his spine and penetrated his heart. The wound was not survivable and Kenny died. The shooter had obviously been waiting for an opportunity to perform the cowardly act and when the perimeter Officers left their positions, the coward fired the fatal shot.

I still have THE yellow phone message handed to me by Gwen on September 1, 1976 in that hallway outside the DEA classroom. I kept it in the top middle drawer of every desk that I occupied, in every position that I have held since that day. I inserted a copy of the note into every Lesson Plan and every PowerPoint presentation that I have used to teach Officer Safety classes since that day. Before each of the hundreds of high risk operations that I have participated in and/or managed since that day and in each Officer Safety class that I have taught since I was handed that note, I read THE note and reminded myself and each of my students that "It ain't over till it's over"!!! One must always make certain beyond every possible doubt that no more potential threats exist, in everything you do, before you let your guard down or…

"let your perimeters collapse"!

I hope that Kenny would be proud to know that lessons learned from his tragedy have helped thousands of Officers for more than forty years…

To get home safely at the end of their shift!

In the Academy we attended class from 8:00 am until 5:00 pm from Monday through Friday and had weekends off. We had ample time for sightseeing in the Capital and we all saw many sites! From the monuments, to the Smithsonian, and from Arlington to the White House, all were visited and re-visited by most of the students of Class #13. As the academy came to a close, we began making plans to return home to our regular jobs. In our class we had Investigators from every corner of the country including local and state agencies as well as the military. Many of the students went on to become heads of their agencies. One student became the head of his state's narcotics enforcement agency in Idaho for example, while our own Steve Mallory later became the Deputy Director of MBN and after his retirement became a Criminal Justice Professor at both the University of Southern Mississippi, and the University of Mississippi, also known as Ole Miss.

Doctor Mallory was and still remains one of my most trusted friends and confidants. The ten weeks that we spent together in Washington and the many years that we worked together with MBN created a strong bond of friendship and trust that has been significant throughout my career.

Graduation day and awards presentations for DEA National Academy Class #13. Fred is at far right holding "Firearms Award".

Finally at 9:00 am on September 24, 1976 it was graduation day. In a formal setting, the administrator of the DEA, Mr. Peter B. Bensinger, assisted by the academy Staff, handed out framed certificates to each student, and then handed out the "class awards". The "Academic Award" was handed out to a student who bested Mallory with his overall academic average by only two points, and the "Firearms Award" was presented to me. After comments and speeches by several of the academy Staff, the graduation was completed by about noon.

After graduation, Mallory and I returned to the Burlington, and finished our packing and moved out of our rooms. While I was to drive back to Mississippi, Mallory had decided to fly home and had asked me to transport his luggage back for him to Jackson. I took him to the airport and once he was boarded onto his plane, at about 4:00 pm I began the eleven hundred mile trip back home. After stopping in Bristol, VA to spend the night, I arrived in Jackson at about 8:30 pm the following day. I met Mallory long enough to give him his baggage and then continued south and to my home in Picayune. I finished my drive and my trip to the DEA Academy when I arrived at my residence at about midnight on September 25, 1976.

Once again during my experiences with the DEA Academy, I had met and come to respect many new friends in Law Enforcement. Both the students with whom Mallory and I studied and trained, and the academy Staff had become new partners with whom we would communicate and share resources for many years. They all earned a special place of honor in the hearts of two ole country boys from Mississippi!

Upon returning home from DC, I also made sure that a much more significant obligation was attended to. Immediately upon my return, Beverly and I held a previously planned, although a bit tardy, "first Birthday Party" for our son Chad. With family and friends around the kitchen table, we sang "Happy Birthday" to one of my greatest Heroes...

For the first time ever!!!

Back on Duty in Gulfport

Over the next several months I rejoined the R-5 team and re-acclimated to the MBN world of drug enforcement along the Gulf Coast. Arriving back in R-5, I realized that Souder and the Agents were just as busy as ever. I fell back into the very "un-routine routine" of surveillances, undercover operations, search warrants and arrests that were now the trademark of MBN Agents across the state. We assisted other Agents, Deputies, and Officers from all across the Gulf Coast with numerous investigations and they in turn, did the same for us.

By now it was early 1977 and there were very few days that were not filled with activities that carried us all well beyond the "normal" eight hour work day. Twelve to sixteen hour days were much more the "norm". At that time in the history of the MBN, there was no legal mechanism for the Agency to "pay" Agents for earned overtime. The only compensation for the hundreds of hours of overtime accumulated by each of our Agents was "compensatory time", a form of vacation time. The problem for the Agents (other than the obvious absence of monetary compensation) was that we all worked so frequently to support ongoing investigations that demanded all of the R-5 manpower, we seldom had a time when we could use any of our "Comp Time". So, we all just kept accumulating and accumulating hours and hours of Comp Time.

It was very common to begin an investigation upon reporting to duty in the morning, that lasted for several days and covered several states without the benefit of time off or the comfort of a bed. We became

Sam Owens driving a seized pick-up truck full of cocaine during a "controlled delivery" to suspects in Georgia

quite adept at eating fast food in the "driver's seat" of our state vehicles while conducting continuous mobile surveillance over many miles and multiple states. That same "seat" provided the platform for the closest thing to a good night's sleep that we might get for several nights in a row while conducting these surveillances. We would follow the suspects involved in the "investigation *du jour*" until they "went down" for the night in a residence or hotel. Then we would quickly establish "shifts" for our surveillance team to take turns sleeping "in place" while other members watched to insure the suspects did not leave unexpectedly and escape from our ongoing surveillance. This might, and often did, go on for days.

Once we followed the suspects to a point where the investigation ended in an arrest or seizure, we would return to the R-5 offices, write necessary reports from our notes made during the investigation, get some rest and begin the process again. In addition to the wide variety of "Narc Equipment" that each Agent carried routinely in our trunks, we each developed "kits". We meticulously maintained these kits which included extra clothes, toiletries, cash, non-perishable food, water, and other personal effects that we most frequently needed on "overnight trips" into our normal world of unknown and unpredictable circumstances. We learned to "keep our *stuff* in one sack" so to speak! Most of the guys and gals that I worked with in those days still have a "kit" in the back of their personal vehicles. I have mine!

Through the months that followed, we participated in a wide range of investigations involving numerous high level drug violators and a variety of types of drugs and other contraband. Along with the long hours working with MBN, we all dealt with events in our personal lives that added the necessary "seasoning" to insure that we maintained an adequate taste of excitement in our lives. One such event for me occurred in this time frame on January 22, 1977. It was the event described earlier involving Mississippi Highway Patrol Trooper, J.L. Johnson and the injury of his son while duck hunting in Pearl River County. What a day and what an event!

Also in January of 1977 my Papa Weston died from a massive heart attack. As with Papa Mac, and Mama Nina, I was out of town when Papa Weston died. I was, however, able to return in time for his funeral which was attended by most of our family and numerous Law Enforcement Officers from throughout the region. They had come to say goodbye to a much loved Papa Weston and a highly respected fellow Officer. After the graveside services, I remained when the crowds left. With permission of the funeral home staff, I covered Papa Weston's casket and filled his grave with a simple shovel. I knew that he would appreciate that! While it was a spontaneous act, it is a highly cherished memory of my last minutes with my role model and Hero, Papa Weston! Although I was certain that he was in a much better place, my world would never be the same again without Papa Weston!

What a remarkable Hero!!!

During the same time frame, the R-5 crew was busy and, as usual, there was no shortage of "seasoning" on the job. In late January, we conducted an undercover operation which yielded the purchase of over one half pound of cocaine from two well documented suspects for a negotiated price of $14,000.00 OSF, in the Jackson County area of R-5, near Pascagoula. On March 15, both suspects were bound over to the Grand Jury by Judge McCloud in Pascagoula and they were both later convicted and sentenced to several years in the state penitentiary at Parchman, Mississippi.

Also on March 15, after testifying in the above preliminary hearing, the Agents of R-5 travelled from Pascagoula to New Orleans and met with two Detectives with the NOPD Narcotics Unit. The two Detectives were close friends from my time with the NOPD. They were Detectives Louie Dabdoub and Andy Haab. These men were Legends within the NOPD for their many heroic acts and arrests of notorious and dangerous narcotics dealers in the New Orleans area. They were the "real deal". After a two day surveillance and undercover negotiations we seized over one hundred forty seven pounds of marijuana and arrested two suspects who later were convicted and sentenced to the Louisiana penitentiary at Angola.

Leaving New Orleans around noon on March 16, the R-5 Agents drove to the R-5 office. After a brief meeting with Souder, we drove to a classroom near the National Guard firearms ranges in Gulfport and met most of the other MBN Agents from around the state. It was an event for which most of us had been waiting and almost begging, for a long time. The MBN had recently acquired rifles for our Agency. Each Agent was to be issued a new Colt AR-15, .223 Caliber semi-automatic rifle. Because of the continually increasing threats to our Agents posed by more and more heavily armed suspects, Mr. Fairly had agreed to the wishes of the Agents and most of our supervisors and purchased the weapons. He had directed Jim Walker to establish a training and qualification program that would insure that each Agent was proficient in the use of the AR-15 before these rifles were issued to the Agents. That's why we were at the classroom. For

"Qualifications" with newly acquired AR-15's just being issued to MBN Agents for the first time

two days we participated in classroom and practical exercises that insured that each Agent was qualified to receive and employ their new weapon. We were then issued our new Colts and went back to work.

Quarterly Firearms Qualifications for MBN. Managed in part by... "The Four Amigos"... (L-R) Jim Wallace, Fred Macdonald, Dempsey Newman, and Steve Ford

On May 5, while working undercover in Picayune, I made what was a somewhat unusual case. Assisted and surveilled by Picayune PD Narcotics Officer Jim Luke, at about 1:06 pm, I purchased a quantity of drugs from a young female in Picayune. The drugs were depressants and were in capsule form. While the quantity of drugs was not overly impressive, the location and circumstances of the purchase certainly were. I had grown up in Picayune as previously discussed and knew almost everyone in town. Officer Luke was a Uniformed Officer employed by the PPD, and was also known by virtually every person in town. With Jim parked directly outside the front window, I walked into the local "Cable Television Company" offices on Canal Street, walked up to the counter wearing my MBN baseball style cap and purchased the drugs from an employee of the Cable Company while she worked behind the counter. Well... go figure! Jim and I both were absolutely amazed by the eagerness of the female to sell the drugs and her ability to ignore the obvious... a LOT of "obvious"!

Fred and "infamous" MBN baseball cap

After several more undercover purchases in the Picayune area during May and early June, I was offered the opportunity to go to another school. This time, it was one that I was eager to attend. Having obviously been interested in firearms for some time now, when I was given training orders to attend the Smith & Wesson Armorer's School in Massachusetts, I was more than excited. This was to be the first of many armorer's and firearms instructor schools that I would attend over the next several years. I was already an MBN Firearms Instructor and enjoyed this corollary duty a great deal. Little could I have imagined the many paths that this first armorer's school would propel me down in the years that would follow.

Then on June 21, I received a memo from Headquarters with a personnel order attached. The documents were quite concise and right to the point. The memo "explained" the attached Personnel Order which was a change in my "Post of Duty". I had been approached several times by Souder asking if I would consider moving closer to the Gulfport R-5 office. *His concern* was the expense involved in my travel back and forth from Picayune and the time that it took (about one hour) for me to travel to the R-5 office when needed there quickly. *My concern* was the expenses that I would have to bear that would be generated by another unsupported move by me and my family within the first three years of being employed by MBN. This would be our third unfunded and unsupported move in three years. I had explained that we had just really gotten settled into the house that we bought for our move from Jackson, and that there were other considerations including my wife's teaching job that she would have to quit. I explained the fact that in Picayune my parents and grandparents were assisting with the "babysitting" of our son while my wife taught school each day. This resource would be lost if we moved fifty miles away to the coast and in turn would cost us even more money. The justifications not to move went on and on and on...

These "discussions" had gone on for several months but were terminated by my receipt of the Personnel Order regarding my new "Post of Duty". I was more than a little upset! As fate would have it, I had been approached by several political leaders in the Picayune area on several occasions for more than a year asking if I would be interested in a job with the Picayune Police Department. After several of these "approaches", and after the receipt of my new "Personnel Order", I had finally called and requested a meeting with the City Manager, Mr. A.L. Franklin. Because of my dad's business and because he had been a City Councilman for several terms, I knew A.L pretty well. I really had no idea what position with the Police Department was open. So in my meeting with him in his office when he asked, after a lengthy discussion, "would you accept a job here as our Assistant Chief of Police?"... Yep... lost my breath! I was not expecting that.

Well, considering all things, this seemed at that moment to be a very timely and appealing offer! I told A.L. that I would have to consider it for a few days but I would give him an answer within a couple of weeks. He said that would be fine and after brief discussion about benefits, salary, and the like, I departed his office.

Over the next few days I engaged in some mighty serious head scratching and discussions with some of my closest friends and family. On June 29, all MBN Agents were in Jackson to attend an in-service training program at the Jackson Police Department Training Academy which was to be concluded with a "General Assembly". During the meeting late that afternoon, Mr. Fairly addressed the agency's Agents and staff concluding the day's session. During the final minutes before we were dismissed, he asked if there were any questions. By now, Mr. Fairly and I had established a very close bond and friendship that was appreciated by very few of the other Agents. Because of the original introduction by Larkin Smith, who we both respected very deeply, and many private conversations over the last several years we had developed a deep respect for each other that we had pretty much "kept to ourselves".

So, when the Boss asked for questions, I thought I'd throw my new "Post of Duty" thing out on the floor in front of the whole group. I raised my hand and with the "Fairly look", he said "What is it Agent Macdonald"? I said "I've been ordered to move to Gulfport". He said "Yep... that's what I hear". I asked if that was his decision and he replied, "I've heard that you'll be moving". Then I smiled at him and asked "Well then... are you gonna bring your old ass down there and help me move"? He looked at me again with the "Fairly look" and then *turned his head* and said, "You know if you need me, I'll bring a truck"! I knew then... He had nothing to do with my "Post of Duty" change! And so knew the whole Agency!!! The assembly was dismissed and we all went back to our corners of the state.

On August 16, 1977, I called Mr. Fairly and told him that I had accepted a job with the Picayune Police Department as Assistant Chief. I told him that I would be at Headquarters the next day to turn in my MBN issued equipment. He said to come to his office when I arrived at Headquarters. The next day at about 10:00 a.m. I walked into the office where I had first met Mr. Fairly some four years earlier and sat down in the same chair that I sat in during that first visit with one of my all-time favorite Heroes, Kenneth W. Fairly! We visited much like Henry Morris and I had when I left NOPD to come to the MBN. We talked about how the MBN had evolved and why. We shared some of our favorite "war stories" and poked fun at each other over dozens of historical events in which each of us could claim superiority over the other. We talked about the "sinking" of the Gulf Stream" and how the Captain of the boat must have looked when he "swam" out of the swamp straight to Pat Cannulette. I laughed with him about how Larkin had "bested" the Boss during the early days when Mr. Fairly was running the LEA and buying equipment for small agencies. He said "yep... that rascal wound up with the best of everything"! It was, once again, a great visit with a true Icon of the Law Enforcement History of our State! And... it would be the last meeting that I would ever have with Mr. Fairly as the Director of the Mississippi Bureau of Narcotics.

Section VI
Working for the
Picayune Police Department

Picayune Police Department,
Assistant Chief's Badge
(Fred's)

Within days of my last official meeting with Mr. Fairly, I was sworn in as Assistant Chief of Police with the Picayune Police Department. This was the Department with which my Papa Weston had worked when I was a small boy and with which I had worked many joint investigations since being employed by the MBN. Having worked closely with the Officers of the PPD in recent years, I had developed close professional relationships with its men and women, many of whom I had known since grade school. I was more than a little excited to be a part of the Department. I was also very eager to make any possible contribution that would better the Department. I was particularly interested in improving the working conditions for the Officers, Supervisors, and Staff.

My Assignment

During each of my meetings with City Manager A.L. Franklin prior to being hired, A.L. had made it abundantly clear that he was hiring me to help manage the Department, but also to assess the Department structure, its personnel, and its daily operations. A.L. repeatedly stated that he wanted me to evaluate the entire Department, and determine what needed to be fixed or upgraded. He had instructed me to make any necessary changes that would correct all deficiencies that might be identified within the Police Department. He pledged his full support for me in these efforts. During a final meeting before I was hired, I met with A.L. and Chief Lavigne in the City Manager's Office. During that meeting, A.L. explained to the Chief why I was being hired, the tasks and instructions given to me by the City Manager and the parameters of my authority once I was hired. The Chief agreed to all conditions enumerated by the City Manager.

*Old City Hall in Picayune with Police
Department in "ground level"*

By now, I had had the opportunity to work with many Officers and Agents from the largest to the smallest Departments, and from local, state, and federal agencies across the State and Nation. I had observed some of the best and the worst of policies, employees, and other assets that can make an agency great or keep an agency from being great. I wanted to bring all the best of resources, policies and conditions to the Picayune Police Department that would enable its employees to lift the Agency to the stature of "the best of the best"!

So when I arrived, full of big ideas and ready to go to work making improvements, I was more than a little eager to make a whole lot of great things happen as quickly as possible. Having been given full authority to make any and all necessary changes by the City Manager, and the Chief having been made aware of the authority and tasks assigned to me, I quickly realized, on arrival, that the concept of change and improvement within the Department was not exactly met with "universal enthusiasm"! The word that immediately comes to mind is…

"Friction"!

While many of the members of the Department were totally supportive and trusted me to only make changes that would benefit the Department, some were not at all supportive. For them, the *Status Quo* provided comfort and confidence and the mere idea of change in their world gave them great anxiety and disintegrated their "comfort zone". While this was never my intention, and I made efforts to reassure the resistors that my ideas for change were in everyone's best interest, most of my attempts to win "conversions" were unsuccessful. I hoped that as change occurred and improvements were made, some of these resistors would begin to trust me and support subsequent changes.

A few did… most did not.

By the time I was hired by the PPD, Hooper Lavigne had been Chief for just over one year and had succeeded Chief Kenny Bounds. Hooper had worked with the Department for several years before becoming Chief and we had worked together for some time. We had always been friends and had worked together well. Hooper's closest and most trusted ally on the Department at that time was Junior Penton. Junior and I also had been good friends and shared an interest in shooting and reloading ammunition. We all had worked closely together in many instances.

Crisis in the First Grade Classroom

O ne such instance had occurred almost exactly one year before I was hired by the PPD. On August 17, 1976, I was on my way out of town and received a call on my personal radio that the PPD had been summoned to a barricaded subject with a gun at the West Side Elementary School. While school was not in session, the environment in which the event was unfolding created its own set of significant circumstances. The subject had forcefully entered the school and then entered one of the first grade classrooms. He then entered the small bathroom in the corner of the classroom and had fired several shots from a shotgun. The shots had been heard by persons nearby and the Police were summoned.

When I arrived, I was met by Hooper and Junior and numerous other Officers who had responded to the school. The shooter was making demands of the Chief (Hooper) who was in the school hallway just outside the classroom. As the Chief responded and communicated with the individual, it became obvious that the shooter was very distraught and angry. Both Hooper and Junior tried to calm the shooter and were offering concessions intended to convince the shooter to surrender. The shooter was having no part of the "put down your gun and come out" scenario! As he shouted demands to the various Officers present, he would occasionally fire a shotgun blast toward the classroom door, outside which the Chief and others were standing. Twice during these aggressive displays, several of us who were outside the classroom, were hit by splinters from the door and door frame as the heavily painted wood was peppered with buckshot from the shooter's shotgun. The shooter's main demand was that the

Chief allow the shooter's wife to enter the classroom and join him in the bathroom for a "discussion".

The Chief asked what I thought, and I responded that allowing anyone into the bathroom with the shooter would undoubtedly be a mistake. I felt that such a concession would only increase the potential for injury or death to any persons allowed into the classroom. Instead, we brought the shooter's wife closer to the classroom door and allowed her to talk back and forth with the shooter from a safe position. It immediately became obvious that the shooter was extremely angry with his wife and would have done her great harm had she been allowed to enter the classroom.

After being refused again in his demands for his wife to join him, there was a long pause in conversation. Then... the muffled report of a last shotgun blast was heard coming from behind the closed bathroom door. The shooter stopped responding. After several minutes with no response from the shooter, we entered the classroom and looked through a broken window in the bathroom door which had earlier been shot out by the shooter. He had placed the shotgun in his mouth, pulled the trigger and ended the situation, his demands, and his life.

It was over!

With one brief radio call my night off and a planned evening out for dinner with my wife had been up-ended. A normally kind, mild family man, who was known to every officer present at the school that night, had committed a very violent suicide. He shot himself in the classroom where I had started grade school some twenty years earlier in the West Side Elementary School... *my first grade classroom*. Every Officer there was stunned and sickened by what had happened. I saw tears coming from grown, hardened, tough men and sadness in every eye present. It was a horrible situation that could have only been made more horrific had an Officer been seriously injured or the shooter's wife been allowed to enter the classroom and become another fatality.

Because of the courage and concern of each Officer present, a more tragic outcome was avoided. In our small hometown in south Mississippi, the Officers of a small, under-manned, under-trained, under-paid Police Department had gone into harm's way just as bravely and just as selflessly as any Officer in any "Active Shooter" situation, in any major Police Department anywhere in the nation! They joined the ranks of the bravest of the brave. There beside them was their Chief, Hooper Lavigne. Although none of the other Officers present had ever dealt with a similar situation, they all immediately used their common sense, and hometown experiences to respond to, contain, and manage a very sad and hazardous event.

First Grade classroom at the "West Side Elementary" school in 1957.
(Young Fred seated under clock with arm on back of chair)

Expectations

Having shared this and many other demanding situations with both Hooper and Junior, I expected them to trust me in my attempts to improve the Department. In some instances they did, but in most they resisted the changes that I made. In hindsight now, and from a more experienced platform more than forty years later, if I made a mistake, it was *not spending more time educating them to the reasons, mechanics, and benefits of the changes.* During that time I suffered not from a shortage of testosterone, adrenaline, or attitude and I most always operated from the "frame of reference" that I was accurate in my assessment of just about everything. Frequently, I was absolutely correct, but on rare occasion, I was not. It is possible, perhaps, that if I had spent more time educating Hooper, Junior, and others, they might possibly have become more supportive of my ideas for the Department. Instead, as instructed by the City Manager, I set about developing plans for the changes that I felt I could accomplish, and implemented those during the time that I was with the Department.

A Matter of Rank

During the short time that I was with the PPD, I was able to create the Department's first "Rank Structure". Prior to this time there was the Chief's position and a few supervisory positions but no defined rank structure or "Chain of Command". I created a Department Organizational Chart that depicted positions and ranks descending from Chief down to Patrolman with a defined supervisory structure for the Staff, Patrol, and Investigative Division. Each person in the Department could look at the chart and identify his or her individual position within the Departmental hierarchy, who was their immediate supervisor, and exactly where they fit into the "Chain of Command". While this surely seems like a condition that would be a "given" within any organization, it never had existed for the PPD. Upon the creation of the "Chain of Command", there then existed a system of responsibility and accountability within the Department.

For the Record

A lso non-existent for the Department at that time was a standardized reporting system. The closest thing to a standard report form was a "speeding ticket". Everything else was pretty much documented upon the closest available note pad or coffee shop napkin. Upon a search in the "Records Section", which was any one of several file cabinets scattered throughout several offices, one might find related reports written on any combination of substances that may or may not resemble a note pad. When Investigations were completed, the "files" were stored thusly until time for the case to be presented to the Grand Jury. Then the "files" were retrieved and taken to the Grand Jury where the Officer "presented" the case for consideration for indictment. Most often the "case file" was at best a compilation of notes that aided the investigator in his testimony.

Drawing on my experience with several departments and what I knew to be their excellent report systems, I created a set of standardized report forms for the PPD. Copied primarily from the NOPD, I created report forms for all major offenses as well as generic forms to accommodate unusual crimes of various categories. The forms had multiple pages or "copies" and pre-loaded "carbon" inserts. Yep… the phones still had wires connecting them to the walls and the computers were still *typewriters*… they still made loud noises and had no monitor.

So after each incident report was typed and corrected, using an adequate amount of "white-out" on each page, a corrected and approved copy of the report was filed in each of three specifically designated file cabinets. The reports were stored in the appropriate cabinet until time for grand jury or court and were then retrieved by the testifying Officer for use in the proceedings. Like the "Chain of Command", it seems pretty amazing now that standardized reports were a new element within the Department, but they were. It made a significant difference in the quality of cases that we presented and prosecuted. The quality of the Investigators also became more obvious.

It's All About Training

Training was another area that offered much room for improvement. Up until this time, many if not most of the Department's Officers had never even attended a basic recruit class. Remember, this is still 1977. It was not until April of 1981 that the Mississippi Legislature passed the "Law Enforcement Officers' Training Program" into law. The law was signed by Governor William Winter and went into effect on July 1, 1981. After that, it was required that all sworn Law Enforcement Officers within the state attend a state approved "Basic Academy" within one year of their initial date of employment.

None of that had occurred yet. Consequently, many Officers were hired with no training or experience and went straight to work on the streets as uniformed officers. Their "training" consisted most commonly, of "on the job training", or OJT, conducted by other Officers already employed by the Department. Often these "Trainer Officers" were "trained" through the same process. While some Officers on the PPD had attended a basic academy, most had not. Many of the deficiencies in this process are quite obvious... some were and still are, more subtle! The dangers facing the Officers in those days were just as real as they are now. They were magnified by the absence of quality training being provided to the Officers of Departments throughout the state, including the PPD! These brave Officers were out on the streets every day, going into harm's way, with almost no training at all!

Within a short time after arriving at the PD, I had implemented an "In Service Training Program" for the Department. Starting with

"Officer Survival" classes, I taught weekly classes to the entire Department. I also asked favors of other Law Enforcement trainers who generously provided training programs for the PD. We conducted the classes in repetitive intervals so that everyone could attend while not "on duty". This system allowed the Department to function at full strength and still provided the opportunity for everyone to receive the training. Within a few months we had the whole Department trained in a number of topics and had established our own training program. They had never had that either. We taught topics including report writing, evidence handling, arrest techniques, use of force, firearms training, officer survival, and others. The response to the training was probably the most positive of any of the changes that I made while there. The Officer Survival classes were among the most well received by our Officers. These classes taught the Officers important safety considerations and techniques designed to protect the Officers during the most dangerous of circumstances.

Time and Money

Among my many ambitions while at the PPD, was a desire to increase the salaries for all the employees of the Department. After only a short while, I became convinced that this would be one of my biggest challenges. I was told quickly, immediately, and without hesitation, that the City simply had no room in its budget to compensate for an increase in the Police Department Budget that would be necessary to accommodate the salary increases that I requested for the Department's personnel. It wasn't going to happen!

So... I set about looking for alternatives. My options were very limited to say the least. I decided to "go outside the ole box". I knew that many of the employees had "outside jobs" that they worked in an effort to make ends meet. I also knew that because of the rotating shifts worked by the members of the Department and the forty hour per week schedule, it was very hard for them to schedule outside employment while they were "off duty". The availability of jobs that would match their scheduled time off was extremely limited.

My idea was to make them more marketable by giving them more time off at more predictable intervals. This in turn would widen the outside job opportunities and give them more options for work. I put pen to pad, so to speak, and designed a Departmental work schedule that generated more days off per week for each employee by working longer hours each day. This allowed each employee to more comfortably acquire and work an outside job, if so desired, and in affect, gain a second income. It also insured that the employees continued to work a full forty hour per week schedule with the Department to maintain "full time" status so they could retain their insurance and other benefits with the City. Most of the employees loved the new schedule whether they had outside jobs or not.

The Machines

Throughout the time that I was developing and implementing the changes to the structure of the Department, the Officers and Detectives of the PPD constantly responded to a wide variety of crimes, complaints, and requests for assistance within the City. One of the frequently recurring complaints was of a somewhat different nature than most other daily calls from the citizens. Several times each week, we received complaints from citizens regarding illegal gambling machines or gaming devices that were commonly referred to by their generic nomenclature… "Slot Machines".

It seemed that these slot machines that were, at the time, illegal by definition under state law, were being offered for entertainment at one of the local semi private "clubs" in the western outskirts of the city. While all gambling was also strictly prohibited by state law at that time, these "semi private" clubs, in some instances in the past, had been allowed to "entertain" members and guests with such devices without intervention. This *historic* precedent created a significant legal dilemma for the *current* PPD. Once I was made aware of these devices' presence, I had a legal, ethical, and professional obligation to intervene. Remember, these devices were "illegal by definition", as in "contraband"! To interpret for the non-contraband-aficionado, what that means is that any duly sworn Law Enforcement Officer with jurisdiction local to the observance of said contraband, must seize, remove, and expeditiously destroy said contraband forthwith! In even more succinct verbiage… If you are a Cop and you *see it* you better immediately *grab it, haul it off,* and *destroy it* at your earliest convenience.

Now as one might imagine, in a small town, the presence of a "private club" probably would connote the involvement of persons local to the community who might both be members of the private club, AND be of some significant political and/or professional importance in the fabric of the community. One would be correct in one's imagining thusly in this instance!

So…. When members of the Picayune Police Department pulled up at the "club", seized all of the said slot machines from the establishment, promptly hauled them off, and within a very short time

"The Machines"… slot machines and other contraband seized in raids in Picayune in 1977

Jim Luke, Don Frierson, and Charles "Bogie" Stockstill destroying slot machines and other seized items pursuant to a Pearl River County Circuit Court Order.

Fred destroying slot machines in Picayune. With Charles Stockstill, Don Frierson, and Hooper Lavigne in background

went forthwith to an appropriate site, and destroyed the machines beyond repair or recognition, it was without great surprise that the Chief, the City Manager, all Officers involved, and I were enjoying a much diminished popularity in the local polls! Those who had even the slightest "interest" in the machines were annoyed beyond consolation. Some have never recovered!

The Officers who participated in the "destruction" with me were Don Frierson, Jim Luke, Anthony Gill, Charles Stockstill and the Chief, Hooper Lavigne. While we destroyed a great deal of other seized evidence from other cases that day, pursuant to court orders signed by a Circuit Judge, the primary focus of the community was firmly placed upon "The Machines". The political backlash, while completely predictable, was quite palatable for a long time from every corner of the City. We anticipated that to be the circumstances after the destruction. With that expectation, the men who participated in the destruction with me, did so eagerly, and just as bravely as if walking into an armed confrontation.

It WAS a *"political gunfight"*.

These men participated because they were…

W*ho they were* and W*hat they were*…

Heroes!

Calling all Cars

W hile at the PD, I had the opportunity to work with many outstanding individuals. Among those were the ladies who comprised our staff of dispatchers. One of these was Francis Lott... affectionately known within my family as "Aunt Frank". Aunt Frank was a sister-in-law to my... you guessed it... Papa Weston. She had been a dispatcher for many years and constantly watched over the Officers of the PPD, as did all the

Dispatcher Frances Lott at her post in the Picayune PD radio room in late 1970's

dispatchers. She communicated timely information to Officers as they performed their official duties each hour of each day, and monitored each Officer like a "mother hen" insuring that each Officer's requests were handled quickly and efficiently. In a time when there were no portable radios much less cell phones and the like, she and the other dispatchers were our only link to the world and our only resource for summoning support in times of crisis. They were our "life-line", and they all took their jobs very seriously!

Among the other dispatchers were ladies like Esther Doolittle, Shirley Culpepper, and Brenda Smith. They, like Aunt Frank, had been with the department for years. They were all highly respected by the Officers and Staff of the PPD.

Dispatcher Shirley Culpepper on duty in the radio room at the PPD in the late 1970's

They too had received only limited "On the Job Training", or *OJT*, and were often required to stretch their imagination to enable them to cope with circumstances which arose in the "Radio Room" of the PPD.

The Dispatcher and the Chief

Soon after I arrived at the PD in 1977, Brenda Smith had approached Chief Lavigne and asked if there was a chance that she could become a Police Officer for the City. Hooper told her that she could, but only if she would meet strict physical requirements as defined by him during their discussion. Brenda immediately went about losing a massive amount of weight and meeting all the requirements as set forth by the Chief. After several months, Brenda again met with the Chief with accompanying Doctor's documentation verifying that Brenda had met all of the Chief's requirements. With documents in hand, she again asked to be hired as a Police Officer with the PPD.

Instead of immediately elevating Brenda to the position of Police Officer, the Chief declined her request and told her he would not hire her. She was understandably devastated. As she was leaving the Chief's office headed to her vehicle to go home, I met her just outside the front door of the Department. During a brief conversation, she explained the outcome of her meeting with the Chief. I left Brenda and went upstairs to the City Manager's Office and walked into his private office. He was in a meeting and I interrupted and told him that I needed to speak to him immediately. He asked the other individuals in the meeting to excuse us for a few minutes and they exited the room. I closed A.L.'s office door and turned to see a somewhat "flustered" City Manager seated behind his desk staring at me with that "what the heck" look.

I explained the situation in which Brenda had found herself. I also expressed my strong opinion that due to the promises made by the Chief several months earlier and the fact that Brenda had met or exceeded all of the Chief's requirements, she should be immediately elevated to the position of Police Officer. While, in actuality, there was a somewhat longer version of my description of events, circumstances, and obligations, suffice it to say, A.L. quickly and completely agreed with my assessments. He told me he would instruct the Chief to hire Brenda immediately as a Police Officer for the City. Well... A.L. did, the Chief did, and in late 1977, the Picayune Police Department had, for the first time ever in its history... *its first*... female Police Officer, Brenda Smith!

After being hired Brenda didn't stop there, nor did she ever fail to continually "out-do" herself at every stage of her career. In addition to being an outstanding Officer, over the next several years she rose to the rank of Captain and attained the position of "Patrol Commander". In 1985 Brenda became the first Officer ever from the Picayune Police Department to attend the prestigious FBI National Academy.

Dispatcher Brenda Smith at the Picayune PD in late 1970's. Throughout a career of demonstrated courage and fortitude, Brenda became one of my Greatest Heroes!

After returning to the PD and working for several more years, in August of 1996 Brenda was appointed as Chief of Police for the Picayune Police Department as its first ever female Chief. She served as Chief for almost seven years... and remains one of the longest serving Chiefs in the history of the Department.

In 1990, Brenda helped create a "Police Explorer" Post at the PPD under the supervision of then Chief, Freddy Drennan. This is a program that exposes youth to the responsibilities and duties of Police Officers. In 1991, Brenda was approached by one of the young men who had been in the "Explorers" for several months. His name was

Joseph "Joey" Coleman. After a discussion with Brenda, Joey told her that he had something he wanted to share with her. Brenda immediately encouraged the young man to "tell her anything"... Joey said, I just wanted you to know that my dad, Philip Coleman, was one of the NOPD Officers killed at the Howard Johnson in 1973.

Brenda almost lost her breath... After that, Brenda and Joey enjoyed a special friendship that still lasts even today. And as a side note... Joey later became a Police Officer for the Slidell, Louisiana Police Department by whom he is still employed today. When Brenda told me this story, it was difficult not to become emotional. In 1973, standing in the bitter cold outside Charity Hospital during that thirty-six hour siege, I could never have imagined that some seventeen years later, the infant son of one of my fellow NOPD Officers murdered at the Howard Johnson Incident, would be mentored at the Picayune Police Department by one of my biggest Heroes... Brenda Smith.

After originally being hired as a Dispatcher for the Picayune Police Department in 1973, Brenda retired as the Chief of Police in 2003 after a model career with the PPD. Throughout her entire career, Brenda continuously distinguished herself as a true professional and one of the finest and bravest Officers ever to wear the badge of the Picayune Police Department!

She had been *"The Dispatcher and The Chief"*, and just about everything in between!!

Brenda is, and always has been, a true Hero!

What About MBN

S oon after going to work with the PD, I started receiving calls from several of my MBN friends who kept me abreast of current events within the Agency and the many personnel changes that were beginning to occur statewide. I returned several times to testify in the trials of suspects in whose arrests I had participated. Invariably, I would be questioned as to when I would leave the PPD and return to work for MBN. For a while I deflected the queries and would jest with the curious by stating that I had "found a home" with the PPD. However, in learning of some of the changes within the MBN, I continuously had my interest elevated until it was eventually hard to suppress.

About six to eight months into my time with the PPD, I received several calls from my good friend Jim Wallace with MBN. Jim was still the Agent in Charge of the Technical Services Division of the MBN in Jackson. His calls were to inform me that he expected to soon be promoted to "Region Commander" for the northern region of Mississippi for MBN. This was to be a promotion that would cause him to move his residence to the Oxford area and would also leave a vacancy in the command of "Tech Services" as his current unit was most often referenced. Jim's calls eventually moved in the direction of encouragement for me to return to the MBN and assume command of Tech Services". Knowing that his promotion was eminent, this prospect was extremely difficult for me to ignore.

To Stay or Not To Stay...

While gaining some ground within the PPD regarding support for my ideas and changes, several of the strongest resistors, including Hooper and Junior were staunch in their positions of non-acceptance. I knew that these and others were going to make it very difficult to move very far forward of where the Department had advanced up to that time. Without their support or the full support and authority of the City Manager, future "improvements" would be impossible.

While the changes that I was trying to implement made all the sense in the world to me, these "old friends" simply were not buying into the "big picture" that I was trying to paint. As stated before, had I possessed the experiences then that I collected in the many years that followed, I would possibly have handled things a bit differently than I did then. Would it have made a difference...? Maybe, and maybe not...! I simply had done the best I could with what I had to work with at the time.

During a series of long conversations with the Picayune City Manager, I had asked many direct questions regarding how he felt about the condition of the Police Department and what he was willing to support as I moved forward to accomplish all the "changes" that he had encouraged when he hired me. While he was extremely pleased with the improvements already accomplished, his answers to my questions indicated some hesitation to support other much needed modifications.

In addition, the time frame of six months from my original date of employment had come and gone. This was the period during which A.L. had insured me that there would be a command structure re-alignment of the top positions within the PD and I would be made Chief. Although a condition for my acceptance of the job as Assistant Chief, my promotion to Chief had not happened. At this juncture, I believed that my ability to make much needed improvements to the Department was about to become static. So, after weighing all my options carefully, I came to the unchallenged conclusion that returning to the MBN offered an awesome career enhancement opportunity!

In leaving the Picayune Police Department, my thoughts were once again directed to the outstanding men and women who comprised the Agency. While there were those with whom I held deep differences of professional opinion, I believe that most of the Officers and Staff were outstanding people and Law Enforcement Officers! Men and Women like Don Frierson, Jim Luke, Danny

McNeil, Danny Goynes, Charles Stockstill, Rochelle Marx, Anthony Gill, Brenda Smith, and others, worked tirelessly for many years to *Protect and Serve* the citizens of Picayune.

They worked long difficult hours for low pay in what were frequently the most adverse of circumstances so that the people of the community could go about their daily activities and sleep safely in their homes at night. They went often into harm's way because they were and are made of the same "stuff" that was the core fiber of all the other Heroes with whom I have worked for fifty years.

They are all "the real deal"!!!

And they are all great Heroes with whom I rode!

Officer Jim Luke and others lower the flag at the Picayune PD and City Hall. Jim later served as the Chief of Police in Picayune and is currently the City Manager. Jim remains a close friend and has been a Hero to many.

Section VII
Back to Stay, at MBN?

During my visit with Mr. Fairly just before leaving the MBN in 1977, he asked several questions in an attempt to guide me in the direction of a good "decision" regarding my planned career move to Picayune. One of the questions has stuck in my mind since the words left his lips! Looking over the top of his half-frame reading glasses he asked... "Son.... Do you know what the professional life expectancy of a Chief of Police is, much less an *Assistant* Chief of Police...?"

For clarity and proper emphasis, each of those bold and underlined "O"s was uttered with the ever present distinction of a Fairly "*long* O", grammatically speaking of course. His unique conversational tone and method of "delivery" set most of his comments, and especially his admonishments, widely apart from any other Boss for whom I have ever worked! He was just simply... THE BEST!

So when I responded honestly that I had no idea what the life expectancy was, he was as usual, short and to the point! He simply said "Well son... It ain't long!" He was, as usual, correct. At the time that Mr. Fairly had issued that admonishment, there was no way that he could have known that before I would leave the PPD, he would be leaving the MBN.

After the most recent gubernatorial election, the position of MBN Director became a much sought after state government position. Shortly before I left the PPD to return to MBN, a new Director had been appointed by the new Governor to replace our highly respected and highly trusted first director, Mr. Kenneth W. Fairly. The new Director was Chester Quarles, PhD. He had been a professor at the University of Mississippi at Oxford more commonly referenced as

"Ole Miss". Along with him came a new Deputy Director/Chief of Enforcement, William "Bill" Turcotte.

Other Agents and Supervisors had also departed the Agency since I left less than a year earlier. Among these were Larry Burris, John Souder, Steve Ford, Louis Guirola and many others. The fabric of the MBN, comprised of the original Agents hired by Mr. Fairly, was beginning to fade. While the Agency would continue to be manned by some of the most professional and competent Agents and support staff anywhere in the nation, with Mr. Fairly gone, the MBN was also changed forever! The "Boss's Office" would never be the same again!

On May 1, 1978, I returned to work as an Agent for the MBN. I was allowed, this time, to continue to reside in the Picayune area. Going through a divorce at that time, I had moved into a gated community just north of Picayune called "Hide-A-Way Lake". I had rented a house in this community and would live there for about a year before moving back into town. Knowing that I was to be taking command of the Tech Services Unit for MBN, I had accepted the fact that I would be working "statewide" and would be required to travel constantly to meet the requirements of that position. While I was fine with that, it would have been impossible to have predicted just how accurately "travel constantly" described my next several years. But… as they say… there was *never* a dull moment! *NEVER!!!*

After barely settling back into the job, I was hurled into a variety of investigations throughout the state. Having had a long time interest in many aspects of Tech Services, I had developed adequate skills in some of my responsibilities including photography, audio and video recordings, tracking devices, surveillance and such. With new "tools" at my disposal, I sought the mentoring of my great friend and "high tech guru" of the time, James R. "Jim" Wallace.

Fred about to enter an MBN surveillance van "on assignment" during an undercover operation in southwest Mississippi

Having created and developed the Tech Services Unit, Jim knew how to use, build, repair, and design equipment that I had only seen in brief glimpses as he would open cabinets deep within the confines of the most protected of MBN spaces at Headquarters. These were the "Top Secret" areas of MBN. If there was an equivalent to the US Military's *"Area 51"* At MBN Headquarters, this was it. In those cabinets were stored surveillance devices that most other agencies would have given many treasures to possess and employ in their efforts to gain useful evidence with which to prosecute the "bad guys" that they pursued each day. We had surveillance equipment that even the federal agents, with whom we worked, coveted!

The Tech Services Unit provided many tools and skills in support of ongoing investigations by Agents around the state in the various districts and regions. Working under Wallace's wing for several months upon returning to MBN, he "opened the cabinets" for me. I learned not only what our equipment resources were, but he also taught me the proper application, use, and maintenance of these highly technical and sensitive devices. I had not had so much fun since Papa Weston gave me that old "broken radio" years earlier. I think, like Papa Weston, Jim was shocked that I could get some of his high tech toys to actually work... Little could I have known more than twenty years earlier that Papa Weston had discovered a future "Tech Guy" and cultivated an interest that would last an entire career and beyond! *Technically*, it has been an adventure!!!

We were regularly called upon to conduct surveillances in the most demanding of circumstances. Providing support to Agents in both urban and extremely rural areas, our imagination and the versatility of our equipment was constantly being tested. It was not uncommon to drive one of our surveillance vans for hours to arrive in an area of the state where an undercover purchase was to occur. We might set up for long periods waiting to take photographs of the drugs and OSF exchanging hands between one or

Inside the surveillance van in which Fred spent many hours monitoring and recording hundreds of investigations

more of our Agents and the dealers who were selling the drugs. After documenting these transactions, we might drive back to Headquarters only to again drive or fly into another District at the other end of the state to repeat the surveillance process for other Agents. With Agents throughout the state constantly initiating high level undercover investigations involving major drug traffickers, and an increasing demand from prosecutors for more and better technical surveillance documentation of these cases, there was no shortage of requests for our services.

Cookin' with our New Microwave

One of the investigative challenges that was just starting to reveal itself was the presence and increasing frequency of *drug labs* within the state. While there were many types of clandestine labs for sure, the most frequently encountered were either "PCP" or "Amphetamine" labs. In late May of 1978, Jim and I were summoned to Meridian... the same town where J.C. Denham's house was shot into.

It seemed that DEA and MBN Agents had followed a known lab builder and operator to a mini warehouse business on old Highway 45, in the northern edge of town. The DEA had gotten a tip that the suspect was acquiring a very large quantity of "precursor" chemicals from a chemical company in Illinois. The suspect had been located and then was followed by DEA, MBN, and other Law Enforcement Officers to the mini storage, in Meridian. Once there, he had unloaded all the chemicals into a unit that he had obviously rented earlier. Upon unloading the chemicals, the suspect had locked the unit and departed the area. He then drove to the Jackson, Mississippi, area where he was lost by the surveilling Agents.

We knew that the suspect would have to recover the precursors from the mini storage in Meridian before he could operate his lab and manufacture PCP. We knew also that if we watched the mini storage, we could intercept the suspect and follow him and the precursors to the location of the lab. Our job, was to install a camera at the mini storage facility that could be transmitted back to a surveillance location manned by Agents who would watch the unit day and night until the suspect returned for his stash of chemicals. Sounds easy enough, *right*? Well… in 1978, it was definitely *NOT* an easy job!

To accomplish this seemingly simple task, Wallace and I would need to employ one of our most recently acquired surveillance options… our "Microwave" video and audio transmit/receive system. While that also sounds like a simple enough chore, one must again remember… *1978*, and the word *"system"*. Back then, any technology that included the word "system", probably required a full sized pickup truck to transport the containers in which the "system" was normally stored. Our "Microwave" system was no exception.

What can now be accomplished with a smart phone, with much higher quality audio and video, wirelessly from one phone to the other from anywhere in the world, in 1978 it took us four full days to set up, test and activate our system. Installing the system involved physically climbing local radio towers, up to heights of one thousand feet, to install and align both transmit and receive "microwave dishes". Then we would deploy up to a quarter mile of hard wire to or from the tower. We had to run Coax cable from the camera at the mini storage unit to the transmit dish on one tower. Then we ran cable from the receive dish on another tower to the monitor in our MBN motor home/command post which, in this instance, had been parked in a campground about a mile away from the mini storage. After aligning the dishes, connecting all necessary cables, and crossing all of our fingers and toes, we fired that puppy up! And to the amazement of all Narcs present, the dang thing worked like a charm! *We were "Cookin"...*

After a well-deserved celebration, Wallace and I swapped shifts over the next five months... yes...five months! We kept watch over our "system" making sure that a live video image remained displayed on the monitor, in the motor home, at the campground, down the road from the unit, which contained the precursor chemicals for the PCP lab. Over those five months, MBN and DEA provided manpower for the twenty-four hours per day surveillance that was conducted without interruption. We established shifts and set up schedules by which Agents from across the state were rotated in and out of Meridian on regular intervals. The motor home/command post was manned by at least two Agents at all times for five months. We also maintained a mobile surveillance team of at least four additional Agents at a local hotel a short distance from the mini storage. A mouse couldn't have surprised the surveillance teams at the mini storage unit without being observed, identified, recorded, and followed.

Then, we watched and waited. We waited more than five months for the "Lab Man" to return to his unit and lead us to his lair where we would undoubtedly seize many pounds of recently manufactured PCP plus all of his lab tools and equipment. One morning, in fact, he did return. He showed up, parked his truck and walked briskly to his mini storage, all of course, while being monitored and recorded at the command post. After unlocking and opening the door on his unit, he backed his truck up to the door and quickly loaded all six large containers of chemicals into the bed of his truck. He then closed the door on his unit and got back into his vehicle, cranked the truck and drove to the exit lane at the front entrance of the mini storage facility.

With surveillance teams in place both north and south of the mini storage units, the suspect turned north onto Highway 45 and in about two blocks quickly turned east off of the highway onto a back road. The surveilling Agents, seeing him make an unexpected turn, quickly drove to the road upon which the suspect had turned and likewise turned east off Highway 45.

After more than five months of physical surveillance, thousands of man hours, twenty-four hours per day video surveillance, and thousands of dollars in motel, food, and fuel expenses, the "Lab Man" had returned, recovered his stash from the mini storage, and **vanished**! The Agents searched back roads and highways for some time after the "Lab Man" turned off Highway 45. He was never seen again!

Unfortunately…

We didn't win them all,

Most… but not all!!!

Which Hat Today?

Over the next several years, assignments, requests for assistance, and a variety of responsibilities would insure that my parameters were constantly broadened, stretched and tested. By now I was the Technical Services Unit Commander and was working out of my offices at Headquarters in Jackson. Wallace was now the *Northern Region Commander* and had moved to Oxford where that Region's offices were located. He continued to tutor me in the use and application of our special investigation tools as my learning curve slowly flattened.

In addition to my technical support duties, I also became more and more involved in training within the MBN and also for outside agencies upon request. I constantly was called upon to provide classes or blocks of instruction regarding various topics including counter smuggling techniques, arrest procedures, use of force guidelines, burglary investigation, firearms training and qualifications, and others. In addition, I was constantly offered the opportunity to attend specialized training programs all across the nation. I seldom turned down an opportunity to go to a special school.

My weeks and months were a mixture of supporting fellow Agents in their covert and non-covert investigations, attending schools, teaching various classes across the State, providing technical support to outside Agencies, maintenance of equipment, and administrative duties. The Agents, Officers, and Deputies that I came to know and work with in those years were unsurpassed in their dedication, professionalism, and bravery.

Whether watching an undercover Agent through a camera lens while he or she purchased drugs from a heavily armed and dangerous drug dealer, or providing and installing a body wire on an undercover Officer about to meet with a known armed and highly dangerous murderer, I watched these men and women risk their lives daily to take dangerous criminals off the streets of communities throughout our State. I constantly met and worked with the "best of the best" of Law Enforcement from every corner of Mississippi for many years. Now, many years later, I still recall investigations and operations throughout the state in which *I watched Heroes become Heroes, up close and personal!*

Another Responsibility of the Tech Services Unit was a task known as "ECMS" or Electronic Counter Measures Sweeps. ECMS is the process through which we employed both electronic and mechanical devices as well as highly detailed and systematic physical searches to determine if a specified area had been "Bugged". One might assume that the skills associated with these sweeps would probably require a great deal of specialized training by competent instructors as well as an ample amount of On the Job Training under the tutelage of a competent ECMS expert. Once again, one would be absolutely correct in both assumptions. While under the wing of former Tech Commander Wallace, I had assisted him with dozens of ECMS sweeps and upon assuming command of Tech Services, he had sent me to several of the best and most highly respected "spy schools" in the Nation.

For example, shortly after coming back on board with MBN, Wallace had arranged for me to attend a special class with a highly respected company in San Francisco, California. It was a ten day school designed to meet training objectives and specifications enumerated by Wallace, and was designed specifically for me. I was the only student. Not only was this a very rare structure for a school, I would learn upon arrival in San Francisco, that my instructor and mentor for those ten days would, to say the least, be a rare individual! His name was John. He had been contracted specifically to conduct my class. We met in numerous locations during the class including my hotel room and other venues that supported the topics du jour.

John was remarkable. He taught me many techniques associated with my new responsibilities and I came to respect him highly for his knowledge in many areas of Tech Services!

I also came to learn from our many conversations, that John was "the real deal"! After learning about some of his background, I was not only in awe of his skills and knowledge, but was honored to be in his presence as a student. As I would learn throughout the school, John had served in our military during World War II. Some of his assignments were, one might say, *of significance*. During that war, John served in Europe as a personal body guard for Dwight D. Eisenhower.

While *officially* in that position, he also worked in and ultimately supervised the "Lab" which designed and built most, if not all, of the "spy tools" used by our military in Europe during the war. The vast majority of the records regarding what John did for our country during the war are still classified. The knowledge that I acquired from John and many other world class trainers over the next few years from every corner of the nation, would assist me in many aspects of my job for the rest of my career. I applied skills learned from these trainers almost daily while managing the MBN Tech Services Unit as well as in many other assignments.

Because other Agents and I were routinely involved in Smuggling Investigations, we regularly attended counter smuggling schools and conferences at every opportunity. Many of these classes were sponsored and taught by the DEA, US Customs, and "ASIA" or the Air Smuggling Investigators' Association". I was fortunate enough to attend ASIA conferences in Virginia, Florida, New Orleans, and other locations around the nation. On one occasion, I was offered an opportunity to attend a one week Smuggler Investigators' Conference in San Antonio, Texas. I accepted.

Along with three fellow Agents from MBN, we drove to San Antonio for the school. The other Agents were Jerry Gardner, Dempsey Newman, and James "Jay D." Moore. That's right… my old friend and partner from college and the NOPD Vice Squad was also an Agent with MBN. Jay had actually come to work with MBN before I did and had worked numerous undercover assignments throughout the State for several years by this time. The classes were great. We learned of new techniques being used by both air and water-borne smugglers and valuable countermeasures for defeating and capturing these modern day Pirates.

During the week, I met and visited with a close friend of Mr. Fairly, Mr. Bill Pruitt. Bill was a high ranking member of the Texas Department of Public Safety. During discussions with Bill, he invited the other Agents and myself to follow him back to Austin at the conclusion of the smuggling class for a tour of the Texas DPS Headquarters. While Jerry opted to return home after the school, Dempsey, Jay and I headed for Austin.

When we arrived at the DPS Headquarters complex, we were treated "like we were somebody", as Papa Mac used to say. Bill gave us the grand tour showing us everything from his offices to all that lay "downstream". Then after about an hour or so of meeting most of Bill's team, he said "y'all come with me, I have some other guys I want y'all to meet". We had no idea where Bill would lead us next or what sites we might behold. Already having been shown numerous display cases full of memorabilia gleaned from a hundred years of western "Lawman" experiences, this ole cowboy was approaching sensory overload!

After weaving through several corridors, we came to a special area of the building that I did not expect to be invited into. It was the Texas Rangers Headquarters. Having worked closely with several Texas Rangers while in New Orleans and with the MBN, I was more than a little excited to be meeting the Heroes of some of my greatest Heroes! When brave men reference other brave men with whom they would be proud to "Ride the River", these are the kind of men about whom they speak! The reputations of some of the Rangers who I knew worked behind these doors, were what cowboy legends were made of.

Inside we were introduced by Bill to several of the most Senior of Rangers! These men comprised most of the command structure that was in charge of all other Texas Rangers. Among them, Senior Ranger Captain Bill Wilson accepted us into his office and we visited with him and the other Senior Rangers as if we had known each other for twenty years. They were great guys and impressed us all as being everything we would have ever expected them to have been.

In the years that followed, I have always remembered and appreciated everything that Bill Pruitt did for us throughout that trip to Austin. I especially appreciate his efforts in providing us an opportunity to meet and visit with the Texas Rangers at DPS Headquarters. They, like Bill, were the real deal! Before retiring, Bill was to hold positions within the Texas DPS including "Chief of Criminal Law Enforcement" and "Commander of the DPS Narcotics Division". Later in my career I would have numerous opportunities to work with, train with, and provide training for many Texas Rangers. They have always lived up to and exceeded their reputation and all of my fondest expectations.

They are, and always have been, among my greatest
Heroes!!!

Hanging in a prominent position* in Mr. Fairly's office, while he was Director of the MBN, he had a painting that was given to him by Bill Pruitt years earlier. It was the portrait of a lone cowboy wearing the badge of a Texas Ranger.

The caption on the bottom of the painting simply said,
"One Riot, One Ranger"

The Technical Side of Smuggling

In late March and April of 1979, MBN's Jackson District Agents developed information on a group of suspects operating in the Jackson area who were believed to be air smugglers. After following the group for several days and running license plates and names of members of the group through state and federal computer systems, the MBN Agents acquired several "hits" on members of the group. At least three of the suspects had records in the computer systems indicating that they were, in fact, known smugglers. Other information developed indicated that the group's members were associated with several aircraft that had been known to fly large quantities of drugs into the United States from foreign countries...

That's smuggling, and that's wrong...!!!

Armed with this knowledge, the Agents were able to ask for, justify, and receive the costly manpower and other resources needed to conduct an investigation and related surveillances associated with a counter smuggling operation. Along with other Agents from across the State, I responded to the Jackson Agents' request for assistance in monitoring the group's activities.

The Agents had determined that the group was staying in a hotel near the intersection of Interstate 20, and Ellis Avenue, which was a major four lane road in west Jackson. This was a busy intersection with several hotels, various businesses, and a shopping center in all four quadrants of the "crossroads". With the suspects' hotel in the north eastern quadrant, we set-up the MBN command post motorhome on a hill in a parking lot in the south east quadrant of the intersection. From here we could observe the suspects' activities at the hotel.

This location also gave us the advantage of elevation which greatly enhanced our communications with mobile MBN Agents as they conducted moving surveillances of the suspects. For over a week, I supported the other Agents in their efforts to monitor the suspects and follow them as they prepared to smuggle drugs into the nation and our state.

During the process of following these suspects, we determined that they were communicating with each other on citizen band or "CB" radios. Not knowing what channels they were utilizing, I requested that my boss, Bill Turcotte, approve the purchase of a special CB radio that would allow me to *scan* all CB frequencies. Bill approved the purchase, and I acquired the radio from a local radio shop. With this device, I quickly determined which frequencies were being used by the smugglers to coordinate their activities. From the elevated position where our command post was situated, we could monitor much of the communications between the smugglers over the next several days.

Due to the fact that the smugglers had the ability to communicate among themselves as they moved about in their vehicles, the Agents also requested another form of technical support. To effectively follow the smugglers from a greater distance, the Agents needed the advantages provided by the installation of a tracking device on one or more of the suspects' vehicles. The tracking devices that were most commonly used by Law Enforcement in that era were called "Bird Dog" systems. These were systems that were comprised of several components... and yes... they came in some of those large containers like the microwave system. Everything was "big" back then.

The Bird Dog systems consisted of a "transponder" that was about the size of a large box of matches and had strong magnets mounted to its bottom side. Once batteries were installed and the switch was activated, it was ready to go. The receiver for the system was a device about the size of a small lunch box and was connected to a magnetic antenna array which was meticulously mounted to the roof of the tracking vehicle. There were no moving maps on a monitor or smart phone nor were there any GPS location indicators. There WAS a needle in a center module on the front of the receiver that simply swung *left* and *right* within its "bubble". Left meant the target vehicle was moving left and right meant it was moving right. While this was mighty crude technology compared to the mapping software and GPS location providers of today, the ole Bird Dog was used by hundreds of Officers to successfully follow many outlaws to their ultimate criminal demise, back in the day.

The biggest drawback, and dangerously challenging task associated with operating a Bird Dog, was that someone had to physically go to, crawl under, and attach the Bird Dog transponder to... the suspect's vehicle. At that time, no court order was required for such placement of a tracking device on an individual's vehicle. However... imagine the difficulty one might have in trying to explain to the vehicle's owner what one was doing attaching a magnetized black box to the underside of their vehicle at 2:00 am in the black of night. It was a situation that we made every effort to avoid.

In the early morning hours of March 31, 1979 yours truly, with the assistance of several fellow Agents went to the hotel in which the suspects were asleep... we hoped. As the other Agents watched for any sign of the smugglers, I crawled under one of the suspects' vehicles and implanted the Bird Dog transponder. After carefully, quickly, and quietly insuring that the device was installed correctly, I retreated with the other Agents to the command post to activate the receiver for the system. It was working perfectly.

Over the next several nights, the Bird Dog and the CB receiver were used to listen to and track the smugglers as they moved about the area. On two separate nights we successfully followed the suspects from their hotel in Jackson to an airport near Vicksburg. This was a distance of more than sixty miles each way, and involved travelling on both busy highways like I-20 and small rural roads in Warren County south of Vicksburg where the Airport was located. With the smugglers making every effort to identify any possible surveillance by Law Enforcement and talking constantly on their CB radios, the task of following them for well over one hundred miles per trip was a formidable challenge. Watching the MBN Agents manage this highly complex surveillance, I thought several times of how proud Mr. Fairly would be of these Agents' skills and professionalism. Having personally handpicked most of these Agents himself, the Boss would undoubtedly have been displaying a "Fairly smile"!

The surveillances continued 24-7 for the next several days. During those days and nights the Agents were doing more than just following the smugglers around the State. Knowing now where the load was most likely to be brought in, Agents had met with Sheriff Paul Barrett of Warren County and requested his support in the investigation. As always, he was anxious to help. He arranged for a flight in a helicopter owned by a local business man that enabled me to get an aerial view and photographs of the airport and surrounding area. This helped us tremendously as we planned for surveillance positions which would give us strategic advantages to observe the smugglers while landing and unloading their plane.

We also planned to position our Agents and Deputies in specific locations around the airport that would give them cover and concealment prior to and during the arrest of the smugglers once they met the aircraft and took possession of the load of drugs. The Sheriff also arranged for us to use a nearby vacant building for an onsite command post and surveillance post prior to and during the suspects' arrests.   During our preparations and planning for the arrest of the suspects and the seizure of the plane and its load, Sheriff Paul Barrett was tireless in his support of our Agents. It would have been very difficult to have been successful without his help. Paul was a great friend for many years and a true Hero!

Another required duty during the employment of many of our specialized technical surveillance devices was the dreaded *changing of the batteries*. Most "portable" devices depended upon one form or another of a power cell or battery. In 1979, batteries were, like much other technology, *antique* by today's standards. There were no nickel cadmium batteries, much less the power cell of today, the "Lithium Ion". The best that the world had to offer at that time was the old reliable but not too long lasting "Alkaline" battery in its many shapes, forms, and power ratings. How this information relates to our story with any significance is that the Bird Dog transponder was one of those much depended upon devices that had batteries… batteries that "ran down"… ran down quickly.

Because the transponder could not remotely be disabled to conserve battery life, it "ran" constantly as long as it was installed upon a suspect's vehicle. The life expectancy of the transponder batteries was even worse than that of a "Chief of Police"… much worse. One could count on batteries in this type of application to last about two to three days, depending upon the age and condition of the batteries upon their initial deployment. Well… in this instance, we lost signal from the transponder on the third day of deployment.

Hoping that the problem was in fact a battery problem and that the transponder was still attached to the suspects' vehicle and not in a dumpster or along the road somewhere, I went to the vehicle again in the dead of night under the cover of darkness and several other trusted Agents. Upon finding the transponder still in place, I switched batteries and after a stealthy retreat, we were back in business. Or as we say "in the business" we were "back on the air".

After having made all preparations possible to insure our success in capturing the suspects and their load of drugs from a yet unidentified aircraft, the Agents continued to surveil the smugglers and their vehicles for several more days. Then on April 5, they made their last trip to the Airport in Vicksburg. As the smugglers made their way from their hotel to the airport late that evening, they were again followed by the Jackson Agents.

They drove their rented load truck to the area of the airport, stopped a short distance from the runway, and awaited the arrival of the load. It was obvious that the load was about to arrive because this was the first time that the load truck had stopped at the airport. During previous trips, the smugglers had driven to and then immediately departed from the airport and returned to Jackson. After having again successfully followed the suspects to the airport without being detected, the surveilling Agents took up preassigned fixed positions and waited for the load to arrive.

Other Agents and I were positioned in the vacant building near the north end of the runway. As we waited for the aircraft to arrive, I sat with Bill Turcotte and listened to the CB as it scanned frequencies in an attempt to tune in on possible conversations between the smugglers. The channels were all quiet. We sat and listened for what seemed like days but which was actually a relatively short time. As I sat with Bill, my boss, I was having a hard time sitting still. My job in this instance was quite different than it had been during several previous smuggling operations. In all previous cases, I was on the ground with the Agents involved in the apprehension and seizure. I was not at all comfortable with sitting and listening to a CB radio. I wanted to leave the command post and travel down the ditch outside that led to the position of one of the arrest teams and help arrest the smugglers as they arrived. I was about to miss the excitement of the arrest and seizure, but more importantly I felt that if the other Agents met opposition from the smugglers, I would not be there to back them up.

Realizing how anxious I was becoming, Bill put his hand on my shoulder and said, "you have a job to do here too Fred... get it done first". I knew what he meant, and he was right. It didn't make staying there any easier, but it at least helped me focus... and he was the boss! So I mentally "came back inside" and went to work.

We talked to the teams of Agents positioned in wooded and grassy areas near the runway who were prepared to arrest the smugglers and seize the aircraft and its load upon arrival at the airport. We talked to the Agents still in their vehicles who were positioned and ready to respond in support of the arresting Agents and Deputies. They were also prepared to apprehend any potential fleeing suspects who might try to escape arrest by the Agents on foot around the airport. We had made every preparation possible to insure that we safely and successfully caught and arrested the smugglers as they received their load of drugs from South America.

Then, we received a call from one of the Agents on foot near the runway. He said that he thought he had heard a faint rumble of engines in the sky south of the runway but could no longer hear the sound. In fact the pilot of the aircraft had cut back on all power to the engines and had coasted onto the runway to avoid being heard by residents living near the south end of the runway. Just as he stopped talking, another much more excited Agent came on the radio and said, "I just heard wheels hit the runway... It sounded like something big landed"!

DC-3... Load Aircraft on ground in Vicksburg, MS, area

Then suddenly, another Agent reported, *"They're here... Damn... It's a DC-3 and it's pulling up right in front of me"*. Immediately one of the mobile units reported, "The trucks are cranking up out here and moving toward the runway..." Within seconds, the DC-3 was on the tarmac at the north end of the runway and the trucks, including the large rental truck, were all pulling up to the DC-3 that had now stopped and killed its engines. The doors flew open on the side of the aircraft and the crew inside the plane started throwing bales of marijuana out of the plane and into the load truck which had backed up near the plane. Within a few minutes, the plane was unloaded.

As the smugglers were busy unloading the plane and loading the truck, Agents and Deputies swarmed the suspects, vehicles and aircraft. In moments, it was over. The bad guys were under arrest and more than five thousand pounds of smuggled marijuana had been seized by MBN Agents and Warren County Deputies. As the

Members of arrest teams around rental/load truck and DC-3 just after seizure

reports of the vehicles meeting the DC-3 had come into the command post, Bill looked at me and said..."OK Freddy, I'll take over the radios, you can head out there now... I don't want you to miss your plane". We both laughed, but I was out of the Command Post and headed to the plane before Bill had even finished saying the words.

As I reached the tarmac where the load had arrived, I was met by the Agents and Deputies who had all begun the process of inspecting the plane and vehicles as well as the cargo of drugs. I assisted with the follow up activities related to the seizure and investigation throughout the next several days. During the inspection

"Jake" Jacobson (DEA), Steve Mallory and Alvin Eddie Berry (both MBN) outside DC-3 just after seizure

of the plane, we observed several things that would help us in future smuggling operations. Inside the plane, in the main compartment, seats had been taken out to allow for the loading of the bales of marijuana into this area.

The interesting observation was that the smugglers had also installed an inflatable bladder tank in this area to increase the plane's fuel capacity. This in turn increased the plane's range or distance it could fly without refueling. The crew would fill up the bladder tank before departing for South America. The plane would then be flown to the location from which the load would be obtained using the fuel in the bladder tank. By the time the plane arrived at the pickup location in South America, it would have used all the fuel in the

DC-3 with "bladder tanks" in cabin area... Tanks are deflated in floor of cabin area

bladder tank. The bladder would by then be completely deflated and would be flat on the floor of the aircraft cabin area.

After loading the cargo of marijuana on what was now an empty and flat bladder tank, the pilot would fly the DC-3 back to the United States using the fuel stored in its normal wing tanks. This way the plane had ample fuel to make the entire trip without the need for refueling. This was a huge advantage for the smugglers and now added to our knowledge regarding their methods of operation.

Bladder tanks would be observed by Agents during many smuggling investigations far into the future. Using the knowledge of their presence in aircraft, we predicted the activities and plans of dozens of smuggling groups for many years to come.

After the plane was secured, the suspects, their vehicles and

Agent Larry James, Sheriff Paul Barrett, and Fred seated in rear door of rental/load truck full of marijuana smuggled into Vicksburg, MS, aboard the DC-3

the load were transported to the Warren County Sheriff's Office. The suspects were locked up, their vehicles were seized and inventoried, and the load of marijuana was subsequently burned and destroyed. In all, six smugglers were arrested, several vehicles were forfeited to the MBN, and over five thousand pounds of marijuana and a well-worn DC-3 were seized. The Bird Dog Transponder was recovered from the smuggler's vehicle and along with the MBN motorhome/command post were all returned to proper storage awaiting our next assignment.

Many Agents participated in the investigation regarding the DC-3. These included Eddie Berry, Bill Marshall, Doug Cutrer, Mickey Robbins, Steve Mallory, Larry James, Sara Neil, Barry Newsome, and Region Commander Charlie Lindsey. Also involved was my boss and then Deputy Director, Bill Turcotte. By then I had known most of these Agents for years and had worked closely with

MBN Agent Doug Cutrer sitting on left engine of DC-3

them during investigations that were very demanding physically and in some instances emotionally as well! Having watched them all work tirelessly to apprehend drug dealers throughout the state in a wide variety of investigations and circumstances, I sometimes took their individual and collective expertise for granted.

MBN Agent Sara Neil standing in cabin area of seized DC-3

MBN Agent Mickey Robbins stands in door of DC-3

They were all so dang good at what they did,

They made it all look simple!

None of it was… ever…simple!!!

Working past the point of pure exhaustion in highly threatening situations involving the most dangerous of suspects, these brave heroes glided smoothly between the borders of crisis and success, bumping shoulders with pure evil around every corner, and they always won!!! They always outsmarted the bad guys through the use of their individual experience, skills, intelligence and bravery…

They made many bad guys "wet their pants"…

figuratively and literally.

It was a "win-win"!!!

They were and are among the best of Heroes!

Technically, It's Just Another Hat

Throughout the several years that I managed the Tech Services Unit, assignments continued to vary widely. From ECMS sweeps, to various electronic surveillances, to dignitary protection details, to specialized training, I responded to numerous requests from Agents as well as outside Agencies as approved by the Director and or Deputy Director. Hardly any request was ever refused unless I was already committed to an assignment that conflicted with the newer request. One request involved a skill set which was commonly employed, but which came from an unusual "customer".

In late 1978, we received a request from the Mississippi Highway Safety Patrol to assist them with a dignitary protection detail in the Natchez, Mississippi, area. After talking with members of the Patrol, we agreed to support them and over the next several weeks, we alternated shifts with members of the Patrol and Agents from around the State. It seemed that a Television "Mini Series" was being filmed in Natchez and the "Stars" of the series required protection while filming their parts in the production. Upon arriving in Natchez, I was met by several MHP Investigators who gave me a tour of the "Set" at which the filming was being done. I also was shown the residence and other areas being used by the stars during the filming.

Later that afternoon, I was invited to the temporary residence for a barbeque dinner and to meet the stars. As the sun was setting on Natchez that day, I found myself sitting on my cooler full of ice and refreshments, eating a hamburger and visiting with Mohammad Ali, his family and Kris Kristofferson. With Ali's young daughter sitting on my knee and entertaining us all with her precious laughter as we visited, it was not a bad way to end a day. Neither the Champ, nor Kris could have been more friendly, hospitable, or appreciative throughout the time that we provided protection for them in Natchez. It was a great break from chasing bad guys through the swamp!

Back in the swamp... things were always hopping, as they say. I remained occupied with my normal duties around the State including those recurring ECMS sweeps. I regularly responded to calls for sweeps from various heads of agencies throughout the State including District Attorneys like Mike Moore of Jackson County, Sheriffs like my old friend Larkin Smith, and State Government officials. At the

State level, I routinely performed sweeps on the offices and residences of Senators, Legislators, and even Governors. On numerous occasions, I "swept" the current Governor's offices as well as his residence in the Governor's Mansion. Some of these sweeps were relatively brief in duration due to the size of the space being swept, but some took several days to complete.

When Mike Moore was elected Attorney General, we had been friends for some years. He immediately requested that I perform a detailed ECMS sweep of all offices under his control. That took a few days! In the years that followed while he was involved in the court proceedings involving the tobacco industry, I swept both his offices and the presiding Judge's offices in Laurel, Mississippi, numerous times throughout the course of those proceedings.

Because of the frequency of the sweeps, our presence became somewhat of a deterrent to would be "buggers", but on several occasions over the years we did find several listening devices implanted within various offices. It was an interesting area of enforcement which required a skill set that, as stated before, brought me in contact with many world class trainers and Tech Services Legends. It also brought me in contact with many executives and leaders for whom I have great respect still today.

A by-product of ECMS was that the better one became at *detecting* "Bugs", the better one became at *installing* and *hiding* "Bugs". Along with hundreds of ECMS sweeps conducted through the years, I also received an equal or greater volume of requests to "Bug" rooms and other locations where important meetings or undercover transactions were expected to occur. Wallace and I frequently mused that by the time we retired, there wouldn't be a hotel room in Mississippi that we didn't have a preinstalled pinhole for a camera or microphone from an adjacent room. We found ourselves quite frequently in the early years, as I found myself many times later, responding to requests for assistance from numerous Agents assigned to MBN Districts from every corner of the State.

"Surveillance Kit" used by MBN Technical Services Unit to monitor and record hundreds of undercover investigations in various locations all across the state for many years, including Hotel Rooms.

We would often go to a preselected motel and rent two adjoining rooms. One would be for the undercover transaction and the other would be the "listening post". After moving what was often an assortment of baggage large enough to meet the definition of a "system" into the listening post, we would set about our covert installation. Through any combination of numerous techniques, we would either inject an audio transmitter into the undercover room or hardwire a microphone through a wall or under the carpet that was usually joined by a *seam* under the adjoining doors of the two rooms.

However, if we required "video", we were channeled into an entirely different realm of technical expertise. Still in the 1970's, one must try now to envision a camera and lens "system" that required at least one and probably two *substantial* tripods to support. The obvious problem, I think, is that trying to "hide" a camera of that size and weight in a motel room and then route the necessary connecting cables back to the listening post presented some pretty daunting challenges. The main idea, other than gathering useable video and audio *evidence* of the undercover transaction, was NOT TO GET CAUGHT!

The most common option therefore, was to remove a small section of the wall material in the wall between the two rooms. From the listening post side of the wall, we would carefully shave away fractions of the wall material on the inside of the undercover room's wall until we had created a small "pin-hole". By using this very small opening we gained visual access into the undercover room through which a well-placed pinhole lens could view all activity. After a normally tedious process of mounting lens to camera, and camera to tripod, and meticulously placing the assembly against the newly created pinhole in the wall, we were ready to record any and all events in the adjoining room as the undercover Agent negotiated and consummated the upcoming transaction.

WE would be "ready" that is, after a few loose ends were tied up... At this point in the preparations, we connected all of the required cables from microphones and cameras to the related recording devices. Then we placed the proper recording medium, i.e. "tapes", into the correct recording devices. It was further required that we "pack" the tapes by winding them completely forward and then rewinding them back to their original condition to insure that the tape was not going to break or snag as we actually recorded the undercover event.

At this point in time, the "video" recorders still "recorded" on *tape* that was stored on "reels"... that's right... *reel-to-reel video recorders.* Oh... and the recorders only recorded in "black and white". We had a few color recorders, but those were for "special" events! They were also about three times the size of the black and white "systems". Considering the size of the black and white systems, that was significant! We only had "one shot" at capturing the transaction... we couldn't afford for a faulty piece of equipment or tape to fail during the meeting. That would be a really bad thing!

Then, after hours of preparation, we would wait until the appointed time for the undercover Agent or Agents to arrive. At that time we would initiate our documentation process that would provide needed corroboration of the criminal activity about to occur in the adjoining room. We would sit only inches away from the negotiations where we would watch, listen to, and record the Agent's and the Outlaw's every word and every move.

Also, always present in our listening post, was adequate weaponry with which we could respond quickly through the adjoining doors to rescue the Agent if, in the not too uncommon event, the outlaw decided to do bad things to the undercover Agent. Always ready for the unexpected, we were constantly ready to switch from observer to rescuer if the circumstances demanded our involvement. We always understood that we were the undercover Agent's closest, and perhaps only, "back up" if the Deal went bad... We took that very seriously!!!

In more than a few situations, we in fact switched rolls to become back up for the Agent in the "other room". Thankfully, because we could usually see a bad situation developing as we monitored the negotiations, we were always able to successfully intervene with no serious injuries to the undercover Agent. Having been on the "other side of the wall" in numerous instances while working undercover, I knew just how good it felt to see the "Cavalry" coming through the back door! It was always an honor to provide technical support to these brave and dedicated undercover Agents. It was an even greater honor to be their "Cavalry" when they needed to hear the bugles blowing!

We constantly provided similar support throughout the State. While the process and techniques were usually similar to the "Hotel" installations, the locations varied greatly. On one occasion, I was requested to assist Jim Wallace in the Southaven area. Jim called and explained that Jerry Dettman, a fellow Agent and extremely close friend, was working undercover in a local *Bar and Pizza Parlor* in Southaven and was involved in high level transactions with various drug dealers in the area.

Wallace went on to explain that most of Jerry's transactions and negotiations were occurring in the bar. While they had tried to inject a video recording system into the bar to document the transactions, they had failed due to the lack of adequate secure space in which to conceal the camera and associated recording "system". Within a couple of days, I drove to Southaven and met Jim and Jerry at the bar during the hours that it was closed for business.

Armed with all necessary tools and supplies, we spent the next six hours constructing a "closet/storage room" behind the bar. The closet, while small by household standards, was more than adequate to store assorted bar supplies and yes… a video recording system, complete with pinhole camera. We built a "box within a box" type enclosure and to anyone entering the closet to retrieve bar supplies, the camera system was completely invisible. It would have taken a keen eye for detail and a good measuring device to have deduced wherein the camera "hide" was located. Since most of the patrons were at least somewhat inhibited by the consumption of one or more mind altering substances, our secret was never detected!

Over the next several months, Jerry purchased a variety of controlled substances from many significant drug violators from the Southaven and Memphis areas. Each transaction was "systematically" recorded by a camera in a closet behind the bar in Southaven. The recordings were properly sealed and stored as evidence. The Defendants were prosecuted using the taped video recordings of their transactions and the testimony of Jerry and other surveilling Agents. After completing the investigations at the bar, Jerry was off to a long successful career with the MBN during which he and I would work together many times. I was always proud to "Ride the River" with my good friend and hero, Jerry Dettman!

A short while after the Southaven installation, I was contacted by Director Quarles. The Director told me that he had received a request for technical assistance from a Law Enforcement Agency on the Gulf Coast. It seemed that they were working an investigation regarding threats to a prominent individual in the Pascagoula area and had asked that MBN help by installing listening and recording devices on the victim's phones and in his offices. He instructed me to go to the Coast and meet with the Law Enforcement Agency and provide whatever help I could to support them and the victim.

Within hours I was in Pascagoula and meeting with all involved. I was taken to the victim's offices where I assessed the environment and selected the devices that would best accomplish the needs of the Investigators involved in the case. After several hours of work installing and testing the equipment to be employed by the victim, I also provided adequate in service training for the victim to be competent in the operation of the devices. He was ready to go. During my time in the victim's offices, I was able to visit and get to know him and a little of his history. I had come to respect the skills and heritage of his ancestors many years earlier when I was a young boy. He was quite friendly and we immediately formed a mutual respect for each other. He became, and remained a friend for years to come.

The "victim" was Chief Sam Kinsolving...
Apache Chief Sam Kinsolving!

The *Law Enforcement Agency* that I had been dispatched by our Director to assist, was an element of the *Apache Tribal Police* who were, like the Chief, very appreciative for the assistance of a young cowboy from the MBN!

Because the investigation was conducted by the Tribal police, I left the equipment under their control as instructed by our Director. It would be more than ten months before I would be informed by Chief Kinsolving that they no longer required the use of our recording equipment. I returned and removed the devices and after servicing them, they were placed back in storage awaiting their next assignment. The Chief nor his Officers ever informed me as to the outcome of their investigation. My job was done… I assumed theirs had been as well!

I suppose that with all the history involved,
They would trust a *pale face* only so far!

Ice on the Inside

Another of our newest additions to the tools employed by the MBN Tech Services Unit about this time were Night Vision Devices or NVD's. Once more, one must remain focused on the time frame and the contemporary concept of "space" as it refers to the volume of area required to contain any given technical device. Just keep thinking "LARGE"!

On a "VERY" cold day in December, shortly after having been allowed a generous few hours to celebrate Christmas, other Agents and I were summoned to assist with an ongoing counter smuggling investigation in the Hattiesburg, Mississippi, area. Jim Kelly, another fellow Agent and good friend, along with other Hattiesburg Agents had been working on a group of suspects believed to be air smugglers. I had been requested to assist with a surveillance operation at the Hattiesburg airport where the Agents expected the smugglers to perform modifications to their aircraft before it was to travel to South America to obtain a load of drugs.

After working with Jim and the other Agents including Kent McDaniel and Danny Blackledge for about a day and a half, we had acquired all required components of the equipment needed to record the suspects' activities at the airport upon their arrival. While at the Hattiesburg District Office or HDO, the "system" needed to accomplish the recordings of the smugglers had been assembled, mounted onto tripods and tested. It was a sight to behold. The "system" consisted of a video camera, a night Vision device, and a lens system. The components were interconnected with a series of adaptors, bellows, brackets, and spacers that were designed to allow each independent device to function properly with the other components that made up the "system".

With each component being a "unit" in itself, it required three tripods, and a specially designed "parallel rail" support device to mount and support the "system" in a useable configuration. In this instance, "useable configuration" only indicates a level of probability and should not be perceived as an indicator of certainty! In the office, *under controlled conditions*, the "system" had successfully operated... intermittently. Not only was this all new technology, it was being assembled and tested by novices to the world of night vision assisted video recordings. We were pretty much winging it!

The next consideration, now that the "system" was assembled, was transportation and concealment for the "system" that would allow our new monster to be deployed to the area of the airport and employed during the clandestine activities expected to be engaged in by our smuggling suspects. The logical and obvious choice was one of our MBN surveillance vans. So, after carefully transferring the "system" from the HDO into the *company van*, my close friend and fellow Agent Dempsey Newman and I boarded the van and drove carefully to the airport. Having watched the smugglers working on and around their aircraft previously, Kelly had told us specifically where to park the van so that we would be able to clearly observe the activities of the smugglers when they arrived later that night.

Dempsey and I drove unnoticed into an unoccupied area of the airport and positioned the van so that we could see and record the suspects upon their arrival. We parked alongside a hangar building and after securing all doors, crawled into the back of the van to await the arrival of the smugglers. While waiting, we insured that the camera/NVD conglomeration was still intact and still upright on the tripod-trio. As far as we could determine through close visual inspection, it was still standing and hopefully operational.

Over the next several hours, Dempsey and I sat quietly in what we hoped would look like an unoccupied company van and waited for the outlaws to show up. Did I mention at the beginning of the story that it was COLD? I thought that I did... that was what is known as a "gross understatement"! The temperatures continually dropped until the little red line in the glass tube said 20° F. As the waiting continued the temperatures plunged down into the low teens, Fahrenheit. That's just past cold and approaching painfully uncomfortable... especially considering the fact that we could not run the engine in the van to warm up the interior where Dempsey and I were occupying space. We had no mechanism to reintroduce warmth into our space and very little in the way of resources to even retain the warmth that we brought with us. As the temperatures continued to drop, so did our comfort level. It was very *cold*.

Now some who read this will undoubtedly pontificate as to the absurdity of the concept that thirteen or fourteen degrees Fahrenheit should ever be considered as an indicator of any condition approaching the status of "*cold*". May I admonish thee thusly...? In south Mississippi with the humidity hovering in the range of ninety percentile, and the two cowboys in the van adorned only in blue jeans and long sleeve shirts, possessing no mechanism with which to create any form of artificial heat, please indulge me in my claims that the "low teens" was plenty *cold* to accommodate the applicable definition for the purposes of this story!

Thank You!

After a couple more miserable hours, a crackle came over our frozen radio and we heard Jim say, "The plane's landing". Kelly has always been a man of few words. After a minute or so, over the sound of our teeth chattering, we could hear the plane. It taxied up, in total darkness, and was immediately met by several vehicles in front of another hangar that was straight in front of our van's windshield. As the DC-3's engines went silent we could see the crew and the men from the vehicles meeting outside the aircraft and hear them talking. We knew that if we could hear them, they could hear us. *Quiet* was a mandatory requirement for Dempsey and me for the next couple of hours.

I fired up our *onboard magic video machine* and all its components. It powered up and promptly displayed an image on the small monitor that gave us, after some adjustments, a "close-up" night vision view of the outlaws working on the DC-3. How cool was that...? The images by the standards of that day and time, were remarkable! In the green tint of the night vision device's image, we could see every move of the suspects on our monitor and upon switching to a view through the windshield with our naked eyes, could see absolutely nothing.

As we quietly sat and recorded the smugglers activities, Dempsey and I, in very low whispers, discussed what we were seeing the smugglers doing on and around the DC-3. They were installing auxiliary fuel tanks, or bladder tanks. We could see the bladders being removed from the vehicles that the smugglers had arrived in and could see the collapsible fuel cells being carried onboard. We watched as the crew made numerous trips into and out from the DC-3.

Watching and recording the smugglers, we began to notice that our image on the monitor was becoming less clear. I checked the lens on the front of the system and saw that it was unobstructed. I checked all points where components were interconnected and they all still seemed perfectly aligned. What we came to realize was that as we watched the monitor in order to be able to actually see the suspects, we had not recently looked through the windshield. Upon an inspection of said windshield, we observed approximately one half of an inch of solid ice covering the entire INSIDE of the windshield. As our breath was condensing on the inside of the front glass, it was immediately freezing and becoming thicker and thicker.

Have I mentioned that it was a somewhat brisk evening?

As fate would provide… as we were noticing the condition of the windshield, the smugglers seemed to be completing their work on the DC-3. After only a short time, they began securing the plane and their equipment. The ground crew departed the airport. The DC-3 was fired-up and promptly taxied out onto the runway and departed the Hattiesburg airport.

After the smugglers had departed the airport, Dempsey and I cranked the van, allowed it run long enough to warm up the interior, and when we could see through the windshield, we too departed the airport. The surveillance of the smugglers continued for several days. During that time we followed the ground crew to Montgomery, Alabama where we watched them meet the DC-3 at another local airport. The crews seemed to become stalled in their preparations to complete a smuggling venture, and our surveillances were terminated.

After almost a week of surveillance, and having endured a bit of extremely unpleasant weather conditions, we had waved goodbye to a group of known smugglers and had placed them in the "another time and another place" file. We had all gained experience in dealing with this crew of outlaws and had also gotten some really good recordings of the installation of bladder tanks in a DC-3. It was, to the best of my knowledge, the first time that one of our reel-to-reel video/NVD camera systems was used in combination to record anything similar to the bladder tanks being installed in total darkness…

especially in the *COLD!*

Simply Alarming

A nother form of new technology was a portable alarm system that Wallace had acquired to assist with the ever increasing number of drug store burglaries throughout the State. The devices purchased by Wallace were known as the "Simdac" system. These "portable" units met all the requirements to be designated and defined as a "system". Each unit was about the size of a "family sized suitcase". It was, however, self-contained with its own power supply (batteries) and could be set up quickly and discreetly in most warehouse size environments like large drug stores.

The good news was... they worked pretty darn well. They were basically a remote transmitter that could be triggered by a number of devices that could be hidden throughout the recipient drug store. Upon being activated by a burglar during the hours that the drug store was closed, the unit transmitted a unique coded signal to the system's receiver which was usually in our command post or in a local Agency's radio room.

Each unit had its own identifier within the code so the person monitoring the system's receiver immediately knew which location was being "burgled". With over a dozen of the Simdac units available, we could "alarm" most of the drug stores in a town or city and increase our likelihood of catching burglars operating in the area. When I took command of the Tech Services Unit, the Simdacs were new hardware in the Unit. They needed to be tested and evaluated. I often worked with members of the Jackson Police Department including a good friend named Jimmy Dixon. Jimmy worked with me deploying the Simdacs throughout Jackson where they remained deployed for several months. I moved between various assignments throughout the State while the Simdacs were in the field, and Jimmy and his team of Detectives responded numerous times to alarms generated by the Simdacs. As a result of the use of the Simdacs, the

JPD Detectives were able to apprehend several suspects who were responsible for many burglaries around the area and throughout the State.

Down the Drain

Then... on April 15, 1979, it happened. The "Easter Flood" of Jackson. Our Headquarters building located near the Pearl River just off Lakeland Drive in East Jackson, was devastated by flood waters that reached well into the second floor of our offices. Our Headquarters building *was a two story structure*. My office, store rooms, "cabinets" and all of those items that we had used so frequently to protect Agents and put outlaws in jail... were destroyed and rendered useless. The flood had occurred without notice. I was at my home in Picayune and by the time other Agents and I arrived the whole building was under water. When the flood waters subsided, we started the heartbreaking process of wading through the slush and slime that previously was the MBN Headquarters. It was a mess!

I had just finished remodeling my offices a week earlier and had been provided all new furniture, carpet and decorations. I had hung many of my training certificates and commendations. I had training manuals and reference books in my office that were priceless and used regularly to insure the proper procedures and maintenance regarding the equipment with which I worked daily. It was all destroyed along with almost everything else in the building.

Our records division which was full of the documents that created the basis for all the Agency's records checks by our Agents was also destroyed. Records Division personnel would, for months, try to "dry-out" and restore thousands of files in an attempt to recreate any possible portion of our records system. The "Property" section in which was housed all supplies that were used in support of almost every function of the MBN, was destroyed. Everything from paper clips to ammunition and weapons had been submerged in the filthy backwaters of an overflowing river.

Thousands of other buildings were also destroyed during the Easter flood and the area of the city where MBN was located, remained dark for weeks before the power could be restored. Our Motorhome/Command post was parked in front of our building and teams of Agents took turns providing security for Headquarters until the mess was finally cleaned up. It was a slow, miserable, filthy process. It would change MBN in many ways, but it would change Tech Services forever.

With most of our resources destroyed, at least for the foreseeable future, there would be very little that I could do to support the Agents in the field with technical assets. Except for the items I kept stored in my MBN vehicle, and those assets which were at the time deployed in the field to support current investigations, most of the remaining sophisticated items that still existed were those that we had placed in Region or District offices around the State for redundancy. This placement of resources had allowed me, in many instances, to avoid having to return to Jackson to retrieve a piece of equipment needed in one area of the State only to have to drive directly back to the same area to deploy that equipment for a local Agent. Even with this pre-staging of these resources, the majority of our technical capabilities had been literally washed away in the flood!

Not only were many physical assets and resources destroyed in the flood, it would be months before we could move back into MBN Headquarters… if ever. We moved into temporary space in the Department of Public Safety (DPS) Headquarters and remained there for some time. With office space and resources quite limited the MBN was still able to function, but at a much reduced capacity. We "limped along" for some time after the flood.

Repositioning our Technical Assets

By August, less than four months later, I met with the Director who at that time suggested that I begin working out of the Gulfport District and from there respond to requests for technical assistance for which we still had the capacity to provide the requested support. I agreed completely with this arrangement and within a week had been assigned an office in the Gulfport District Offices of MBN. I would remain in the GDO for some time and within only a few months, The MBN would have a new Director and Deputy Director.

I would learn in all the years that followed, that I would never be completely absent from the technical support activities of MBN. For most of the rest of my career I would continue to participate in and conduct technical training, ECMS sweeps, technical support to MBN Districts around the state, and other functions required to augment investigations conducted by MBN Agents and Officers from hundreds of other Agencies. Wallace and I were to meet in many more "hotel rooms" far into the future. Purely on a professional basis of course!

Major Losses

Also within a very short time, the MBN would lose one of its most respected Agents ever to wear the badge designed by Mr. Fairly in 1972. The Agent was the former establisher and commander of the MBN Intelligence Division, Claude Stuckey. Claude died after a long battle with cancer. He was admired by every Agent who ever worked with, for, or near him. He was a Vietnam Veteran, a true American patriot, and an amazing Hero to every Agent and employee of the MBN!

Within a month of Claude's death, we would also attend the funeral of the first MBN Agent to die in the line of duty. While assisting the local Police Department with a vehicle stop on a street in Corinth, Mississippi, Agent Lane Caldwell was shot by the suspect being stopped during a struggle in the suspect's vehicle. Lane died a short time later. Lane too was loved and respected by all fellow Agents and was another Hero of the MBN.

A New Boss in Town

In January of 1980, Governor William Winter was inaugurated in Jackson. Along with a new Governor, there were many new "Bosses" in most State Agencies. MBN was no exception. Our new Director was a former DEA Agent with whom I had worked for many years, Thomas Dial. Tom took immediate control of the MBN and began assessing the status of our Agency and what needed to be accomplished to move the mission of the MBN forward.

For more than a month, Wallace and I would be involved in numerous ECMS sweeps throughout Jackson. The Capital, Governor's Offices and Mansion, the Research and Planning complex, Sillers Office building, and many other locations were swept electronically and disassembled physically during intricate searches by Wallace and me to insure that no "spy" devices would compromise conversations among our State's leaders as they managed our State's business. By the end of our sweeps and searches for all these executives, we knew where every cockroach was in every building in Jackson!

Because I was still "stationed" in Gulfport, I also was able to again become involved in the investigative activities of the District. With Steve Ford and most of the other original Gulfport Agents gone from the MBN by this time, I was working with other newer Agents who were conducting challenging and exciting investigations almost daily. Among those Agents were two men who would become and remain some of my closest friends and trusted working partners for many years. Their names are Jay T. Eubanks and Samuel Owens. In the years that followed, Jay would leave MBN and ultimately become a Group Supervisor in the Amarillo, Texas office of the DEA and Sam would rise to the position of Director of MBN. But at the time, we were "chasing outlaws, and taking names" together in Mississippi.

For the next year or so, other than an occasional Tech Services assist in another part of the State, or a training assignment, I would work with Jay and Sam regularly. In many cases I would help conduct surveillance for one of them to make an undercover purchase of controlled substance. On other occasions, I would act in the undercover role and they would provide surveillance for my transactions. We bought a wide variety of drugs including dilaudid, PCP, heroin, cocaine, assorted amphetamines and barbiturates, marijuana, hash, and many other drugs and concoctions in use and in demand by that era's version of the "crack-head". This dependent, user, customer mentality that would later be described as an involuntary "Illness", created a "market" for millions of dosage units of scores of drug categories which were being manufactured "in country" or were being smuggled from abroad. In my opinion, this condition was and still remains one of the greatest existential threats ever to face our Nation.

Our job, *and we had accepted it*, was to impede and/or eliminate this threat by any means necessary and legal. We all were and are committed to this mission, even today! Along with Jay, Sam and other Agents including Dean Shepard, we worked daily to identify, locate, and arrest drug violators from every corner of the Gulf Coast. We worked with other Agencies constantly to interdict drug trafficking throughout our area of the State and Nation. Between ourselves and other Local, State, and Federal Agencies, we built an extremely effective drug enforcement Team all along the Coast from

Texas to Florida. These boys and girls meant business and they were exceptional in their skills, dedication, and tenacity!

We all *"Rode the River"* a lot for many years together!

Give Me Your Gun

In March, 1980, I was still living in Picayune and had only been married to my wife, Gayle for a little over a month. I had taken a couple of weeks off from work in February and after our wedding, we had gone to the Great Smoky Mountains with my son, on our honeymoon-vacation. I was enjoying an evening at home with my new wife late in March when I received a phone call from a local business man. This business man was a bit more unusual than some of the other store owners and retailers in town. Lonnie was a "Class Three weapons dealer".

A Class three dealer is a federally licensed business owner who is empowered by law to engage in the sale of Class Three items which includes fully automatic weapons, suppressors and things of the like. The sale and purchase process includes a lengthy detailed application to the ATF and an in depth background investigation must be conducted regarding the intended purchaser. The process usually takes several months to complete, and the purchaser can only complete the acquisition and take possession of the weapon or item, after the process is completed and approved. One does not simply walk into a Class Three dealer and buy a machine gun and take it home.

When I answered the phone and Lonnie immediately said "Fred... I need some help... now!" he had my attention! My thought was that someone was holding a gun on him or there existed some equally threatening circumstance. It was not quite that pending, but he was right... he needed help.

He quickly explained that he had been contacted by a person we'll call Billy from Oceans Springs, Mississippi. Billy had requested that Lonnie meet him at the Picayune airport at about 10:00 pm that night and bring all his "machine guns" to the meeting for Billy and a couple of his friends to "look at". Billy went on to explain to Lonnie that Billy and his friends would be flying into the airport in a small plane owned by yet another friend of Billy who was from out of State. At this point Lonnie asked me, "Fred ... you think I ought to meet these guys...?"

After pondering all the above facts and circumstances for a lot less time than it takes to read my answer... I said, "Hell no!" I quickly followed up with an offer that would not only make Lonnie much more comfortable, but would also launch me into an investigation that would last for more than a year and a half. I said, "Why don't you let me go with you to meet these guys and just sit in your van while you talk to them...?" Lonnie jumped on that offer like the proverbial "Duck on a June Bug"... For those who earlier took exception to my evaluation of "Cold", the "Duck on a June Bug" thing means... real fast, quick, and in a hurry!!!

I told Lonnie to come by my house and pick me up at about 9:00 pm which I thought would insure that we arrived at the airport far ahead of Billy and his friends. This, in turn, would give us ample time to get "set-up" before they arrived. I then called my good friend Jim Luke with the Picayune Police Department and asked him to meet me at my house as soon as possible and explained the situation to him. After talking with Lonnie and having a "Gut Feeling" that I had experienced many times in the past, I concluded that it would likely become a great advantage to have additional back-up and more witnesses to what might occur when I responded to the potential outcome of Lonnie letting Billy and his friends "look at" and most likely fondle his machine guns. I knew that the viewing, at the least, had a better than average chance of becoming "very nasty"!

Luke arrived at my house followed shortly by Lonnie. After a hug and a brief good bye with my beautiful new wife, which would be repeated a thousand times over the next many years, I was off to the airport with Lonnie and Luke leaving Gayle on our couch alone to anticipate the outcome of another unplanned night at work for her new husband.

I had left my closest lifelong friend and Hero at home!
Thank God for our Heroes at home!!!

Arriving at the airport in Lonnie's van, we parked it so that we were set-up in a position from which we could provide protection for Lonnie during his meeting. We sat back and waited for Billy and his friends to arrive. At a few minutes after 10:00 pm we heard the plane land on the runway with a sharp but brief screech of its tires. Then after Lonnie flashed his lights on his van, the plane pulled up about fifty feet behind the van and its engines went silent. We had already planned for me and Luke to stay in the van while Lonnie met Billy and crew. We intentionally had parked so that the back of the van would be facing the plane. In this position Billy and his friends could not see through the windshield and into the back of the van where Luke and I were seated. We wanted Billy to think Lonnie was alone.

As the plane's engines quieted and the doors of the aircraft opened, Lonnie stepped out of the van with his ever present stub of a cigar clenched tightly between his front teeth, and walked, with his own unique cadence, toward the plane. He was carrying a large "satchel" that contained all of the treasures for which Billy and his friends had made their trip to Picayune. As Luke and I sat quietly in the van, we watched through a tinted side window while Lonnie displayed several of the weapons that he had brought for Billy to inspect. Anticipating evil to occur at every moment during the meeting, we remained "fully operational" throughout Lonnie's long meeting with Billy and his three friends.

It was about an hour into the meeting when Billy and one of his other compadres suddenly stopped talking, inspecting, and laughing. Billy made a motion toward the van and he and his *interested friend* exchanged a few words that were inaudible to Luke and me. We didn't need to hear their words to read their non-verbal communications and body language. It was obvious that they heard or saw something in or about our van that had caused them some concern. Again, Billy pointed to our van and asked or said something to Lonnie. Lonnie left the group and walked to the van and opened the side door where I sat. He explained that Billy and "Ted" had heard some sound come from the van and wanted to know who was in the van.

Luke and I had no idea what they had heard but one of us must have moved just enough that they had heard something. At this point, it didn't really matter who did what… it was time for me to get out and do a little "soft-shoe". Leaving Luke in the van, I hopped out and joined Lonnie. We walked back to Billy and crew and I introduced myself as Lonnie's close friend and fellow weapon enthusiast "Frank Gray".

After I left the van and joined the "party", Billy and his crew never looked at the van again. They completely accepted our story that Lonnie and I were alone in the van. Still expecting that the whole visit might be a well-planned "robbery" to acquire several fully automatic weapons after which Billy and his friends would simply fly away into the night for a quite theatrical but completely successful escape, I remained most vigil as I listened to Lonnie's brief discussions that followed my joining the group.

During those minutes that followed, I could tell that Ted was constantly looking about the area quite curiously. It was obvious that he might have had evil in his heart, but he just couldn't convince himself that there weren't others present in discreet locations around us who might rain on his picnic if he were to commit some overt act in furtherance of his criminal intentions. He was absolutely correct. As we continued to talk, my trusted friend Luke sat only a few feet away in the van, still "fully operational" and heavily armed. He was more than ready and completely capable of intervening in whatever plans Billy, Ted and the others might have had in mind. In opting not to go through with whatever plan they had arrived in Picayune to execute, they chose wisely to abort and return to base!

Ted became quite conversational just before leaving and asked me several questions in an attempt to determine who "Frank" really was. I was able to swap inquiries with him and had piqued his curiosity enough that when I told him that he and I might possibly be able to "do some business", he told me to come by his "shop" and we could talk. He told me where he owned a business on the Coast in Jackson County, and I told him that when I was in the area, I would drop in and see him. He said that would be great and shortly thereafter, Billy, Ted and two yet unidentified male subjects re-entered the plane, taxied out onto the runway and disappeared into the black sky above Picayune. They departed however, with none of Lonnie's highly controlled merchandise.

There is no doubt in my mind that they departed with a lot less armament than they had anticipated when they first flew into Picayune! Lonnie explained after the plane left, that before they asked who was in the van, he had expected them to rob him at any moment throughout the hour long meeting. We would never know whether Billy or Ted actually heard something or not, but whatever caused them to ask "who's in the van", might have averted quite a historic event that night at the Picayune airport. As we drove back to my house for Luke to get his car and for me to rejoin my wife, I was already planning a future meeting with my new friend Ted.

Over the next several weeks, I met with Agents of the Federal Alcohol Tobacco and Firearms Agency or ATF. I had worked with the local ATF Agents who were stationed in their Gulfport Offices, on many occasions. These and other Agents of this outstanding Agency proved themselves over and over for many years to be among my most trusted Law Enforcement partners throughout my entire fifty year career. I still work closely with former ATF Heroes even today as we travel all across the Nation! Together we have crossed and ridden many rivers!

Meeting with Ronnie Baughn and Skeet Waites in Gulfport, I was able to gain valuable information regarding Billy and Ted as well as the other two previously unidentified men that I had met with Lonnie at the Airport in Picayune. Not only were these men known to the ATF, they were suspects in a great deal of criminal activity over which the ATF had jurisdiction. The ATF Agents "knew who they were". With the registration of the plane which met us at the airport, and other identifiers that we were able to obtain through subsequent investigation, the ATF Agents became very interested in the group's aspirations, and initiated a parallel investigation to the one that I had begun for the MBN.

Over the next several weeks, I made contact intermittently with Ted and finally in early May, Ronnie, Skeet, other MBN Agents and I met at our offices in Gulfport to plan for my first undercover meeting with Ted at his business in Jackson County. As we met, Ronnie told me that their "procedures" required that I wear a "body wire" during my meeting with Ted. He was referring to a *small* transmitter/microphone that can be worn on the body of an undercover Agent that allows surveilling Agents to listen to the conversations between the Agent and the suspects involved. In this case that would be me and Ted. This was no new concept for me or MBN. We had dozens of these devices in use in every corner of the state. After all I was now a "*High Tech Guru*", I knew these things!

What was unusual was that they required "*Their Body Wire*" to be worn so that the ATF Agents could listen directly to the conversations. The suspects involved were significant enough to the ATF that they wanted everything done perfectly. Since we were all still anticipating some sort of illegal weapons case to develop involving Ted, the ATF wanted to be certain that they could record every word of every conversation to insure that if and when Ted was arrested, he could be successfully prosecuted and convicted in Federal Court. I was not at all excited about wearing a "wire" during our first meeting. There were just still too many unknowns about Ted and his friends. But, reluctantly, I agreed.

The next day, we met again to discuss final plans for my meeting with Ted. The plan was for me to travel to Ted's shop in a "high dollar" undercover vehicle, meet Ted and see what happened. We hoped that Ted would open up and I could overwhelm him with my loving personality and charming wit which would cause him to be overcome with a deep desire to sell, give, or otherwise transfer warehouses full of illegal weapons into my possession for which he would be incarcerated for many years to come…. Not exactly! I just hoped that he would talk to me and not start shooting as soon as I walked in his shop!

As I made final preparations for the undercover meeting, Ronnie and Skeet showed up at my office with *their* body wire. As they started to retrieve it from its storage container, I saw that it was encased in some sort of shoulder holster apparatus that I instantly thought Dirty Harry would have been proud of. With the "system" finally in full view… I was now certain that it would fit and transport a full sized .44 magnum! I asked Ronnie, "Does that belong to a guy named Harry?" We all laughed and I crawled into the leather contraption. It was awful! As I stated, we used 'Wires" all the time, but ours were normally "taped" to an unobtrusive portion of our body and covered with ample garments to disguise its presence. In this case, I was wearing blue jeans, cowboy boots, a tee shirt and a cowboy hat. With the device donned under my tee shirt, I added to my apparel. I put on my leather vest. With this addition, I was a bit more comfortable.

With the body wire tested and known to be working as advertised, we all departed the GDO and drove to Jackson County and to Ted's business. Being a thirty minute drive, we tested the wire several times in route. Ronnie and Skeet would pull up beside me on the highway and I would "sing a little Willie" for them and they would give a thumbs up. I think that after the first couple of tests they just wanted to hear me sing… By the time we arrived in the "target area", I had actually become a lot more comfortable with my ATF buddies' body wire system.

Ronnie and Skeet pulled into a predetermined position near Ted's place to listen to our meeting. I drove right up to the front door of Ted's shop, smoothly exited the Continental that I was driving and walked in the front door of the shop. Ted was behind a counter and when he saw me standing there, he came straight out, shook my hand and asked me to sit down on one of a couple of stools that were in front of the counter. He sat on another and we began to talk.

There was no one else in the front area of the shop, and Ted was not shy about commenting on his eagerness to purchase and/or sell weapons through any channels available that were not traceable by the ATF. As we continued to talk, he asked if I ever dealt in any kind of drugs. I told him "I've handled tons", and asked what he had in mind. He said he also had contacts for just about anything that I might want and he could even get small quantities for samples if I wanted to test his products. I said "Yep... I always test everything I buy... I have people who will test anything I bring them" He seemed impressed.

The meeting was going better than I could ever have hoped and suddenly... his eyes fixed on the area near my armpit under my right shoulder... with expletives deleted, one can certainly imagine what had just gone through my mind. He was only seated about a foot from me and reached right over and put his hand under my vest and tapped the bottom of my all leather body wire containment and transportation system.

With a couple of taps, he smiled at me and now with a much less friendly tone in his voice asked, "What the hell is that?" Having been in numerous "testy" undercover situations which had caused more than a few elevations in my adrenaline levels and related heart rate, I immediately felt a familiar surge in anxiety normally associated with a near catastrophic bodily release commonly referred to in more polite circles as "an unplanned, spontaneous, defecation"! Well... it wasn't quite that bad... but the level of concern and concentration has now been properly demonstrated!

Knowing that Ted had been a great host up to this point, and there seemed to be a better than average chance that I could negotiate some large purchases of a variety of controlled substances and weapons, I took a deep breath, because I had again lost mine, and said with a smile, "that's my gun". I thought that might satisfy him. It didn't! He smiled again and said, "Can I see it?" I said *sure*, and I knew beyond any doubt that Ronnie and Skeet had just lost *their* breath!

I always carried a gun. Usually, I carried one of several revolvers in my waist band on my right side. Today it was a Smith and Wesson .38 special model 60, five shot, stainless steel revolver, and it was inside my pants just below where the body wire was dangling. Still wearing a big smile, I reached under my shirt as if to retrieve a gun from the "Dirty Harry Rig", and turning the right side of my body slightly away from Ted, I grabbed my revolver instead. Just like that I pulled out my gun and held it in front of Ted. He loved it. He asked, "Can I hold it?" and as I said *sure*, I knew that by now, Ronnie and Skeet needed CPR. Ted looked at the gun and in admiration, commented on his desire to possess the pistol. As he handed it back to me he said, "I'm gonna trade you out of that thing one day".

I recovered the pistol from Ted, turned again as I placed it back in my waist band and feigned placing it back in the "shoulder holster". Repositioning myself on my stool, I talked to Ted for some time and by the end of our first visit, we were conversing as though we had grown up together as cousins. After the meeting I told Ted that I would be back in touch to begin negotiating for quantities of drugs and weapons. As he walked with me to the front door, he seemed very excited about our future together. Still wearing a "Cowboy Smile", I departed his shop. I drove onto highway 90, and after driving around the County for a while to insure that I wasn't being followed by Ted or one of his friends, I returned to the GDO where I met Ronnie and Skeet.

We discussed the conversations regarding the weapons that Ted said he could produce as well as the drugs he wanted to sell to me. We began to plan for subsequent meetings and my ATF buddies said they were sure that their agency would provide all funds necessary to purchase ample quantities of weapons from Ted to insure that he would remain behind bars for many years. They commented numerous times on how well they thought the first meeting had gone...

But... that was all **after** our *first topic of conversation* at the GDO... The *first discussion* was limited exclusively to the "*body wire* *double reverse"*. They could not believe that I had actually handed my gun to Ted who they and I knew was fully capable of turning the gun on me with the intent to do great bodily harm. They repeatedly exclaimed… "That's the wildest thing that we ever saw or heard of… What would you have done if he turned it on you?" I smiled and said, *"I had my knife in the other hand, I never give up my knife"*! Nor did I ever wear the "Dirty Harry Rig" again! We sought other options!

Over the next year, I met with Ted numerous times. Many of the meetings were intended to collect information that would assist the ATF with various other related investigations. We negotiated for a variety of illegal weapons and identified many of Ted's sources for those weapons. I was able to provide a believable channel through which Ted expected to make his fortune supplying hundreds of weapons to unknown purchasers, none of whom actually existed.

Also during this process, I purchased several of those "samples" that Ted had suggested that I "Test". They were in fact tested by "my people"… the Mississippi Crime Lab. With our talks about weapons declining, we opted to prosecute Ted on State drug charges and after the purchase of a sizeable quantity of cocaine, he was arrested and incarcerated in the Jackson County Jail. During the entire investigation concerning the weapons, my good friends with the ATF provided hundreds of hours of manpower support and other resources Ronnie and Skeet proved over and over to be the outstanding investigators and heroes that I had known them to be for many years before we worked together on Ted. They were and still are considered to be close and trusted friends with whom I left many tracks along the rivers of the Gulf Coast.

A few months later we tried Ted and he was convicted of the drug sales. During the trial, Ted's attorney constantly questioned me time and again as to the identity of the informant who introduced me to Ted. At first, I thought he was asking about Lonnie or Billy. Then

I realized that he was trying to build a fake alibi for Ted. As Ted's attorneys began to present their defense, it became obvious that they were arguing that some unknown individual had taken me to Ted's shop and had given the drugs to Ted to simply "hand to me" and that Ted was an innocent party just "doing a friend a favor". Placing Ted on the stand as a witness, he testified to the same fabricated scenario. His attorney then demanded that I disclose the identity of the informant and explain exactly how I came to meet Ted.

He nor his attorney liked my answers! With the attorney having opened a door beyond which he had no clue where it would lead, I began to explain. I told the Attorney, the Judge, Ted, and the Jury how a legitimate business man had been summoned to the airport in Picayune months earlier and Ted along with other known gun violators had attempted to illegally purchase or steal fully automatic weapons in the dark of night from this businessman. I told all present that Ted himself had invited me to come to his shop and after meeting with him we had discussed potential illegal gun deals for months.

Then I explained that the quantities of drugs that I had purchased from Ted, although significant, were only samples of what Ted intended to sell to me at later dates. I re-emphasized that there was no informant involved. Ted's attorney asked no more questions. The defense rested and the trial was soon over. After less than an hour of deliberation, the Jury returned guilty verdicts on all counts against Ted. He was subsequently sentenced to many years in the State Penitentiary at Parchman, Mississippi.

Oh… and he was also convicted of perjury!

Assignments Vary

Throughout the remainder of the year, we constantly were involved in investigations varying from small undercover purchases to large scale counter smuggling operations. During one week, I purchased four hundred Quaaludes for a "negotiated price" of $800.00 in OSF, from a well-known suspect while sitting in the parking lot of the "Pine Tree Plaza" shopping center in Picayune. During the purchase, Sam Owens, Jay Eubanks, and Jim Luke sat in various hidden locations a short distance away from my location and provided surveillance and back-up while the money and drugs exchanged hands between me and the outlaw.

Within a few weeks, and after other similar transactions, Jay and I worked with other Agents in the Biloxi area to support Sam as he purchased cocaine from a significant violator who owned and operated a business inside the "Edgewater Mall" on the beach in Biloxi. While other Agents and I walked unnoticed through the ever present crowd that filled the corridors outside the suspect's business, Sam entered the shop, met the suspect and did his magic. A few minutes later, the purchase was complete. Sam had purchased *ten ounces of cocaine* from the suspect. The Outlaw was immediately arrested by Sam and other Agents who were inside the shop acting as customers during Sam's purchase. Another ounce of cocaine was found during a subsequent search of the shop and all of the OSF was recovered from the suspect and shop. Another bad guy would soon face serious criminal charges and a potentially long prison sentence as a result of the quantities of drugs he was "marketing" and due to the quality of investigation conducted by Sam and the other Agents of the MBN.

We all knew that a drug dealer of his caliber should be going
away...
For Many Moons!!!

The other Agents and I also remained highly occupied with other duties that fell equally under our job description at the time. I constantly taught and attended training classes covering a wide range of drug enforcement topics at academies and other temporary or permanent training facilities. We all attended a "conspiracy" course taught by the DEA in Jackson. The course was designed to give us knowledge that would assist with the investigation of "upper level" drug violators who distributed large quantities of controlled substances through lower level dealers while the upper level drug kingpins seldom came close to the actual drugs. With the conspiracy laws, we could attack these upper level outlaws!

I also continued to provide technical support throughout the State upon request, as did my good friend Jim Wallace. On one occasion during this time, I was dispatched to the Hattiesburg area to perform an ECMS sweep for the Mayor of Hattiesburg. The requesting official was an old friend, Chief of Police Dempsey Lawler. On arriving at the Mayor's offices, I was met by the Chief and another old friend who I had not seen for many years. After several hours I completed the sweep and gave a clean bill of health to all of the Mayor's "most private spaces". All of his private places were clear and he was safe to go forth and communicate!

Oh, and the old friend travelling with the Chief... that was my first Law Enforcement "boss" for whom I had begun working undercover in the 1960's at the University of Southern Mississippi, just across town from the Mayor's office. It was none other than MHP Investigator Bruce Rogers... Did I tell you earlier what his official radio "call sign" and badge number was at the time?

I didn't think that I had...

It was B-*13*.

Back in the Enforcement saddle, we also continued to be involved in numerous smuggling Investigations. The most prevalent form of smuggling that we intercepted was "marine smuggling". The "air smugglers" like the ones in Vicksburg and Hattiesburg were probably more common, but carried much smaller payloads. They were much harder to intercept because they were able to divert from their primary landing site at the last minute, and simply fly to another preplanned alternate airstrip to unload. If they flew only for a few more minutes, they would be many miles from our arrest teams. By the time we could respond to their alternate site, if we even knew where they had diverted to, they would be long gone.

Vessels used by marine smugglers, on the other hand, could carry a much larger cargo of drugs because they had much larger cargo spaces. In some instances we would see large vessels like the "Gulf Stream" shrimp boat travel deep into the marshes of Hancock County, and offload directly from the "load Vessel" that actually brought the load from South America. In other investigations we would often see operations in which smaller boats would meet the "mother ship" far offshore and bring in smaller quantities of drugs to load sites far inland along intercostal waterways. These smaller "go-fast boats" would meet trucks that would haul the cargo from the drop point to an inland distribution location where the drugs would be disseminated to buyers from across the country.

These investigations were constantly being conducted by MBN and many other Agencies all along the Gulf Coast. With the "network" that we had helped establish with Agencies all across the Coast, we shared information and helped piece together clues that led to the surveillance and apprehension of numerous smuggling loads and resulted in the seizure of many more tons of drugs. Just as with our earlier investigations involving the Cigarette and Gulf Stream, when a smuggling group was located and identified along the Coast, all of the Agencies involved in our ad-hoc counter smuggling team would provide support and manpower for the surveillance that would inevitably be initiated.

Priceless Admonishments

S ome of these surveillances were short in duration, and some went on for months. During March and April of 1980, the MBN GDO, along with the Louisiana State Police, US Customs, DEA, the Coast Guard, and other Agencies began a smuggling investigation that centered in the Pearlington, Mississippi, area. Having rented a large house on a deep water bayou just off the Pearl River, the smugglers intended to bring a multi-ton load of marijuana to the house aboard their Yacht, the "Destiny V". By the size of the yacht, we knew that it was capable of

Destiny V, after seizure, about to be unloaded

transporting several thousand pounds of marijuana and also that it was able to travel far off-shore to meet the "mother boat".

Having followed the smugglers for several weeks, their activities began to indicate that the time for the load to arrive was near. Customs had several of their surveillance vessels pre-staged in the waters of the Gulf of Mexico just off- shore near the mouth of the Pearl River. The Coast Guard was positioned farther off-shore. They all were prepared to intercept the "Destiny V" as it left the river and travelled out into the Gulf to acquire its load from the larger vessel. The River was the only access to the Gulf for the smugglers. Unknown to these Pirates, they would have to travel through the surveillance net created by the Customs boats. With surveillance being conducted on the house, we would know when the "Destiny V" left and the Customs boat crews could be alerted.

After watching the house for several more days, finally, the "Destiny V" pulled out. As the smugglers piloted their yacht out into the Gulf, Customs intercepted them and cautiously followed from a

Miss Yvette, shrimp boat seized with over 20,000 pounds of marijuana

distance that would insure they could not be detected by the smugglers. Soon, the load vessel was met by the smugglers on their yacht and they quickly began to transfer the load from the "Miss Yvette" to the "Destiny V". The Miss Yvette was an eighty foot open water shrimper and had brought the multi-ton load of marijuana from South America across the Gulf. As the load was being transferred, Customs Agents and the Coast Guard, descended upon the vessels. Blinding lights from aboard the Coast Guard and Customs boats illuminated every inch of both the Miss Yvette and the Destiny V. The Pirates had gone from creatures of the night to a gaggle of scampering cockroaches with the flip of the switch on both of these high intensity flood light systems. They were quite literally *"Lit-Up"*!

As "our team" approached the smugglers, several of the Pirates picked up weapons from the deck areas of the yacht and for a moment, the Coast Guard and Customs Agents felt that the smugglers would fire on them. Then from the speakers on board the Coast Guard Cutter came an often heard and always welcome *hair raising admonishment* from the Captain of the boat...

"Occupants of the vessel "Miss Yvette", This is the United States Coast Guard! Heave to and prepare to be boarded! We will not ask again!"

An occupant of any vessel that floats, is not required to have "Sailed around the Horn" to be completely capable of comprehending the substance and seriousness of those instructions nor the implications thereof! The question always is, "are they going to be smart enough to comply"!

Just as the Customs Agents prepared to fire upon the armed bad guys, and some really bad things were about to emanate from the Coast Guard boat, the Pirates threw all their weapons overboard into the deep waters of the Gulf, and complied with the commands from the Coast Guard Captain.

The Customs Agents described the Pirates' weapons as appearing to be short barreled, compact frame, large caliber weapons known as the "Mac-10". They had seen at least four of these weapons being thrown overboard during their approach to the vessels.

The "Destiny V" and the "Miss Yvette" were boarded and seized. All subjects on both boats were arrested. The arrests were made without incident except for a couple of minor scuffles with temporarily non-compliant deck hands on the "Miss Yvette". All were quickly taken into custody. After being processed at the US Customs offices in Gulfport, all were locked up in the Hancock County Jail awaiting various hearings.

A search warrant was obtained by MBN for the house in Pearlington and was soon executed by Sam, Jay, other Agents, Officers and myself. While several suspects known to be part of the group were still unaccounted for, the house was unoccupied except for the Pirates' dog. The other suspects were never caught.

Mac 10 and other weapons, etc...found in smugglers' house

After securing the house and insuring that it was not occupied, a thorough search was conducted. During the search, we found two weapons and a large stash of ammunition and magazines. A Smith and Wesson semi-auto pistol and one previously described "Mac-10"

.45 caliber, fully automatic weapon complete with suppressor were found hidden in the house.

Neither the suppressor, nor the Mac-10 were adorned with a "serial number". In the weeks that followed, we would learn that the Mac-10 was among a shipment of approximately two hundred Mac-10's that the ATF had ordered to be destroyed in south Florida almost two years earlier. The guns were, in fact, destroyed pursuant to the order. However, the "pieces" were later purchased as "scrap metal" by a local entrepreneur who subsequently welded them back together and "recreated" the Mac-10's.

The "kicker" was that the newly re-assembled fully automatic weapons now had no sign of a serial number. The specific areas of the weapons where the required "cuts" were made, happened to be exactly where the original serial numbers had been located. When the guns were cut into pieces before being re-incarnated, the original serial numbers were demolished and obliterated. Thus, the Mac-10 that we found in the smugglers' house and undoubtedly the ones thrown into *"Davy Jones' Locker"* by the occupants of the "Destiny V" had no serial numbers. The Mac-10 that we found and seized was later re-inscribed with a serial number by the ATF and was awarded to the MBN. I carried it for several years in my official capacity until I turned it in to MBN Headquarters to be issued a more modern and more reliable weapon.

As a result of the "Destiny V" investigation, approximately

Marijuana bales being unloaded from Miss Yvette after seizure

ten tons of marijuana was seized along with several vehicles. Six smugglers were arrested and the above described weapons were confiscated. Also seized from the smugglers' house was a Winnebago motor home in which we found a great deal of marijuana debris or "gleanings". The Pirates' plan was to bring more than five thousand pounds of marijuana to the house via the "Destiny V". Then, using the motor home, they planned to haul varying amounts of the "killer weed" out to purchasers until the entire load was sold and disseminated.

They would then repeat the process when the next "mother lode" arrived. Had it not been for the Agents and Officers who were willing to go into harm's way on

Diesel fuel being sprayed onto marijuana bales at "burn site" hundreds of bales of marijuana from the Miss Yvette and Destiny V about to be consumed in smoke and fire

land and on sea to apprehend these dangerous Pirates, they would probably have been successful in their smuggling ventures far into the future. With the weapons that these maritime outlaws possessed, it

would have only been a matter of time until an innocent citizen or an unsuspecting Officer was perceived as a threat to one of these thugs and would have become a victim of a burst of .45 caliber rounds from a fully automatic "Mac-10"! Instead, the Pirates and their weapons were

The load from Miss Yvette and Destiny V just beginning to burn

removed from the community by a group of unsung Heroes!

Hardly anyone had noticed the efforts of the Heroes!
Hardly anyone had noticed that another band of deadly outlaws was gone!
The Pirates went to jail and the Heroes quietly went back to work!

Part of the "burn crew"... (L-R) Sam Owens,
Ken McMillan (US Customs), Jay Eubanks,
and Jack Taylor (DEA)

A Matter of Interpretation

Within a few months, another very similar Smuggling Investigation conducted by the same team of Law Enforcement Agencies yielded another multi- ton seizure of marijuana. After being surveilled for several months in a rural area north of Covington, Louisiana, and at the "Gulf View Motel" on the Mississippi Coast in Long Beach by Narcotics Agents with the LSP, DEA, and MBN, a well-organized group of smugglers again tried to bring their load into south Mississippi. This group possessed "go fast boats" with which to travel out into the Gulf to meet larger load vessels and retrieve bales of marijuana. The load would then be brought into a load site along an inland waterway.

They also had two four-wheel drive pickup trucks that they were using as "tow vehicles" to move their boats from the Covington "hide-out" to the Coast and then back to their rural retreat. The pickups were also equipped with long range communication systems. These *Ham radios* enabled the load crews to actually talk to the load vessel as it made its way back across the Gulf of Mexico to meet the group's "go fast boats" just off-shore. The group's "go fast boats" were two flat bottom skiffs that were twenty feet in length and were powered by 200 HP Mercury outboard engines. Because of the boats' design, they could navigate very shallow waters. These "skiffs" could also travel in excess of sixty miles per hour while loaded with two thousand pounds of marijuana.

For those who questioned "cold" and were unfamiliar with the "Duck and June Bug" thing, the act of travelling over sixty miles per hour in a flat bottom skiff that is simultaneously occupied by two thousand pounds of anything, is commonly referred to where I grew up as... *"Haulin' Booty"!*

Over the next several weeks, we followed this newest band of Pirates during many high speed trips to various inland waterways. We had also established a stationary surveillance post at the "Gulf View" Motel to watch a few of the Pirates who were occupying rooms 26 and 27. While watching the smugglers at the motel,

4 wheel drive pickups used by smugglers in "Wolf River" operation to pull "flat boats" and run counter-surveillance against Law Enforcement.

Agents including Sam and Jay had seen our newest bad guys moving several AR-15 style weapons between their vehicles and their motel rooms. We knew that they were heavily armed.

Also during the investigation, US Customs and the DEA had learned from surveillance assets off the coast of Columbia, South America, that the likely "Load Vessel" was the St. Ann, a ninety foot long open water shrimper. The load crew who we were now watching at a farm north of Covington and at the motel in Long Beach, continued making preparations to meet the load vessel. We knew that because of the capacity of the St Ann, our Pirates planned to acquire a large quantity of the "green leafy substance" known as marijuana from the load vessel.   After several more days, their ship finally came in.

On or about August 11, the members of the crew at the farm in Louisiana left their hideout, with their "skiffs" in tow, and headed to the area of Harrison County, Mississippi, known as Delisle. The members of the crew staying at the Gulf View also moved into the areas along the Wolf River. They seemed to be activating all of their resources. Being the highly trained and skilled investigators that we were, we concluded that something was about to happen…

Arriving at a boat launch on a bayou just off the Delisle-Pass Christian road, they launched their "skiffs" and travelled upstream on the Wolf River.   As the boats went up river to their load site, the trucks pulled the trailers which had previously carried the boats, to the same load site. Once there, all were hidden in a wooded

Bridge over Wolf River as seen from wooded surveillance position

area near the Wolf River. This was the site to which the "skiffs" would later that night bring load after load, from the off-shore vessel, to the large load truck which had also been brought to and parked near this offload point or load site. The load site was on a small bayou just off the Wolf River and was in an area that was not heavily traveled by other boaters. The Pirates had chosen wisely.

20 foot long aluminum "Flat Boat" with 200 horsepower outboard motor, used to transport more than 2000 pounds of marijuana per trip from the Saint Anne in the Gulf, to the load site on the Wolf River.

With the "skiffs", the load trucks, the pickup trucks and trailers all positioned and ready to go to work, the load crew sat back and waited until it was time to put their plan into action. With MBN, Customs, DEA, LSP, and other Agencies involved, there was plenty of manpower to handle almost anything that the smugglers might initiate. The problem was that the area around the load site was so lightly travelled and so remote that stationary surveillance was impossible.

With Customs and MBN boats off-shore watching for the load vessel and the "skiffs", the weather was not cooperating. It had become very foggy and was drizzling rain. This combination caused it to be very difficult to observe events both on the water and on land. The DEA and Customs Aircraft that had been providing aerial reconnaissance for us for several days, were grounded. We knew that the Pirates were heavily armed and we knew that they were running counter-surveillance along the roads near the load site. We couldn't afford to be compromised from an investigative nor from a safety standpoint. Any mistakes could have deadly consequences.

Instead of stationary surveillance positions, Agents were conducting periodic "drive-byes" throughout the area trying to determine whether the smugglers were still at the load site or had gone. Other Agents were driving across and parking near several bridges that crossed the Wolf River downstream from the load site. They were trying to monitor the river closely enough that they could see the "skiffs" as they sped under the bridges either going out after a load or returning to their camp with a load. On several occasions Agents saw one or more of the "skiffs" pass under the bridges but it had become so foggy and was so dark that they could hardly see the boats at all. By the sound and speed of the "skiffs" they were certain that these were in fact the correct Pirates.

After several such sightings, Jack Taylor of the DEA and Eddie Dickey of the MBN decided to go into the area of the load site on foot and see if they could determine to what stage of the operation the smugglers had progressed. They were dropped off on the main

road and began walking into the
area where the smugglers had their
load site. Both Jack and Eddie had
night vision devices (NVD's), but
they were both antiquated and offered
little in the way of useable images.
They were operating in almost total
darkness. After almost feeling their

The muddy trail down which Eddie and Jack walked through fog and rain in the dark to "recon" load site

way along for some distance, they heard a faint sound. Stopping and
quietly listening, they realized that they had walked right into the
middle of the Pirates' camp. All alone and surrounded by silhouettes
of sleeping bags and other unidentifiable objects, in the complete
pitch black of night, they had no way of knowing who, or what, was
where. They could hardly determine each other's location. It was
obvious to them however that the entire load had not been delivered
to the trucks by the "skiffs" or these outlaws would be long gone from
the riverside camp. Jack and Eddie then very quietly exited the area
and returned to brief the rest of us on what they had seen.

After several other sightings of one of the "skiffs" by Jack
who actually saw *bales* in the boat, there was then an absence of the
boats on the Wolf River. We concluded that the load transition must
be complete. With darkness fading and dawn approaching we
decided to swarm the load site and arrest whoever was there. Just
after daybreak we did just that. As we entered the "camp" in
numerous vehicles, we saw several of the suspects fleeing south into
an extremely dense area of the swamp that surrounded the load site.

Seeing that most of the Agents were following the fleeing
suspects in an attempt to apprehend these smugglers, I turned my
attention to the rest of the area around the large truck and other
vehicles. Having rained now for some time, my assumption was that
there may be some of the suspects within the various vehicles trying

to get out of the weather. I was even more concerned that if there were suspects in these vehicles they could possibly pose a serious threat to the other Agents who by now, all had their backs to these vehicles.

As I walked away from my vehicle to inspect the campsite closer, I saw movement in the cab area of the large load truck which was backed into the edge of the swamp to my left. I was armed with my handgun which was in my holster on my right side. I also was carrying in a much more available position, my MBN issue .223 caliber, Colt AR-15. Seeing movement, I focused on the cab of the truck. As I looked toward where I had seen the movement, nothing was visible... then... more movement. A head popped up from behind the dash area of the cab and then disappeared again. Then at the other end of the dash, another head popped up and quickly went back out of site. Within three or four seconds, I had seen at least three different individual heads in the cab of the big truck.

Location at load site where "unwilling" smugglers occupied the Load Truck", just prior to the "interpretation"

In my best "Command Voice", I ordered the occupants to hold up their hands and exit the vehicle. Nothing... I ordered them to come out again... Nada! Then I observed something rise over the dash that definitely was not a noggin. Having voiced my legitimate instructions now at least twice, and fearing that any additional time granted to these non-compliant individuals within the truck might give them entirely too much opportunity to initiate an attack on me or one of my fellow unknowing Agents, I opted to employ another communication asset!

Aiming my AR-15 well above the top of the cab of the truck, I fired about six rounds of .223 ball ammo into the trees behind the truck. The doors immediately flew open on the truck, four wet individuals exited the cab with all their hands extended fully, they marched as if rehearsed to the area in front of the truck, and assumed a kneeling position awaiting further instructions.

Dang... I was impressed!!!

The subjects were all handcuffed and placed into various vehicles to be transported to our offices for processing. All but one of the other suspects who had fled from the pursuing Agents had been captured in the dense brush and briars along the bayou that led back to the Wolf River. The outlaw who had successfully escaped into the swamp filled with bottomless mud pits and vermin of every known species, would later be apprehended along a rural county road by a local Deputy. The Agents who had chased the smugglers into the potentially unforgiving areas surrounding the Pirates camp all returned in varying degrees of discomfort as a result of their experiences with the flora and fauna of the swamp.

As we stood around our vehicles making plans to move all of the seized vehicles and vessels to a location for storage and inventorying, our Deputy Director, with whom I had worked for many years, approached me and in a low voice said, "You know Fred... our policy is that *we cannot fire warning shots...!*"

*Actual Load Site on a bayou just off the Wolf
River, where tons of marijuana were offloaded
from the "Flat Boats" into "Load Truck"*

Feeling that what I had done was completely justified based upon the threat that I perceived, I said, "Those were not warning shots... I asked my interpreter to speak to the non-Anglo individuals in the truck... they didn't speak English but they damn sure spoke .223!"

There was never another mention of policy nor warning shots.

Once again another band of Pirates was taken off the street and off the waters of the Gulf. As a result of the many month investigation, we were able to seize over twenty thousand pounds of marijuana, one "skiff" complete with two trailers and the pickup trucks that towed the boats, assorted paraphernalia, and a ninety foot open water shrimper named the "St. Anne". You caught the discrepancy in numbers of boats and trailers? I'm again impressed. One of the "skiffs", while returning to the load site with about forty bales of the leafy substance, was broadsided and cut in half by a previously uninvolved open water shrimper. The operators of the "skiff" were apprehended, and we picked-up bales of marijuana all along the beaches for several days. The boat, and all pieces thereof, were completely destroyed.

Saint Anne "Shrimper" used to transport almost 30,000 pounds of marijuana from South America to the Mississippi Gulf Coast

In addition to the brave acts performed by Jack Taylor and Eddie Dickey, other Agents also participated tirelessly in the "Wolf River Operation". From MBN there were Jim Kelly, Eddie Berry, Sam Owens, Tim Wilkinson, and Jay Eubanks. From DEA there was

Agent Charlie Park. From US Customs there were Ken McMillan, Ron Hughes, Harold Parker, and Pat Taylor. From the Louisiana State Police (LSP) there were Butch Milan, Corky Dwight, Jack Crittenden, Bob Thomason and many others. And from the Alabama Bureau of Investigation (ABI) there was my great friend and longtime trusted fellow *State Narc*, Ed Odom.

Almost 30,000 pounds of marijuana being burned after seizure during Wolf River investigation. These "burns" lasted for days!

Part of the "Burn Crew" on the Wolf River investigation. Standing by rear of Fred's MBN vehicle is Chief Ken Pell (Long Beach PD), seated are Fred and DEA Agent Charlie Park.

These men and dozens of other Agents, Officers, and Deputies worked tirelessly all along the Gulf Coast to impede and deter the smuggling of massive amounts of drugs and other contraband into our country. They constantly engaged in battle on the Sea, in the Air, and on Land to combat dangerous heavily armed Pirates and other outlaws year after year for well over a decade. The tenacity of these men as they courageously fought weather, exhaustion, political pressures, and various personal hardships to continue the war against a commonly perceived enemy of our nation and its youth was one of the most dramatic demonstrations of courage, patriotism and selfless dedication that I have witnessed by my fellow members of the "Thin Blue Line" in over fifty years.

They were among the best of the best and the bravest of the brave!!!

They were and are some of the greatest of America's Heroes!

Thank God for giving our country Heroes like these!

Up and Over

The rest of 1980 was spent scurrying about the Gulfport District and State chasing Outlaws. Most of my activities and assignments were, as we say in the business, uneventful. However, in the latter part of the year, I was called by our Director, Tom Dial. It was shortly after the conclusion of the Wolf River Smuggling Investigation. Tom asked if I could come to Headquarters in Jackson and meet with him the following day. By then, I had gained enough worldly experience and *Intergalactic Narc Knowledge* to know that a "*request*" by the Boss is a polite professional mechanism used to cleverly disguise a "*direct order*". I said "*Sure*"! I told him that I could be in his office by about 9:00 am the next day, and he stated, "That will work fine".

Arriving at Headquarters early the next morning, I talked with several of the secretaries, staff, and Agents around the famous coffee pot in an effort to see if I could glean some poorly concealed nonverbal indicator from an unwitting source as to what the heck the Boss wanted with me. With all my years of cleverly averting catastrophes and ambushes, I was sure that I could collect enough clues, or what the FBI would now call *indicators*, to walk into Tom's office completely confident and proud as a Brahma Bull.

I have gotten more useable "indicators" from clients of a morgue than from these donors. If any of my "friends" here at the coffee pot were holding any cards in this poker game, they were hidden well "inside their vest". They weren't giving up a particle of useful information, intentionally or otherwise. Feeling like the "Corpus Delicti" in a "Who-Done-It", I decided to make myself *uncomfortable* in the Boss's secretary's office until it was time to meet the Director,

At 9:01, I was invited into the Director's office by the *Deputy* Director. As I entered, the Director spoke politely and invited me to have a seat. As I sat down in the chair that he had pointed toward as the invitation was extended, I was looking for power cords that might be attached or sheets of plastic that might have been carefully prearranged under the chair. So far... so good!

I bet all of you with whom I have previously jested about "Cold" and "Ducks" and such are just brimming with excitement and have concluded that I am about to get my Butt handed to me over the "warning shot" thing. Well... I can't say that the circumstances surrounding that event had not occurred to me a time or two. Especially when the Deputy Director led me into the Boss's office. It had crossed my mind! So when the Director began asking me how things were going and then switched to queries concerning my aspirations within the MBN... I was beginning to hear the faint sound of a whistle that was on the locomotive that was probably coming down the tracks upon which my chair was currently positioned.

After several more relatively meaningless exchanges, and hearing the whistle less faintly, I gave an intentionally subtle glance toward the Deputy Director and then, as I turned my head and the Director came into full view, I asked... "Is there something that we need to discuss Tom?" He calmly picked up a piece of paper from his desk that I was sure contained some form of *Personnel Order*, and handed it to me across the desk. As I took the paper in my hand, he said "Congratulations Lieutenant Macdonald... You are about to become the new Commander of the Gulfport District Office... that is... if you want it..."

One of Mr. Fairly's most revered and most often quoted admonishments from "back in the day" was, *"Boy... if you screw this up... I'll transfer yo ass to Iuka...!"* Iuka is a community in the extreme northeast corner of the State... the most extreme corner. If one were *from* Iuka, this would not be a bad thing. The problem was, that at that time, there were only about four humans who lived in Iuka... NONE of us constituted any of those four! The threat of being transferred there was a condition that more than adequately demonstrated the gravity of consequences associated with whatever assignment an MBN Agent had just been given! It made it very easy to concentrate exclusively on the successful conclusion of the current assignment!

Having had little idea what to expect upon my arrival in Jackson, I now knew that, at least I wasn't going to Iuka!!! However, there was going to be a move... Part of the *promotional opportunity package* was that I had to move into a "local phone call radius". That meant that I had to physically move from Picayune to a new address that could be called from the GDO without using "1" or the "area code", to accomplish the call. This was still a time when "Long Distance calls" *cost extra...* a lot!

I could not be *"Long Distance"* from the GDO.

With the increase in salary associated with the promotion, I accepted the offer. They had finally dangled a "Carrot" in front of me that was hard to resist! They had made an offer 'I couldn't refuse". Over the next few months, with the help of an old friend and former State Legislator, Gayle and I found a small place almost exactly half way between Gulfport and Picayune. This, in my mind, created a "compromise" between moving and not moving away from Picayune. With my Son still living in Picayune with my first wife, I would never have moved any distance from him that would have eliminated or altered our weekends that he and I spent together every week.

That wasn't going to happen!

Having only a short time in which to make our move, we successfully remodeled the house before moving into it on April 1, 1981, and have lived on the property ever since. With few exceptions, Chad, Gayle, and I spent almost every weekend here together for many years! It's been a great place to watch all my little buddies grow up!

The Owner of the property, at the time, became one of the dearest and most highly valued friends of my entire life. He and his wonderful wife and family remain treasures to my family after almost forty years. Mr. Emmitt Niolet was one of my most respected and cherished Heroes of all time. Although we lost Mr. Emmitt a few years ago, the memories that I have of him, walk with me daily as Gayle and I now live on and own the property that his grandfather *homesteaded* many years ago. I would never have known Mr. Emmitt had I not been required to get a *"local number"*. It was exactly the right time to make our move from Picayune! We still have that same number, and to this day, it's still a "local" call to Gulfport... with the phone that has a wire connecting it to the wall!!!

Becoming the new Gulfport District Commander would once again, change the silhouette of the MBN in my mind forever. While some images, created by circumstances caused by my new position, would produce lasting mental frowns, other opportunities would paint smiling portraits of thousands of priceless encounters and would become some of the most rewarding events, and memories, of my career.

It was to be quite a *"ride"*!

Section VIII
Managing a District

The geographic area that comprised the Gulfport District consisted of five Counties. Pearl River, Hancock, Stone, Harrison and Jackson Counties were the primary areas worked by the GDO Agents. These Counties covered the area all along the coast from Louisiana to Alabama and in some areas extended more than eighty miles inland. The area also contained two Interstate Highways, dozens of deep water rivers, bayous, and canals and over one hundred airports, airstrips and private air fields. It was the most densely populated area of the State with the entire coastal area comprising an almost continuous "City" made up of numerous municipalities whose, borders or city limits, were all contiguous to each other. Where one city ended, another began.

While some of these Cities were quite large in geographic size and population, some were quite small. Likewise, the Law Enforcement Agencies associated with these Cities varied directly. The larger the City, the larger the Agency. The same applied generally with the Counties and their Sheriff's Departments. Along with these "Local" Agencies, there were several State Agencies including the Mississippi Highway Safety Patrol or *MHP*, the Alcohol Beverage Control or *ABC*, and the Mississippi Bureau of Narcotics or *MBN*. Federal Agencies included those bearing one of the "alphabet" identifiers with which all are familiar including the *ATF*, *DEA*, and *FBI* as well as US Customs, Border Patrol, and of course the US Coast Guard.

Even with the presence of hundreds of Law Enforcement Officers of varying jurisdictions and enforcement responsibilities, the large population of citizens along the Coast always offered ample supplies of potential victims for thousands of aspiring criminals of varying levels of experience as Outlaws. There was never a shortage of bad guys to go around. One simply never knew what was going to fall from the sky, emerge from the sea, or crawl from the swamp next. With highly talented, brave, and honest Agents working in the GDO, as well as tremendous resources with which to work, it was an exciting time to be a Cop on the Gulf Coast.

Priorities

As I assumed the role of District Commander in the GDO, I had only a couple of primary objectives. I wanted to assist the Agents in the development of cases that would remove as many drugs and associated outlaws from the street as possible. In short... I wanted the GDO to be *successful* in its mission. The second objective that always outweighed the first was that I ALWAYS wanted to do everything possible to keep the GDO Agents *safe* and insure that they got home to their families at the end of each shift. In order of priority, the objectives always were, and always will be...

"Safety and Success"!!!

These are the two primary motivators that have guided me in every decision that I ever made while managing men and women that I led or sent into harm's way. It is also the mindset that I have tried to impart to thousands of other Officers who I have trained or worked with for well over four decades. I could not believe more strongly that one should first plan for "Safety" and then for "Success". Every element of every operational or management plan should support one or both of these two objectives... ALWAYS!!!

It has been my experience that when misguided personal goals and aspirations begin to influence planning in a manner that it directly affects the operational environment, the likelihood for "Safety" and "Success" begins to diminish rapidly. Most importantly, my experience has proven that when these goals or aspirations are present, people usually get hurt! In the Military world, there exists an operational concept that allows for what is known as the "Accepted Casualty Rate". This factor varies from operation to operation and historically has applied even to training programs. In the Law Enforcement world there is "NO ACCEPTED CASUALTY RATE...EVER"!!!

Getting any Law Enforcement Hero injured or killed due to poor planning is *totally unacceptable!!!* Always has been... Always will be!!!

Working within these parameters and with these objectives always guiding me, I assumed command of the Gulfport District Office of MBN and began managing the hundreds of investigations which were to be conducted over the next six years by the dedicated and brave Agents of this office. It was a great honor and provided many challenges and opportunities!!!

Ludes and Goggles

In early 1981, we received a call at the GDO from Agent Dean Shepard who still lived in the Pascagoula area. Pascagoula is in Jackson County and is only a few miles from the Alabama and Mississippi State line. The Jackson County Airport was on the east side of Pascagoula and only a few miles inland from the Gulf of Mexico. Dean had received a call from the FBO (Fixed Base Operator) at the airport. The FBO managed the airport and had observed a twin engine plane fly into the airport and park in an unusual area some distance from the FBO Offices. The pilot and second occupant of the plane had secured the aircraft and had left the area in a vehicle that had come to pick them up.

Being suspicious of the aircraft and it being one with which the FBO was unfamiliar, he approached the plane to see if he could see inside. Upon his inspection of the interior of the plane, the FBO could see numerous boxes and other items that made him even more suspicious. Dean agreed to meet the FBO at the airport and asked that I meet him there with any other available Agents so that we could inspect and/or search the plane. I agreed and left the GDO in route to meet Dean at the airport. The total distance from our office to the airport was about fifty miles and within a relatively short time, I was meeting with Dean, Agent Tommy Payne, the FBO, and others.

By the time that I got there, Dean and the other Agents were meeting with the FBO near the small plane. I also had advised the MBN Regional Commander Eddie Dickey, of the circumstances and he had likewise travelled to Pascagoula to meet me at the aircraft. While Eddie and I were in route, we had notified the Gulfport, US Customs office of the call from the FBO and upon arrival at the plane we were met by Customs Agents Pat Taylor, Ken McMillan, and others. The significance of having our ever present Customs partners present was that they could legally search the plane if it had just re-entered the United States.

Upon visual inspection of the plane, it became obvious that it and its operators had been involved in a smuggling venture. The large cardboard boxes were adorned with various printed words... all of which were written in Spanish. We observed, still from outside the plane, that there were several other items that supported the "smuggling theory". In the cabin area of the twin engine plane were several portable plastic fuel containers that seemed to be empty. There were a pair of binoculars, and a "hard case" that we all recognized to be the container in which dual lens *night vision goggles* (NVG's) were normally stored. We also observed various charts and maps for areas both within and outside the United States.

Having observed these items, the Customs Agents concluded that a search was warranted and they opened the plane. Upon removing the items from the plane, we learned that they had in fact just returned from a remote site outside the US. The operators/pilot had obviously used fuel that had previously been stored in the fuel containers to refuel the plane while it was in flight. Utilizing a makeshift refueling system that had been installed in the cabin area of the plane, they *very dangerously* had poured fuel into the "hose assembly" that was set up to refuel in flight. Pouring fuel in this manner had undoubtedly filled the plane with highly combustible fumes emitted from the high octane aircraft fuel. There is no logical reason why any one of the many electronic devices also installed in the aircraft, had not ignited the fumes and turned the plane into an unintended but impressive "skyrocket".

After removing all items from the cabin of the plane, we also learned what was in the large cardboard boxes that the FBO had first observed. Contained within, and packaged very carefully so as not to be destroyed or damaged while in transit, were 300,000 Quaaludes from a South American clandestine lab. It was, and as far as I know still is, the largest single seizure of Quaaludes ever in the history of the MBN or by any other Agency within the State.

With the registration numbers on the plane, and other evidence collected from the plane and at the scene, the Pilot and his co-smuggler were subsequently arrested and convicted of smuggling. They were both sentenced to long jail terms in a federal penitentiary.

Twin engine smuggling plane seized at airport in Jackson County, MS. Cardboard boxes are packed with hundreds of thousands of Quaaludes

Boxes containing Quaaludes... also "Night Vision Goggles" in black hard case, and "fuel cans"... all seized from smugglers

It was all made possible by the keen eye of an honest FBO who "saw something suspicious", and the skills and experience of the members of our multi-agency counter-smuggling "Team" from the Gulf Coast.

Agents beside seized twin engine and other evidence on ground. (L-R) Eddie Dickey, Pat Taylor (US Customs), Tommy Payne (MBN) with dark cowboy hat and beard, and others

Primary or Corollary?

While enforcement always remained our primary responsibility, the other Agents and I still also had numerous assignments which were sometimes *indirectly* related to our enforcement duties. I continued conducting dozens of ECMS sweeps throughout the State for Dignitaries like the Governor, Senators, Legislators, as well as other heads of Agencies like the Commissioner of Public Safety and District Attorneys.

Another responsibility was training. We all constantly attended specialized training programs that were conducted inside MBN by our own Agent/Instructors. We also had many opportunities to go to schools provided by some of the best trainers in the Nation. Because I had been promoted into a supervisory or management level position, I was required by MBN policy to attend various *Police Management* schools.

Among the ones that I attended were the FBI *Mid-Management Training Program*, the DEA *Drug Unit Managers*

School, a specialized *Mid-Managers' Seminar* conducted by the Mississippi State University, and a two week *Police Managers School* conducted by Babson College in Boston, Massachusetts. I was also fortunate enough to attend various other courses all across the Nation.

By now, I was providing much of the firearms training for all of the MBN Agents from across the State, and managing most of the Agency's quarterly Firearms qualifications sessions. Because of these responsibilities, I was constantly attending Firearms related training including Firearms Instructor classes, Advanced Firearms instructor classes, Armorers' Schools for the various weapon systems that were issued by MBN to its Agents, and special tactical training schools.

All of these programs were taught by the leading training providers in the Nation and the world at that time. By attending these training programs, other Agents and I were able to acquire exceptional knowledge and skills that we in turn passed on to all of our Agents from throughout the State. Through this means, we could expose every Agent to critical but very expensive training that they would otherwise not be able to attend. This training was designed to save Officers' lives in the most deadly of situations and confrontations. Being a part of the process of teaching skills that helped save Agents' and Officers' lives has always been one of the most rewarding aspects of my job. It doesn't get much better than helping Heroes learn skills that will get them home to their families when their shift is over!!! Learning and teaching "Officer Safety" became a way of life!

What an honor it has been to work with Heroes training Heroes!!!

Many other opportunities also exposed themselves at every turn. We very frequently gave speeches to civic organizations, private groups, Colleges, and Universities all along the Coast. These groups constantly requested presentations regarding drug awareness and prevention topics as well as stories about our most recent seizures of contraband. As they listened to our stories and winced at the close calls with disaster that we would describe regarding our most dangerous of operations, they would pledge their support to encourage our State Legislators and Senators to provide much needed funding for our Agency. Many times these State law makers were in our audiences. It was an exceptional mechanism to get our message out to the public and to our State Government Officials! They became proud of their Heroes also!!!

For over six years, my tracks would weave between undercover buys, surveillances, technical support, training programs, and managing the operations of the GDO. I learned that an effective Agent or Manager must be able to prioritize both primary and corollary responsibilities in a way that they all are accomplished... safely and successfully. All are important and contribute to achieving the mission of the Agency! Technically... It's a "system"!

Climbing the Ladder

With the competent Agents assigned to our Office, we were able to make cases on and arrest some of the most significant drug violators ever to operate in our State. We arrested members of the drug underworld who other Agencies and the MBN had known for years were involved in notorious criminal enterprises all along the Gulf Coast from Texas to Florida.

Criminals who had built legendary reputations that they had enjoyed for years were snatched up, one by one by the GDO Agents and sent away for long prison terms in both state and federal penitentiaries. Several of these outlaws died in jail before they could complete the sentences imposed upon them for their crimes. It was a bad time for Outlaws! The Agents of the MBN did more than their part to win the "War on Drugs" during those days!

To get to the top of any structure, one usually must start from

the bottom. That was commonly the way that we approached the sometimes daunting challenge of taking out a drug kingpin. We were never so arrogant as to ignore an opportunity to make a case on a lesser or lower level violator in order to develop a path to the drug dealers at the

UC purchase at residence on Beech Street in Picayune, MS

next level above the current target. Upon making a prosecutable case on a dealer at the next level… we repeated the process.

We would keep "climbing the ladder" until the most current defendant started mentioning names that we recognized as *targets of value* in our next level of investigations. Upon reaching the person who we had determined to be the head of the organization, or the "Grand Poohbah" of the current "Dopers Anonymous" empire, we would usually call in an Agent from another part of the State to minimize the possibility of a compromise. Then, employing the talents of our guest undercover human *weapon of choice*, and with ample surveillance both technical and "in the flesh", we would set about purchasing adequate quantities of controlled substances to put the Poohbah in the calaboose for as long as possible in order to permanently disrupt his or her criminal enterprise.

The ladder would have been "Clum"!

UC purchase by Sam Owens at the Small Craft Harbor in Pass Christian, MS

Starting at the bottom didn't always yield cases of interstellar significance, but the worse that could happen was that we would remove a "street level" dealer from a neighborhood who was, at the very least, endangering the citizens in his or her immediate area of operation. These areas were always full of victims of every size, age, sex and persuasion. Removing a "Doper" from their midst was always a good thing. Anytime we could decrease the amount of LSD, Heroin, Amphetamines, Cocaine, or marijuana from a neighborhood, we felt that it was a job worth doing!

Starting at the "ground floor" the Agents of the GDO and I purchased a wide variety of drugs and widely varying quantities of these controlled substances. One Agent might purchase fifty Quaaludes from a suspect in Hancock County near Louisiana for $200.00 OSF before lunch and by nightfall, while in Gulfport, negotiate and purchase two hundred Quaaludes for $530.00 in OSF. Then following the undercover purchase, execute of a warrant on the house from which the purchase was made. In that Search Warrant, we found and seized over two thousand more Quaaludes, and a half pound of marijuana.

As the sun would rise the next day, we would be out on the ground again arranging our next purchases, searches, and seizures. We often might have an Agent in Ocean Springs purchasing cocaine with two Agents running surveillance while another Agent was in Long Beach buying dilaudid with Agents and local Officers providing cover and documenting the transaction. In one instance, we arrested a well-known dealer at the Gulfport Airport upon his return from a drug acquisition soiree to a City in a northern State. During his arrest and subsequent search, he was found to be in possession of eight hundred "preludin" tablets, six hundred "T's and Blues" (a heroin substitute), another two thousand tablets of assorted illegal drugs, and $6,976.00 in cash.

These types of investigations would be conducted for days, weeks, or sometimes months… and then… we'd hear that name… the name that rang that bell up at the top of the ladder. At that point in the process, we would begin to develop a prosecutable case against this newest *Poohbah* that would remove another top level drug supplier from the streets of our State for many years… if not forever!

Often joking among ourselves, we would proclaim… "We're bustin' Outlaws from *Coast to Coast*… from the backwaters of Bay St. Louis to the mouth of the Pascagoula River…" These brave and dedicated Agents were definitely kickin' butt and takin' names! When the "Bell Rang", it was *all hands on deck*, and the Agents of the GDO brought many pirates' pirogues into permanent "Dry-dock"!

From Cocaine Cowboys
to No Boys Allowed

In August of 1981, a notorious, interstate drug dealer's name popped up on the radar of the GDO. We'll call him Donald. For several years, other Agents and I had tracked this outlaw from location to location along the Coast and knew that he was involved in various high level drug operations that involved many other notable drug kingpins. We knew that he owned a "camp" type house on a bayou just outside Waveland, in Hancock County. We had documented all vehicles and vessels that had been present at the camp for many months. We had followed him to numerous meetings with known top level bad guys at locations throughout a four or five county radius and documented their associations. We had expended many man hours exhausting every possible investigative tool at our disposal and we had not been able to directly connect him to any specific crime for which he could be arrested. We knew he was "up to no good" but so far, legally, he was the proverbial "hounds tooth"… he was clean.

Then, we were given a valuable chip to play. An informant provided by a close friend and local Sherriff was about to "Ring the Bell". Upon meeting with the Confidential Informant or CI for the first time, I immediately knew he was going to be the "real deal". He was straight forward and throughout a long interview, he was not at all hesitant to say three words that most CI's have a hard time uttering and still maintain the persona that they *"know everything"*. When asked a question about which he had no knowledge, he would quickly say *"I don't know"*. I was impressed!

After several interviews with the CI and a few successful "trial runs" in which the CI arranged for the purchase of small quantities of drugs from low level dealers, we pressed the CI regarding his knowledge of any significant distributors in the area. The first name that he uttered was none other than *Donald*. Over the next several hours of the interview that ensued, we learned pretty much everything there was to know about 'ole Donald! We learned many previously unknown but highly noteworthy facts about his criminal enterprises and verified almost every single evil deed for which we already believed Donald to be responsible… and guilty! Donald was an even more significant outlaw than we had suspected!

As we placed several wheels in motion which needed to start rolling, we continued making plans with the CI to arrange for a significant purchase of cocaine from Donald. The CI had explained to us that he had connected several "buyers" with Donald in the past and that it should be no problem to introduce an undercover Agent to him for the purpose of making a "buy" from the outlaw. I contacted a fellow Agent, good friend, and District Commander of the Hattiesburg MBN Office. Jim Kelly quickly agreed to provide the undercover charm for the meeting and purchase of drugs from our most current upper level resident of a significant ladder.

In late August after making all necessary plans and arrangements to purchase drugs from Donald, Lt. Kelly came to the

Coast and final preparations were complete. Working with one of our female Agents, that we'll call Cindy, from the GDO, the couple travelled to a hotel in Long Beach and drove to the room previously obtained by yours truly. Shortly after they entered the room, they were met by the CI as per previous plans. From the room, the CI called Donald, told him where they were and suddenly the "undercover train" was rolling down the tracks.

After about twenty minutes, Donald arrived at the hotel, parked outside Kelly and Cindy's room, exited his car and knocked on their door. Opening the door, Cindy invited Donald into the room. As our outlaw entered the room… *Yes…* Donald became visible on the monitor in the adjacent room that had been set up as our "listening post" several hours earlier. We were "on the air" with properly installed pinhole lens attached to video and audio recorders, with related tapes properly "Packed", and all necessary cables properly routed and cleverly disguised.

Wallace would have been proud!

As Donald entered the room, the CI also welcomed him and introduced him to Jim and Cindy. Within a few minutes after several personable pleasantries, Donald produced an ounce of cocaine from his pants pocket and laid it on the table in front of Jim. Jim withdrew $2,000.00 cash, in OSF, and handed it to Donald, and just like that after almost three years of chasing this high level drug dealer, we had what is known as a "*hand to hand*" purchase of a controlled substance for which Donald could be sent to prison for many years.

After a brief discussion about future transactions, Donald left the undercover room and was quickly gone from the hotel parking lot. Jim, Cindy, and the CI remained in the room until our mobile surveillance team consisting of Jay and Sam verified that Donald was well away from the Hotel. They then all exited the Hotel room and while the CI went back to his lair, Jim and Cindy, along with all surveilling Agents returned to the offices of the GDO. That is, of course, after all the surveillance equipment was removed from the two rooms and they were returned to near normal condition.

Did I give the impression that our "*Tale was Told*" and the story was complete? Not so fast…! This Odyssey is only beginning! You may need another bag of popcorn! Like I said, our friend Donald was even more significant than we had thought!

Within a couple of weeks, and after several direct communications and negotiations between Kelly and Donald, we were back at the Hotel in Long Beach. It's now early September and still quite warm on the Gulf Coast. Everyone was still adorned with short pants and tee shirts. There was more than an adequate presence of perspiration on the brow of most of the local resident population. Regarding our visitors who arrived from the areas that define "cold" differently than we do, most walked around holding the ever present handkerchief attempting to maintain at least a "look" of *being cool* by constantly blotting droplets of sweat from uncomfortably warm faces. We *all* appreciate the same definition of "hot"!

After getting set up in a new pair of adjoining rooms, we were ready to entertain Kelly's newest business associate. This time, Kelly would meet Donald alone in the undercover room and consummate the current transaction. Other Agents including myself, were stationed both within the adjoining room and in discreet locations around the perimeter of the Hotel which would allow them to easily surveil Donald as he exited Kelly's room and left the area.

At about 7:47 pm, the deal was done and a second "hand to hand" was completed between our Lt. Kelly and the now highly documented felon, Mr. Donald. During the purchase, while Donald was handing two ounces of high grade cocaine across the hotel room table, Kelly was taking custody of the drugs and simultaneously handing $4,300.00 cash in OSF to an unsuspecting Donald.

Kelly would state later, as we discussed the purchase that the calm and confident look on Donald's face throughout the meeting was an unmistakable indicator, to the seasoned undercover Agent, that Donald had participated in many similar transactions throughout his long criminal career! We all knew that Donald had "Been Around"! We also knew that he undoubtedly could provide much more cocaine than the MBN could afford to purchase and let the OSF "walk".

Knowing now that Donald was a very capable outlaw, we had begun developing a plan by which we could bring an end to his criminal conglomerate.   The ultimate objective of these initial purchases was to convince Donald that these first transactions were intended only for Kelly to obtain "samples" of Donald's "product". With these samples, Kelly could *decide* if he wanted to acquire much larger quantities that would in turn establish a constant supply of cocaine for Kelly's imaginary customers. Donald seemed to be "all in"!

Now having two prosecutable felonies against Donald, we decided to do more negotiating than purchasing. The concept was that we would attempt to create an environment in which *Donald would try to convince Kelly* to buy from him rather than *Kelly try to convince Donald* to sell larger quantities. For the next several months there were many communications between Kelly and Donald, between the CI and Donald, and between the CI and me.

Communicating regularly with Kelly, we both remained convinced that Donald would continue to attempt to "sweeten the pot" until his greed was adequately stimulated, and he would eventually deliver to us the largest quantity of cocaine at his disposal. At that point, we would thank him for his business and dissolve our partnership. Donald would go to jail for *many moons* as Chief Kinsolving would often quip during our visits. Then, Kelly, the other Agents, and I would go forth in search of our next "Ladder".

It's not always a bad thing that our plans must sometimes be altered!!!

As conversations continued between the CI and Donald, many topics were discussed. Donald constantly provided the CI with a never ending stream of intelligence information about his criminal endeavors. He also spoke of the activities of many other career criminals all along the Gulf Coast and throughout the Nation. Donald was a walking library of "Doper Wisdom".

During one conversation with our CI, Donald spoke of a process for cultivating and growing high grade Marijuana plants. The process was not that with which we had become familiar through the hundreds of seizures that we had made over the years in what were known as "patches". These previous "patches" were "outdoor grows" which had ranged in volume from just a handful of plants to many thousands of plants sometimes covering dozens of acres in rural areas.

While the volume of plants produced in "patches" could be substantial, the quality of the plants was usually only fair to poor. Because of the poorer quality, the grower could only expect to receive minimal return on his or her investment as compared to the higher quality "weed" commonly known as "Columbian Gold" that was brought in from abroad. Growers were constantly looking for methods of improving the quality of their plants to allow them to demand higher prices for their product.

To increase the quality of the plants, the grower needed to increase the level of the active ingredient in their weed. This magical ingredient was, and is, the *pot of gold, pun intended*, at the end of every doper's rainbow. It is *"tetrahydrocannabinol"* or "THC". The highest concentration of THC in marijuana plants is in the female plant. It is nature's way for the plant to encourage pollination by the male plant. In the absence of pollination, the female plants continue to produce more and more THC in an effort to entice a boyfriend. With no available mates, the female plants continue to create and emit THC. The treasured substance eventually covers the exterior of the female plants with a "sticky" film. The value and prices, at this point in our "Floral Courtship", just went through the ceiling for the grower and happiness and love abound!

With this knowledge, and a little additional "book learning" our grower can now identify the male plants and extract them from his "patch" and wait for nature to unwittingly and non-conspiratorially perform her magic. However, if one will step back from the "patch" briefly and ponder all that has been imparted, one might wonder... *"What if there are other "patches" nearby?"*

Upon pondering thusly,
one would be considered an exceptional
"ponderer"!!!

"Boy" plants on back porch of house after being "cut out of the herd" by the marijuana wrangler

Our grower's newest concern, therefore, has just been identified. In an outdoor growing situation, the random presence of a male plant, even at some distance away, creates the highly unwanted environment in which our cultivator's "female" or "*Sensemillia*" highly valued but yet immature plants, might become adequately pollenated so as to devalue these plants and render them just another "patch" of killer weed. This would be devastating to any respectable herb cultivating wizard with any pride whatsoever! It would also negatively affect that grower's profit margin and related "bottom line"! It would create a highly unwanted set of circumstances back at the "patch"!

The obvious remedy was, of course, to go "inside". While this eliminated the *pollination problem*, it also caused a great deal of hardships for the, by now common, aerial reconnaissance being flown by Law Enforcement in most States with much assistance from the National Guard. There were however other complications for our new indoor cultivators as well. These new considerations were the catalyst for countless studies, experiments, and tests that in turn yielded hundreds of publications regarding various remedies for problems which plagued the "indoor growers" and their crops.

Two of the greatest challenges for our new growers of indoor weed, other than lighting, were nutrients and atmosphere. Among the leaders in research regarding these "problems" was our government. In Central America during the 1960's our military continued to conduct experiments regarding the growing of vegetables and other food for our troops. Since as early as 1934, they, along with civilian researchers, studied various methods of growing food indoors, with artificial light and with no soil. They studied various chemical nutrients and methods to introduce these substances to the plants that they were growing indoors. They experimented with a variety of gasses that could be injected into the atmospheres created within their enclosures. Learning that plants could be grown to maturity while suspended in a fluid filled trough, as they are being fed only liquid nourishment, with no soil present, the "*hydroponics*" method of cultivation was born. While many other researchers were engaged in the same endeavors, our Government's efforts in the 1930's were among the first successful programs. Large quantities of various plants could now be grown in completely artificial environments with no sunlight, and with no soil.

Discussing indoor grows with Donald, our CI learned that he had rented a farm in northwestern Pearl River County. The farm was in a community known as "White Sand" and was about twenty miles west of Poplarville. After describing the farm in detail to the CI, Donald finally invited him to the farm for a "show and tell". Our CI quickly accepted. Within a few days, with ample surveillance all around, the CI travelled with Donald to visit the farm. Once there the tour began. After being at the rural retreat for several hours, Donald and our CI returned to the Coast and parted company after a quick meal at a local fast food restaurant in Waveland.

Meeting with our CI later, he gave a detailed account of what he had been shown at the farm. We were all impressed. The farm was a "hideout" for an elaborate indoor grow and was in full production. Listening to the CI, we learned that he had observed numerous marijuana plants in an old garage or shed that was about fifty feet from the house which provided living quarters for Donald while he was at the farm.

On the back porch of the house, the CI had observed a few "plants" laying just outside the back door that "seemed to be fine and had just been pulled-up and tossed on the porch". The CI went on to describe the growing environment as a "bunch of big plastic pipes with plants hanging over them with their roots dangling in the pipes." He told us there were big metal oxygen bottles, gauges, thermometers, and other gadgets all over the interior of the "shed". Finally, he described a strong odor that he sensed when he walked into the "grow area".

The information received from the CI sounded quite familiar as it related to our new knowledge pertaining to *Hydroponics growing*

High pressure "bottles" which automatically injected specific gas mixtures into the atmosphere of the "grow area"

methods, and was more than adequate to acquire a search warrant for Donald's farm, buildings and surrounding property. We were certain that the farm housed an indoor grow, but we could not have guessed, at that time, what its significance would be.

While negotiations were still ongoing between Kelly and Donald for more cocaine, we believed that this unexpected business venture that Donald had branched into would help demonstrate, to any presiding judge, the broad and far reaching extent of Donald's criminal enterprise. We couldn't have been better "believers"!

After providing for adequate manpower for the execution of a search warrant in the rural area of the farm, and insuring that our plan would accommodate the safety of all involved, we obtained a search warrant for Donald's farm and indoor grow. We were about to wrap up our investigation that included many months of undercover interaction with Donald... we thought!

Once all plans and preparations were made, we went to the area of the farm. Meeting at a predetermined rally point about two miles from the farm, we made final preparations to execute the warrant. Eddie Dickey, Jay, Sam, other Agents, and I would go in on foot and secure the house and shed. Jim Kelly would be positioned in a stationary location from which he could give us protection from anyone who might try to ambush us as we cleared and secured all of the structures on the farm.

Kelly went in ahead of the rest of the team and employed skills that he had developed for many years from his days as a Marine in Viet Nam and from his experiences as an Agent with MBN. He found a vantage point about fifty yards from the buildings we were about to search and once there, he prepared to cover us as we went to work. After Kelly was in place, the rest of our group drove to a spot where we planned to park our vehicles. Once parked, we walked quietly and carefully through a wooded area that would allow us to have only a short distance remaining to reach our entry point for the house and shed once we left the woods.

Main house at Donald's "Hideaway", as seen from Kelly's surveillance position prior to the raid on the farm

Once at this "jump point" I checked with Kelly one last time to determine whether he had seen any activity at the house or shed. After he responded "negative", our entry teams simultaneously entered the shed and the house and quickly secured both structures. Although Donald's car was parked behind the house, there was no one on the property. During the search that followed, we located numerous items of evidence supporting our charges against Donald regarding his criminal activities along the Gulf Coast and in other parts of the country. Searching the shed, we found and seized 147 fully developed, extremely high grade *Sensemillia* plants valued at more than $300,000.00, in what was soon to be identified as the *first ever* in the nation's history...

"Indoor Hydroponics Grow"!

The Agents of the MBN Gulfport District Office had just set another record!

Plants being grown hydroponically, suspended in PVC pipes and nutrients

Continuing our investigation at the farm, Agents soon observed a car approaching the house on the dirt road that came into the farm from the highway. As the car approached, we could see that there were two individuals occupying the front seat of the car. Watching the two occupants in the car carefully, they were allowed to drive to the front of the house and exit the car. Seeing that one of the two men was Donald, Kelly stepped into view and said..."Hello Donald". You are absolutely correct... Donald lost his breath. As armed Agents wearing very brightly marked "raid jackets" approached and arrested Donald, and the second suspect from the car, we could all tell that the "sinking feeling" that Donald had just experienced was not going to subside any time soon! At this point, Donald's *"Pucker Factor"* was at an all-time high!!!

Once the searches were complete at the farm, and all evidence was collected and logged, we all returned to the GDO to process the plants and other evidence. We also prepared all arrest documents pertaining to Donald and the second suspect arrested at the Farm. He was Donald's son. Living at the house on the farm full time, the son had kept constant watch over the plants as they grew and matured. They call that an *accomplice* and/or *a co-conspirator*! "Son" was going to jail for a while also!

After processing Donald, he became very eager to contribute in any way possible to carry our Agents and their investigation even farther up the "ladder". He began explaining that he had learned his

Agents in door of "Grow Shed" after raid... (L-R)
Jay Eubanks, David "Chicken" Gorman (DEA),
Eddie Dickey, and Sam Owens

skills as a *hydroponic grower of herbs* while working for our military in Central America many years earlier. He described the program that I relayed earlier and stated that he had managed a large portion of that operation. As he talked, we made notes and asked many educational questions of Donald. It was a very productive training opportunity! We all learned quite a bit about hydroponics and related cultivation skills.

As we talked, Donald also mentioned several other elements of his criminal network. He offered to assist in the apprehension of these worthy suspects and the dismantling of their criminal organizations. The offer that seemed to be of the greatest interest to all present was another Hydroponics lab far from the one that we had just seized.

Donald explained that more than ten years earlier he had created and operated an indoor Hydroponics grow in Cleveland, Ohio. He went on to say that after many years, he had received an offer from an associate to purchase the lab. Donald had subsequently sold the lab to the associate and he was sure that the buyer was still operating the indoor operation. At first the prospect of travelling to Ohio to seize a hundred or so marijuana plants was not very exciting. Then Donald explained further.

The Lab in Cleveland was a warehouse in the old part of town. The warehouse covered a full city block and was four stories tall, not counting a full basement! Donald went on to explain that the entire warehouse, except for a small shop in a corner of the ground floor, was set up to produce high grade Sensemillia plants using the hydroponics indoor process of growing herb. The shop was only there to provide "cover" for the few people constantly entering and exiting what otherwise appeared to be a vacant warehouse.

These "shop people" were watching over the plants as they grew to maturity making sure that the *evil boy plants* were systematically removed from the crop as the unwanted pollinators were identified. Along with all the other responsibilities of the "tenders of the crop", they constantly kept a keen eye peeled for "boy plants" who would, upon revealing themselves, be tossed out of the herd of herbs just as those spotted by our CI on the back porch of Donald's farm house.

Learning of the significance of the operation in Cleveland, we asked our local resident DEA Agent for help. Brian Maas had been tasked with opening a DEA office in Gulfport and was temporarily working from our offices. He immediately became interested in the information from Donald and set about making preparations to travel to Cleveland, Ohio. After an introductory phone call to the current owner of the Hydroponics operation, Donald had convinced his former associate that we were potential purchasers to whom the warehouse operation might be sold for a huge profit.

Making several follow-up calls over the next week, the owner of the warehouse in Cleveland was now anxious to meet with us and consummate the transaction. We were eager also! Brian arranged for the use of a DEA aircraft for our undercover transportation to Cleveland and soon we were on our way to Ohio. Brian, Jay Eubanks, and I were met at the Gulfport Airport by the DEA twin engine aircraft and my old friend and pilot David "Chicken" Gorman. I had worked on many previous undercover investigations and smuggling operations with Chicken and we enjoyed working together. After a brief visit, and boarding the plane, we all were "wheels up" from Gulfport headed to "buy" an indoor Hydroponics "property".

When we arrived in Cleveland, we rented a car and checked into hotel rooms that would be our home for the next few days. After settling in, Brian, who had been communicating with the suspects who owned the Warehouse, called the owner and told him we were in town. As previously planned Brian met with the owner later that night at a local bar with Jay, Chicken and me close by providing surveillance and cover for our "Purchaser" friend.

During the meeting, four local DEA Agents were also seated around the bar and likewise watched as the purchase proceeded. These Agents had been contacted by Brian before we left Gulfport and had agreed to support us in the Cleveland area. As we watched and monitored Brian's conversation with the main bad guy who we'll call Mike, other DEA Agents waited outside the bar to surveil Mike after he left the meeting with Brian. Having seen Mike enter the bar, the DEA Agents had quickly identified him as a major drug trafficker in the Cleveland area.

After the meeting, Mike left the bar and was followed briefly by the Agents outside. Brian explained to us that Mike had agreed to show the warehouse and the Hydroponics operation to Brian the next morning. Mike told Brian that if he liked what he saw, Brian could pay Mike for the "property" and Mike would provide the attorneys necessary to make the transfer legal and official. After all necessary legalities were accomplished to the satisfaction of both Brian and Mike, the deal would be complete and Brian and his "crew" would own the warehouse and inside growing operation. Brian had agreed to the plan and Mike had exited the bar with many more "followers" than those with whom he had arrived.

After a good night sleep we were up and meeting with Mike the next morning at the warehouse. Donald's description of the "Warehouse Hydroponics Operation" that he had created and managed many years earlier had been very "modestly stated". This was a monster! Brian and Mike toured the facility while Jay, Chicken, and I waited for them to return to the shop on the ground floor. When the tour was complete and Brian had walked back to our location with Mike, Brian told Mike that he would go and pick up the money and return to make a deposit on the property. This had been arranged as a show of good faith and would bind the deal until the attorneys could complete all necessary paperwork to transfer possession of the warehouse.

Returning to meet the local DEA Agents at their office, we waited while they prepared a search warrant for the warehouse. As we waited, we mused as to the fact that while Mike talked to his attorneys, we were meeting with our Judge. A transfer of property was definitely about to occur, but it was not going to turn out quite like Mike anticipated. His annual "bottom line" was about to drop into negative numbers.

When the warrant was signed, we all rode with the local DEA Agents and watched as they executed the warrant on the warehouse. Since Jay and I had no jurisdiction in Cleveland, we remained well out of the action and basically "sat this one out". After the building was secured and the two suspects who occupied the "shop" were arrested and secured, Jay and I entered and inspected the new "property" that we had just helped the DEA acquire.

It was a sight to behold. From the bottom to the top of this behemoth of a building, it was set up to grow thousands of marijuana plants simultaneously. Each floor had its own system of four inch PVC pipes which carried nutrients to hundreds of plants which could be suspended into the pipes while they grew. The pipes were all set up to allow their liquid plant food to return to a holding vat in the corner of the huge rooms. In turn the liquid would flow down through pipes to the floor below and be dispersed to all the pipes and plants on the lower floor.

Jay Eubanks standing among high grade
Sinsemilla plants in warehouse in Cleveland

The process would continue from the top floor to the basement where all fluids entered a sump vat and were re-injected with new chemicals automatically that replaced those absorbed by the plants. Upon being refortified, the liquids were pumped back to vats on the top floor and the process began again. High intensity lights at each level provided the needed artificial sunlight for the plants. The lights were on timers which turned them on and off to provide the prescribed amount of light for each day. There were large "gas bottles" on each floor that were also on timers. These bottles automatically injected gasses into the plants' atmosphere that maximized the speed at which the plants could grow and also insured the most potent plants possible. This was indeed the ultimate

Plants, not yet harvested, on one "level" of warehouse in Cleveland. Note sophisticated lighting system... controlled by timers

"herb factory"!

As the warrant was being executed on the warehouse, other DEA Agents arrested Mike and several pre-identified co-conspirators at other locations. All of those who were arrested were processed and placed in the local jail awaiting bond hearings and arraignments. The warehouse was seized. It was later awarded to the DEA and subsequently sold at auction. All of the Hydroponics equipment was seized and later destroyed pursuant to court orders.

Before we arrived in Cleveland to buy the warehouse, Mike and his crew had emptied all but four hundred plants from the *inside grow*. Knowing that he would probably sell the operation to Brian, Mike had decided to make his last profit from what he thought would be his last "crop" from the Hydroponics warehouse. During our search of the warehouse, we did in fact seize four hundred more extremely high quality Sensemillia plants, one ounce of almost pure cocaine, ten grams of high quality "Hash", and two handguns being carried by the two arrestees who had occupied the shop.

Most importantly, we had removed several high level drug violators from the streets in several States, and had successfully seized the first and second Hydroponic labs ever taken down in America. The first was in Pearl River County Mississippi, and the second and Largest was in Cleveland Ohio. The Warehouse in Cleveland remains, to the best of my knowledge, the largest Hydroponics lab ever seized in America.

Once again, a group of unnoticed, unsung Heroes had gone quietly into harm's way for many months to remove significant threats from the communities upon which these outlaws had preyed for many years. The bad guys went to jail and the Heroes again went quietly back to work.   From the

Fred kneeling among "Grow Pipes" in warehouse in Cleveland, OH. Note "cuts" in PVC... identical to those in Mississippi

undercover work done by Jim Kelly on the Gulf Coast with Eddie, Jay, Sam, Cindy and others watching over him as he worked, to Brian and Chicken working in Cleveland to arrest dangerous suspects with whom they had previously only talked on the phone...

For these Heroes it was just another day at the office.

For me it was another amazing opportunity to "Ride the River".

Jim Kelly and Fred in door of "Grow Shed" with crop of hydroponically grown Sinsemilla marijuana plants just seized from Donald

Staying Busy In Between

Constantly negotiating our way through a variety of investigations and other responsibilities, the Gulfport Agents might find themselves involved in cases similar to the one concluded on the Coast on April 2, which yielded 100,000 Quaalude tablets, a pound of marijuana, a gram of cocaine and two arrests. The next day we burned over 100 bales of marijuana which were seized in a previous overland smuggling investigation. The next several weeks was consumed with my providing Officer Survival and Firearms training to dozens of Agents and other Officers along the Coast.

Then upon receiving a brief phone call from an old friend and former boss with the NOPD, Lt Billy MaGaha, I was unexpectedly channeled into an investigation regarding calls from a dangerous member of a radical group responsible for the "machine gun shooting deaths" of several New York PD Officers several years earlier. The suspect, while incarcerated in our State Penitentiary at Parchman, had placed and received numerous phone calls to known dangerous militants in the New Orleans area. An informant had made Billy aware that the militants in New Orleans were planning to initiate a series of violent crimes in the New Orleans area. The suspect being held in Parchman was a main participant in the conspiracy and was acting as the organizer of the planned attacks. With the help of a friend at Parchman, we were able to obtain adequate information to assist Billy in obtaining search and arrest warrants for the suspects and their residences in New Orleans. Together we were able to arrest two suspects for conspiracy to commit murder and kidnapping. They were also charged with conspiracy to commit mayhem. Another violent group of outlaws had been apprehended before they could inflict great damage and injuries upon a completely unsuspecting and unknowing community. Thanks to Billy's swift actions and vast experience, he had organized an adequate response to the group's threat and a serious crisis had been averted. More dangerous outlaws went to jail and another Hero quietly went back to work on the streets of New Orleans.

Weeks later we were again in the "anti-cultivation" business. After receiving adequate information to obtain a search warrant, the Gulfport Agents descended upon a farm in the Saucier community in northern Harrison County. The target was an old "Antebellum" or "Plantation" style house on the farm that was being used for a large "indoor marijuana grow". Unlike the Hydroponics labs, these were indoor grows in which the plants were actually growing in large containers full of dirt. Other than that difference, the indoor grow was just as efficient as the hydroponics labs.

Farmhouse in Saucier, MS, which contained a HUGE indoor marijuana grow. MBN Agent Randy Johnson about to enter house followed by Fred

These growers had also decided to invest their efforts in the growing of high grade Sinsemilla plants and had been very successful... until we showed-up. During the search we arrested two suspects who were charged with *manufacturing a controlled substance*. We also seized one firearm, one pickup truck and 1,320 pounds of Sinsemilla marijuana valued at $2,640,000.00. That's correct... over 2.6 million dollars' worth of killer weed that was grown inside an old farm house being rented for a few dollars per month from an unsuspecting local business man. Also seized outside were numerous partially burned marijuana "stalks" from the previous multi-million dollar crop that the suspects had already harvested and sold. We found an old "pop-up" camper in the back yard and upon further inspection found numerous containers in which the previous crop or crops had been transported to purchasers across the southeast United States. Both the containers and the camper had large quantities of debris or "gleanings" remaining from the previous distribution runs.

The outlaws went to jail and the Heroes went back to work.

Longtime Coastal Characters

From the summer of 1970 when I first came to the Coast to work undercover for the MHP, I heard about a well-known group of Outlaws who had been sought by Law Enforcement for many years. While loosely knit, the group had been successful in building quite a reputation for evil deeds ranging from gambling and prostitution to extortion and murder. Regardless of where the crime fell along the "flow-chart" of legal significance from a prosecutorial standpoint, the group had members who could rightfully claim that category of criminal activity as their *expertise*. For a price, the group could summon experts from their ranks who were highly capable and completely willing to commit any crime necessary to fulfill the mission of the group, and also put higher digits on the "earned" side of their "profit and loss" statement. For the correct number of dollars, they would do just about anything! They were known well, among Law Enforcement Agencies from Texas to Florida, as the…

"Dixie Mafia"

One of the group's members who was most active in the Louisiana and Mississippi areas, owned a business which provided and repaired various gaming machines for bars and other establishments along the Coast. Some of these devices included

"Pinball Machines" and were legal to possess and operate. These provided a "front" for this member and gave him a legitimate reason to be in all the right places along the Coast. From these outposts he conducted his various highly profitable criminal activities. We'll call him "Ellis". Other devices distributed and maintained by Ellis were defined as "contraband" by State law and therefore were illegal even to possess in our State at that time.

Another one of Ellis' enterprises was the sale and distribution of illegal controlled substances or drugs. Ellis had developed an intricate network of drug *sources* over the years and could fill almost any request for any substance in any quantity required by a client. He had done well for himself! While numerous Law Enforcement Agencies had tried for years to develop a case on Ellis and arrest him for his evil deeds, no one had yet given Ellis a "perp walk" that amounted to much more that a hefty fine. He was not only good at what he did, he was very good at getting away with it!

While interviewing a Confidential Informant or CI, who had assisted the Gulfport MBN Office in the arresting of several very significant outlaws along the Coast over the previous few years, the CI mentioned that he had known Ellis for many years. The CI went on to state that he had personally observed Ellis many times as Ellis sold large quantities of various drugs to numerous individuals along the Coast. A lengthy interview followed and we learned much more about Ellis' criminal enterprise.

Fearing that Ellis might know or be able to identify any of the Gulfport Agents, I called a fellow Agent and close friend from the Hattiesburg Office, Mike Tyson. Mike had been with the MBN for several years and had worked in undercover assignments numerous times throughout the State. Mike agreed to provide any needed undercover assistance in developing cases against Ellis. Over the next few weeks, the CI made several contacts with Ellis and slowly convinced him that Mike could be trusted. Having trusted the CI many times before, Ellis agreed to take Mike in as a customer. Notice that word... a*greed*... therein is another of those "indicators". After having foiled, averted, and avoided the clutch of Law Enforcement for decades, Ellis had just waded into a "puddle" that was too deep to walk through and too swift to swim... His pirogue was headed to permanent dry dock.

Within another week or so, the CI had arranged for Mike to make his first undercover purchase from Ellis. After making necessary plans for Mike's presence, as well as surveillance and all other required resources, the deal was set. At the designated time, Mike and the CI began their twenty minute trip to the prearranged meeting location in Pass Christian, Mississippi. Surveilling the area for some time before anyone arrived, Jay, Sam and I watched as the players arrived and the party started.

With surveillance being conducted from discreet corners all around the meeting site, we watched as Mike and the CI arrived and backed into a parking spot a short distance from where Jay was hidden. Within minutes, Ellis arrived and pulled into a spot near Mike and the CI. After a brief introduction of Mike by the CI, Ellis reached into his car and

Photo from surveillance van of Mike Tyson meeting Ellis for first Under Cover purchase of drugs from the notorious outlaw

retrieved a package containing Demerol and Morphine and handed it directly to Mike. Mike immediately inspected the drugs and handed $190.00 OSF directly to Ellis. Ellis said thanks and told Mike to call when he wanted more. He re-entered his car and left the parking lot. Just like that, the first "Hand-to-Hand" purchase of controlled substances from Ellis by an MBN Agent had just been consummated. Unknown to Ellis at the time, he had dug himself into a hole and had only just begun to dig.

Exactly one month after the first transaction between Mike and Ellis, we were again in Pass Christian for a second purchase from Ellis. After making all necessary arrangements, Jay, Sam, and I drove to the parking area in the Small Craft Harbor. Upon arrival, we again established three separate surveillance positions from which we could observe and witness the purchase of drugs from Ellis.

From our three positions, we knew that wherever the transaction might occur within the parking lot, at least two of us would be able to watch the entire process. By arranging ourselves in this manner, we were prepared, even if Ellis arrived early and parked in a position other than the one chosen by our team and described in our briefing earlier. If Mike were able to park as planned, we would all be in positions from which we could observe the transaction. The parking lot was covered.

This time, Ellis was late. Arriving almost twenty minutes after the deal was set to occur, Ellis exited his car apologizing to Mike for his tardy arrival. After several minutes of pleasantries and idle chit chat, Ellis again retrieved the drugs from the front seat of his vehicle. While a relatively small quantity of cocaine, about three grams, it was a second "Hand-to-Hand" with Ellis by Mike and one in which there was no informant present. While Jay, Sam, and I witnessed Mike purchase the cocaine from Ellis, we knew his *hole* had just gotten significantly deeper. As Mike handed Ellis $350.00 in OSF, I heard Sam say, over the MBN radio, "He's gone!" We all knew exactly what Sam meant! Ellis had just committed a felony drug sale as several State Narcotics Agents watched and documented his every move. For that one sale, Ellis would be "gone" for many years to the State Penitentiary. But Ellis's hole was still about to become much deeper.

Over the next several months Mike made numerous calls to Ellis and kept building his interest in negotiating a much larger purchase of various drugs. The plan was to exhibit to Ellis that while

Mike could handle very large quantities of drugs through his network of dealers and users, he was not totally dependent upon Ellis for these drugs. We felt that Ellis' desire to provide drugs to Mike for an ever increasing profit would sufficiently develop the *greed* factor in Ellis and he might become more careless. The plan worked. It often did!

With a plan to complete the excavation of Ellis' hole, Mike convinced Ellis to sell a significant quantity of Demerol and Quaaludes as a *sample*. This sample was to set the stage for a much larger quantity of the drugs to be delivered to Mike within a few days

Aerial view of Ellis' farm during
undercover purchase by Agent Tyson

of the receipt of the sample. Ellis agreed. In late July Mike travelled to a new location at which he would consummate the newest transaction with Ellis. Mike went to Ellis' residence in northern Hancock County in response to an invitation by Ellis. Once there, with surveillance all about, Mike purchased another adequate quantity of Demerol and Quaaludes to insure that Ellis was going away for a very long paid vacation at the State calaboose!!!

Now having serious felony charges against Ellis in two separate Counties, we decided to broaden Ellis' exposure to criminal prosecution by giving him an opportunity to expand his operations into a separate State Judicial District. Ellis had asked several times during negotiations with Mike if they could meet near Poplarville or Carriere, in Pearl River County, to do some of their deals. The area in which Ellis' residence was located was only a short distance from Pearl River County. Pearl River County was in fact another *District*. This meant separate and different Justice Courts, County Courts, District Attorneys, and Circuit Court Judges. We decided to oblige Ellis in his request.

On August 3, we travelled to a prearranged location just off Interstate 59 at the Carriere exit in Pearl River County. In an almost unoccupied parking lot of a nearly defunct truck stop, we once again established several covert and discrete stationary surveillance positions. With Jay, Sam, and me positioned properly all about the area, Mike arrived and parked in his preplanned location. Shortly afterwards, Ellis also arrived and pulled in close to Mike's vehicle. Once there, Ellis hopped from his vehicle and approached Mike who was by now standing just outside his undercover car.

Having already safely *walked away from* several previous sales to Mike, Ellis moved with a commonly observed but misplaced confidence exhibited by drug dealers who have allowed themselves to be overcome by greed and arrogance. Ellis had almost finished digging his hole. As he reached into his vehicle for the last time and retrieved an extremely large container of assorted controlled substances. He had no idea that his digging days were almost over!

Ellis asked to see the money to verify that Mike had enough to cover the deal, and as he looked at the bag full of OSF, he handed the drugs to Mike. Upon accepting the OSF from Mike, the deal was done. With adequate technical documentation of the transaction and having been witnessed by at least three other State Narcotics Agents, Mike gave Ellis some news that would absolutely change the Outlaw's life forever. The surveillance team transformed into an arrest team that now approached from every corner of the truck stop. Hearing the roar of large motors and the screeching of tires on cars now only feet away from the site of the transaction, Mike told Ellis that he was under arrest for sale of controlled substances to a State Agent. As the Cavalry arrived, Ellis was numbed by the sudden realization that he had dug this hole far too deep! As reality sank in, Ellis' face took on an appearance of many I had seen before when the human behind the face knows without any doubt that their "Goose has been Cooked"!!!

Now having Ellis in custody, we travelled to his residence which was about twenty miles away. Once there we executed a search warrant on his home and property. During the search, we seized thousands of dosage units of assorted drugs from Ellis' house. Most of the drugs were prescription or pharmaceutical drugs which had been stolen in dozens of drug store burglaries across the Gulf Coast from Louisiana to Florida. Had I mentioned that another one of Ellis' "expert classifications" within his 'Group" was drug store burglary? I didn't think so. He was a man of many talents, as they say.

Among other items of drug evidence seized from his home were large quantities of cocaine, marijuana, and clandestinely manufactured Quaaludes similar to those purchased months earlier by Agent Tyson. Among the non-drug evidence seized were dozens of illegal gaming devices along with gambling paraphernalia, and dozens of items stolen during various burglaries of homes and businesses throughout the area. After seizing all of the evidence found at Ellis' residence, it was packaged and transported back to the Gulfport Office for processing. Just the processing of the drug evidence took three Agents almost a week to complete. The variety and quantities of drugs were enormous. It was, and

A small sample of the drug "exhibits" seized from Ellis at his farm house

probably still is, one of the largest seizures of Pharmaceutical drugs stolen during burglaries, ever made in our State.

After the search warrant and undercover purchases from Ellis, we compiled necessary paperwork including all related reports of investigation and other required documents. The drug evidence was taken to the Mississippi Crime Lab for analysis. All other evidence was cataloged and stored awaiting the prosecution of Ellis for his felony crimes. Almost exactly two years later after numerous hearings, and Grand Juries in both Judicial Districts in which Ellis had sold drugs to Mike, it was time for Ellis to stand trial.

In both Hancock and Pearl River County Court Rooms before two separate Judges, Ellis pled guilty to all counts of sale, possession and intent to distribute charges. He was sentenced to 30 years in Parchman State Penitentiary for his drug related crimes in both Courts. While being sentenced in Poplarville by Judge Prichard, Ellis stood and listened to the verdict as it was read by the Judge.

Upon hearing the Judge issue the 30 year sentence, Ellis raised his hand and the Judge said "what do you have to say Mr. Ellis?" With a raspy almost aggressive voice, Ellis stated "I'm an old man Judge... I can't do no 30 years!" Without a blink, Judge R.I. "RIP" Prichard looked the notorious "Dixie Mafia" outlaw straight in the eye and said, *That's OK Mr. Ellis... just do all you can... that'll be good enough for me!"* With that, the Judge tapped his gavel, rose from his bench, dismissed Court, and withdrew to his chambers.

After several years in jail, Ellis died in prison. He had finally given the State and "RIP" *all he could* in payment for a life of crime and the untold misery that he had inflicted upon countless innocent victims for many years! The "Dixie Mafia" had lost a significant member to a group of MBN Heroes from the Gulfport and Hattiesburg District Offices. Mike, Jay, Sam, and others had proven once again that they would not hesitate going into harm's way to protect the citizens of our State even when their investigative efforts created great potential peril to themselves!

These Heroes were and are the "real deal"!!!

Watermarks Behind the Scenes

Weaving in and out of various assignments and investigations, we still frequently found ourselves responding to assorted requests for assistance from other MBN Districts as well as other

Agencies throughout the State and region. I might find myself in Tupelo in the extreme north east corner of the State assisting with the covert installation of Tech equipment in a hotel room one day and be teaching a Counter Smuggling class in Natchez in the southwest corner of the State a couple of days later. The variety of opportunities was sometimes overwhelming, but the excitement was hard to resist.

From sitting on a "Shooting Review Board" in Jackson for a group of Agents involved in a shooting stemming from an undercover deal gone bad one week, to teaching "marijuana interdiction" classes to three groups of International Paper Company employees in three different areas of the State the following week, I seldom suffered from boredom!

Another constant "watermark" behind all other duties was the never ending and frequently recurring responsibility of managing the Firearms Qualifications of all MBN Agents each "quarter". That meant that every three months, along with the other Firearms Instructors within the MBN, I would go to Jackson for about a week and conduct the required quarterly re-certification and qualifications of all Agents with every weapon issued to each Agent.

Because each Agent was issued a variety of weapons, this process was lengthy, and tedious. Each Agent was required to fire several hundred rounds of ammunition using each of his or her issued weapons. With total sworn manpower ranging from sixty to eighty Agents within the MBN, the days were full of highly controlled "courses of fire" which required thousands of rounds of various calibers of ammunition being expended daily for almost a week. Doing the math on the number of rounds that I either fired, or managed the firing of, for almost twenty years while acting as lead Firearms Instructor for the MBN, we expended well over two million rounds of assorted ammunition. Can you say, "My ears are both still ringing"? Like I said early in the book, "One does not get good at shooting, or any other skill, by reading or talking about the theory involved…One becomes good at shooting… By shooting!" It was and still is a great honor to work with great Heroes training other Heroes how to defend themselves in the most dangerous of circumstances! I have always taken that honor very seriously!!!

Also within this same time frame, I had been requested by several outside Agencies to provide specialized blocks of instruction to various groups of students from around the country. For several years, I taught "Counter Smuggling" classes for the DEA in their regional seminars, as well as their one and two week advanced training programs. Most of these classes ranged in size from thirty to fifty students. It was a great opportunity to help Officers from a variety of Departments and Agencies learn to recognize smuggling groups operating in their areas and how to investigate these groups safely and successfully! Officers from Texas, Louisiana, Mississippi, Alabama, Tennessee, Arkansas, Georgia, and Florida all responded very positively to the classes.

Another program in which more and more Officers were showing interest was my "Officer Survival" classes. To me, this was the ultimate means of passing along information that would actually help these Officers *get home at night*! I talked about many close calls that I had experienced over the years and what I had learned from each incident that helped me survive the next. I talked about experiences that other Officers had shared and likewise the lessons that they had learned. Accompanied by films and photographs, I put together a presentation that was about four hours in duration. I presented it dozens of times at Academies, In-Service training for various Departments, and for Colleges in the area. It would become the foundation for training that I would provide all across the Nation for the next forty years. It's just as exciting and rewarding to walk into a classroom today and "open" a class for a new group of eager Officers as it was forty years ago. It is and always has been quite a Blessing, and an extreme honor!!!

Cocaine: ver. 2.2

During the course of normal duties, Agents paths frequently intersected trails that led to cleverly disguised opportunities to "climb that old ladder". In the summer of 1983, Gulfport District Agents once again *found a ladder*! While working an investigation on two local Cocaine dealers, Sam and Jay recognized the capabilities of the outlaws to acquire and sell very large quantities of their drug of choice. After a small buy of about ¼ of an ounce of Cocaine, Sam had convinced the dealers that he and Jay had a "Money Man" who might be interested in a much larger quantity.

We'll call these dealers Blackie and his girlfriend, and now co-defendant, Peaches. Sam had told them that his money man lived in Louisiana and was always interested in new sources for his merchandise. Both Blackie and Peaches were all in favor of, and quite anxious to help Sam's friend with the expansion of his market resources. This of course meant that they got to help sell more drugs and in turn… *made more money…* Can one say *Greed…*?

During discussions that followed Blackie and Peaches agreed to meet with their "source" in the Long Beach, Mississippi, area. They planned to begin their preparations to acquire larger quantities of cocaine for what they all hoped would be a very profitable outlet into a new and substantially larger market. With one foot already on the ladder, Sam and Jay returned to the Gulfport office and met with Eddie Dickey and me to discuss the investigation.

Over the next several days, Sam spoke with Blackie and Peaches on the phone and discussed his next purchase of cocaine from the outlaws. Because the age of technology had become *so advanced…* we now were forced to develop investigative skills and resources that would "counter" the technology available to the current generation of "dopers" with which we dealt. There now existed a high tech device known as a *"caller ID"*. While the devices aided us greatly in our daily investigations, they also had to be considered in every undercover phone call that *we made to an outlaw* as well!

Because of the caller ID, we could not afford to call a bad guy

Under Cover calls from pay phones became a necessity after "Caller ID" became available

from our office phones and have the suspect's caller ID post the digits and listing of the Gulfport MBN office! So... we resorted to a more clandestine approach. Remember... just because we had progressed to the age of caller *ID*, one should not forget that *all phones* still had a wire connecting them to the wall! Therefore, we had "Undercover" or UC phones installed in "off-site" locations and listed these numbers to various undercover businesses or individuals that matched our "cover stories". We could then, more believably, convince our outlaw du jour of who we wanted them to believe we were, and what we did.

Phone calls continued between Sam and the two defendants and as a result of their negotiations, Sam arranged a UC purchase that would move the investigation another step or two up the ladder. Explaining to Blackie and Peaches that their money man insisted that he meet them during this larger transaction, the duo agreed to my presence at the sale. In our planning meetings, we all agreed that because of the drug quantities and amount of OSF anticipated in follow-up purchases from the duo and their source, it would be wise to increase our manpower in the subsequent dealings.

This way, we had another "Agent witness" involved directly in the transactions, and additional back up if the outlaws decided to hop from the doper train to the armed robber train at the intersection of "Rip and Run". Remember the rule... "The more money involved and the larger the amount of drugs, the more likely the outlaw is to just take the money and run". Simply put... The more money involved... the more dangerous the deal! It was always just that simple!!!

At the end of August at a prearranged location in a local hotel, Sam, Jay and I went to meet with Blackie and Peaches. Sam was wearing a body wire that was being recorded by Eddie Dickey from a nearby location as he provided surveillance for the transaction. With other Agents also providing surveillance and back up, we went to our rented room and called Blackie. Sam told Blackie where we were, and told him we were ready to make the purchase. We sat back, and with all resources in place, waited for Blackie and Peaches to arrive.

After about thirty minutes they knocked on the hotel room door. Jay opened the door and the duo walked in carrying a small tote bag. As they entered the room, their excitement preceded them! We could tell that while they were somewhat apprehensive due to the quantity of drugs they were carrying, *dollar signs* had created an obvious cloud of greed that made all things Okay! They were certain that they were about to become independently wealthy within the next few days.

As Jay closed the door behind them, Blackie walked to the back of the hotel room and sat the bag on a small table in the corner where Sam and I sat. Peaches sat on the end of the bed watching our every move and never took her hand out of the purse that hung on her right shoulder. Jay stood just inside the door and as he leaned against the wall, likewise kept his hand behind his back where he also gripped his large caliber revolver. As Blackie asked, "can I see the money?" Sam pulled $3,200.00 in recorded OSF from his pocket and laid it on the table by the bag that Blackie had brought into the room. Blackie spread the currency across the table and said, "That looks like the right amount". He then produced a large plastic baggie containing an ounce of what proved to be almost pure cocaine, and placed it on the table. Sam looked at me and said "That looks like a full ounce". He then picked up the OSF and handed it to Peaches and said, "Here, you might want to put this in your purse". Peaches took the money after pulling her hand from her purse and placed the OSF into her shoulder bag.

With Eddie's recorder capturing each incriminating word by both outlaws, Jay, Sam, and I personally witnessed the transaction that now established Blackie's and Peaches' felony sale of one ounce of high grade cocaine to three State Narcotics Agents. These geese were well done, but they were only the *hors d'oeuvres*. The main course was still waiting to be placed in an oven a few steps further up the ladder. After a brief conversation concerning the future purchase of a much larger quantity of cocaine, Blackie and Peaches left the room. In our talks, I had told Blackie that I would call him and finalize plans for our next purchase within a few days.

Because the *Money Man* was supposed to be from Louisiana, we could not use our *local* UC phone for my calls to the duo concerning the next purchase of cocaine. To legitimize the negotiations, Sam, Jay and I drove almost daily for two weeks to Slidell so that our Duo and ultimately their source would see a Louisiana telephonic area code and prefix from which we were making our calls. We would drive to various pay phones in or near Slidell and call the outlaws.

With an audio recorder attached to the pay phones from which we called, we would discuss the upcoming transaction with Blackie and Peaches until every detail was arranged to the satisfaction of all parties involved. Having discussed and agreed to quantities, prices, location and time for the transaction and all other pertinent details, we were finally ready to make what would be the final purchase from Blackie, Peaches, and their source. Arriving back at our office each day, we would listen to the recording of the most recent conversation so that everyone involved knew exactly what the arrangements were for the next transaction. Once we all had discussed the logistics necessary to accomplish the next transaction, we set about making sure every needed resource was in place to accomplish the deal safely and successfully.

I called Headquarters and arranged for an adequate amount of OSF to purchase the requested amount of cocaine. I also talked to Jim Kelly in Hattiesburg and asked that he provide surveillance and close back up during the final negotiations and purchase. Eddie would again record the transaction as it was transmitted from a body wire worn by one of us in the room during the purchase. All other GDO Agents were also briefed on the investigation and had been requested to provide surveillance and cover for our undercover team. All plans were finalized and all resources had been identified and arranged for. We were ready to take the last few steps to the top of the ladder.

On September 15, with all resources in place, we entered and set up in two rooms that we had rented in the Holiday Inn Hotel on the beach in Gulfport. The undercover room was number 226. After several preliminary phone calls with Blackie and Peaches, Sam called them and told them to meet us in our room to finalize the negotiations for the transaction. Blackie had said that his source, who we'll call "Fletch", insisted that Blackie actually see the money with which we intended to purchase the cocaine. Because the quantity of drugs and money was so substantial, we had anticipated that the outlaws might require what was commonly referred to as a "*Flash*".

In a *Flash*, the buyers are required to bring the funds to a meeting location and briefly display the correct amount of money to the seller prior to the actual transaction. This process reassures the seller that there actually are sufficient funds available to make the purchase and that the buyer is not planning to bluff the seller into bringing the drugs just to be stolen by a *fake* purchaser. The problem for the purchaser is that agreeing to a *Flash*, we placed ourselves in a situation where the opposite scenario might be the intended outcome of such a meeting. In other words… They may plan to steal the money with no intention of delivering the promised quantity of drugs. We had therefore prepared ourselves for every eventuality.

With the "Flash Roll" of the required quantity of OSF secured within room 226, and Sam, Jay and me seated comfortably, and well-armed within the room, we watched TV as we waited for the duo to arrive and allow us to *Flash them...* At the agreed time, there was a knock at the door. Again, Jay acted as our "Door Man" and allowed our two associates into the room. Once inside, the meeting was short and sweet. Our money was inside a satchel on the bed. When Blackie walked in, I asked Sam to pour the money onto the bed for him and Peaches to inspect the funds. As the mounds of money poured onto the bedspread, both Blackie and Peaches lost their breath. It was sensory overload for the duo and at that point, we could have all been wearing *Royal Canadian Mounted Police* uniforms and I don't think either Blackie or Peaches would have noticed or cared. I knew at that moment that their subsequent report back to Fletch would be positive and very convincing!

After the duo fondled and inspected the OSF for a few moments, I told Blackie that *show and tell* was over and it was time for him and Peaches to depart and report to their boss. Blackie assured me that he would go straight back and finalize the arrangements for delivering the required amount of cocaine to us as soon as possible. I told him that we would be leaving the hotel room immediately and I would let him know where to meet us for the actual transaction. He said that would be fine and he and Peaches departed the room. Within minutes they were observed leaving the hotel parking lot.

Surveilling Agents followed Blackie and Peaches as they drove directly to a meeting at a local restaurant with... that's correct... Fletch. During the two hours that followed, the Agents were able to follow Fletch and the duo to a house in Long Beach. They subsequently identified the house and car that Fletch was driving as belonging to Fletch. Surveillance was terminated a short while later to insure that our outlaws did not become suspicious of unusual traffic in their area. The investigation was going too well to have it compromised at this point because of an unnecessary surveillance. We now knew who all the players were and where they resided.

After leaving the Hotel, Sam, Jay and I returned to our office and I placed the "Flash Roll" into my vault in the GDO. After a brief meeting with other Agents, Sam, Jay, and I departed the office and went home. We did not want to be inadvertently identified because of some accidental encounter with one or more of our new defendants.

The next day we again met and finalized our plans for what would be our final undercover transaction with Blackie, Peaches and Fletch. We had retained the same two rooms at the Hotel. Everything at the Hotel was set up, ready to go, and "on the air". Knowing now where Fletch resided, Agents set up on him and his vehicle and waited for movement. After all resources were again in place, Sam, and I went to the Hotel room carrying the bag containing the OSF for our purchase. Once in the room, Sam called Blackie and told him we were ready to do the deal. Blackie said he would call "his man" and soon be on his way with Peaches to bring us the Cocaine.

Once again, we sat in our room and watched TV while we waited for the duo to arrive. This time we had brought a set of "triple-beam" scales to weigh the Cocaine and insure that we were not being cheated with a smaller quantity than we were paying for. The "triple-beam" scale was a very common weighing device in use by most drug dealers of that era and was almost expected to be present by any respectable seller of large quantities of drugs. We didn't want to diminish the significance of the moment for Blackie and Peaches, so we brought our scales. We knew that it would make them feel warm and fuzzy!

After almost an hour, our secretary, Brenda Breaux, called us in our room. She had been contacted by the Agents watching Fletch's house. The Agents had asked Brenda to tell us that Fletch was moving and had just met with Blackie and Peaches. We knew that it would only be minutes until the duo arrived with our "package". With Kelly and Eddie close by and other Agents following our duo, we

Brenda Breaux, MBN Secretary, at her desk in the GDO

were all set for our final UC dance with Blackie and Peaches. This time, Dean Sheppard was in the adjoining room managing the recording devices and acting as our immediate backup. It may have also been noticed by the attentive reader that Jay was not in the undercover room for this transaction. Jay was one of the Agents surveilling Fletch while our main outlaw ran "counter-surveillance" for Blackie and Peaches as they made the delivery to our hotel room.

A short time later, there was a familiar knock on our door. As Sam opened the door and revealed our two guests, they happily entered with Blackie carrying a large tote bag. Peaches walked a few steps behind Blackie with her hand, once again, inside her purse. Once they were both well within the room, Sam closed the door. After a brief exchange in which Blackie received an affirmative reply that our satchel on the bed contained the money for the cocaine, he said "here's your package". With that, while he looked me in the eye, he reached inside his tote bag.

During this particular moment in every drug purchase, the UC Agent or Agents, have that growl deep inside their belly that is heard only by them. It is that growl associated with a warily recoiling Tiger which knows that he may be required to pounce swiftly and violently upon a perceived potential threat in order to survive the events of the next few moments. It is a moment of deep concentration and anxious anticipation!

In this instance, although Peaches still had her hand deep within her purse, Blackie produced from his tote, two large clear one gallon Ziploc plastic bags which contained a familiar white powdery substance. Upon weighing the two bags, we determined that the total weight of 2.2 pounds of cocaine that we had ordered, was in fact contained within the bags. Taking possession of the Kilo of cocaine, Sam moved toward the table in the corner of the room to gain a position from which he could "cover" me and the buy money. As I handed the satchel containing the $70,000.00 in OSF to Blackie, we all, except for the duo, knew that nobody was leaving the room with that money other than an MBN Agent.

Blackie took the satchel of money and as he accepted it, I told him that he had better count it. He turned, and as he sat the satchel on the end of the bed, I threw my MBN badge on the bed beside the satchel and holding my revolver in his ribs, softly but clearly said, "You're under arrest". When the members of Sadam's Iraqi Army looked up in the early 1990's and saw US Missiles flying down their streets in Baghdad, those soldiers' faces expressed no more *shock and awe* than did Blackie's face in this previous moment in history.

As Blackie tried to avoid "blacking out", Sam moved quickly and smoothly placed his ever present Smith and Wesson revolver next to Peaches right ear and as he grabbed her hand still hidden in her purse, said, " Don't pull anything out of that bag that's gonna get you in even more trouble... You're under arrest also". As she slowly removed her empty hand from the purse Sam quickly maneuvered her to a position of compliance next to Blackie who was now

Drugs, Triple-Beam scales, pagers, and other items used during the UC transactions with Blackie and Peaches

seated humbly on the bed. Both were advised of their rights and handcuffed. From Peaches' bag Sam retrieved a small frame, fully loaded, .38 caliber revolver.

We were quickly met in the Hotel room by Dean, Kelly, Eddie and other Officers from the Gulfport Police Department. The drug evidence was placed back in the tote and along with the $70,000.00 OSF were taken to the GDO for processing and storage in our vault.

Well over three pounds of almost pure cocaine, money, weapons, and paraphernalia seized during the largest UC purchase of cocaine in the history of MBN

Outside, Jay had singlehandedly apprehended Fletch in the parking lot of the hotel. During the arrest, Jay removed a fully loaded revolver from Fletch's waist band. After he was arrested, Fletch was brought to our office along with Blackie and Peaches.

A search warrant was obtained for Fletch's residence in Long Beach and within a few hours of his arrest, we were conducting a thorough search of the house and property. During the search another one-half pound of cocaine was found. As a result of the UC purchase and subsequent searches, we purchased and seized a total of almost three pounds of nearly pure cocaine, along with two handguns, and other paraphernalia, and arrested three significant outlaws for sale and possession of Cocaine.

Also after Fletch was arrested, he became extremely anxious to give us information which led to an immediate "follow-up" investigation. It seemed that his source for the cocaine was in the Fort Lauderdale, Florida, area. He went on to explain that the source had given the drugs to Fletch without full and immediate payment. He had "fronted" the large quantity of cocaine to him, but insisted that some form of collateral be provided to insure that Fletch would return to make payment for the drugs. Fletch explained that the supplier had demanded that he leave his wife as a "hostage" with these dealers in south Florida while Fletch delivered and sold the cocaine to his new purchasers in Gulfport.

The agreement was that after the sale was complete, Fletch would *immediately* travel back to Fort Lauderdale and pay his source for the cocaine and thus insure the safe release of his wife/hostage. The source had been quite explicit in his description of the fate that would befall Fletch's wife if he failed to return with the funds to pay for the cocaine within a prescribed time frame. Listening to Fletch describe the threats made toward his wife by the source, we could fully understand the anxiety and deep concern that he demonstrated regarding his wife's safety.

Of course this was a "deep concern" that he had for a wife whom he had willingly *"given"* to a group of thug outlaw dope dealers in south Florida to *"have their way with"* while her loving husband Fletch drove a total of almost two thousand miles to consummate a drug deal that was obviously more important to him than his wife! We were overwhelmed with his "deep concern"! I'm sure she was likewise "touched" by her husband's loyalty and love. With the clock still ticking, the time for Fletch to return to south Florida and *pay the ransom* was hastily approaching.

Knowing that he was not going back to Florida with the required funds, Fletch was now quite eager to cooperate in any way that might encourage us to do whatever was necessary to rescue his wife from his outlaw partners in Florida. After a phone call to the local DEA Offices in Fort Lauderdale and an explanation of circumstances surrounding the ongoing hostage incident, the Florida officials rescued Fletch's wife. They also arrested the sources of the cocaine which we had just purchased from Fletch, Blackie, and Peaches on the Gulf Coast of Mississippi.

Once again, the Gulfport District Agents had set a record. While removing several major drug dealers from the streets of our State, they had also made the single largest *hand-to-hand undercover purchase* of cocaine ever in the history of the MBN! This purchase, as far as I know, still remains the largest and holds the distinction of being a record undercover operation. Like I said several times... These guys were among the bravest and the best!!! They routinely went competently and confidently into harm's way to protect citizens from dangerous

Agents Dwight O'Neal, Jay Eubanks, and Sam Owens with the cocaine and other evidence seized during the UC operation

outlaws. In most instances, the citizens never even knew these bad guys were committing felonies all around them every day. These Heroes took the desperados to jail every day and quietly went back to work looking for the next *ladder*.

Old Friends and New Foes

Beginning earlier in the year and ending around the time we started working on Blackie and Peaches, the Gulfport Agents were asked to assist the DEA with an investigation into some well-known members of the "travelling criminal" group that we had known of for many years. As described in the story of Ellis in an earlier portion of the book, the "Dixie Mafia" had managed to establish quite a reputation along the Gulf Coast. This *"Outfit"* had caused their share of heartburn among Law Enforcement Agencies in numerous States. While still working from the MBN Gulfport Office, Brian

Maas had been able to successfully infiltrate a portion of the Outlaws' network with the assistance of an informant provided by another Agency. He asked that we provide support as he proceeded with his investigation. Running surveillance for weeks, we took turns watching over Brian as he drilled deeper and deeper into the criminal "*Outfit's*" workings.

Learning more and more about the members, Brian was able to gain their trust enough that they allowed him to be a part of the preparations for an upcoming expansion of their criminal enterprise. The group was planning an "air drop" of a large amount of drugs onto a rural farm. This was to be an operation in which a large aircraft would fly low over the suspect's farm and jettison large packages of drugs from the plane. As the packages hit the ground, members of the group would collect them and haul the cargo to buildings on the farm to be stored until the drugs were sold to purchasers from across the country. The air drop was to occur on a farm in north central Harrison County. The farm belonged to a prominent member of the criminal group. As with Ellis, putting the handcuffs on any of these outlaws was no small accomplishment. We had no idea at the beginning of the operation, just how far the tentacles of the group actually reached.

As the meetings continued, Brian told the group that flying a large aircraft low over the area in which the farm was located would undoubtedly draw suspicion. The outlaws agreed that such an event would certainly be reported to local authorities, especially after the aircraft made the required multiple flights over the same area within a short period of time. As Brian inquired further as to how the group intended to handle the problem of being compromised, the head of the group, who we'll call Doobie, told Brian not to worry about being caught, they had that *all worked out*.

For the next few weeks, meetings continued and as additional information was gained by Brian, we realized that in fact, Doobie did have it *all worked out*. Then in mid-June it was time for the long planned air drop. Because of the players who had been identified as those contracted by Doobie to "protect" their load of drugs as it was being air dropped, extra reinforcements were called in. These extra personnel would assist with the arrests and searches that were to occur on and around Doobie's farm as the air drop occurred. These extra assets were members of the FBI's SWAT team which worked out of the Jackson FBI Office. With the Agents of the Gulfport FBI Office having been involved in the investigation from the start, the "Team" from Jackson added a great resource to the operation.

On the afternoon before the air drop was to occur, Eddie Dickey and I met with the FBI Agents from their Gulfport Office and the FBI SWAT Team at a rural location in northern Harrison County. The meeting had been arranged to plan for the raid on the farm that would occur as the air drop was being completed early the next morning. During the meeting, the SWAT Team and all other Agents present checked their equipment and verified that all needed resources were present, ready, and functional. As always, with highly trained Agents and *Operators* about to go knowingly into harms' way to accomplish dangerous complex tasks, the preparations were extensive and meticulous. Everyone was very focused and extremely serious!

The plan was for a small group of Agents to go into a wooded area of the farm far before daylight and establish surveillance positions from which they could watch the main farm house and the suspects occupying the house. The rest of the Team would stand by at a safe location from which they could quickly respond at the appropriate time. We knew that at a predetermined time, the "load plane" was to fly over the farm and begin making its drop into a predesignated "drop zone". The Outlaws planned to stay around the main house until they heard the plane passing over. At that point Doobie and his crew would go to the drop zone and begin collecting the duffle bags full of drugs and haul them to the storage areas on the farm. Once Doobie dispatched his crew to pick up the dropped cargo, we knew that the outlaws would be scattered over a wide area. Our timing would be critical. We needed to capture the Outlaws while they were still at the house and preparing to respond to the sound of the plane flying over the farm.

When called, the main element of the SWAT Team would rush into the area, and secure the suspects, the house and other buildings on the farm. Once the buildings and property were secure, and the outlaws at the house and elsewhere on the farm were arrested, they would all be assembled in a central "holding area" while the farm was processed. As the SWAT Team moved close to the farm, other Arrest Teams moving just ahead of the SWAT Team, were assigned to apprehend the *"security group"*, which had been arranged for by Doobie, to protect them during the operation. After all members of the entire group were arrested and secured, a thorough search of the property and buildings would be conducted by additional teams comprised of FBI and MBN Agents.

The meeting lasted for a couple of hours and by the time it concluded, we all knew and understood the plan and also understood what our individual parts were in the overall plan. Eddie would be in charge of the MBN Agents who would conduct searches in various areas of the farm after it was secured. His team would help identify property and evidence to be seized and after the seizures, would catalogue, document, and store the evidence. This would prove to be a monumental part of the operation since there were to be large numbers of items seized.

As the plans for the raid were being explained, the Team Leader of the FBI SWAT Team asked if I would assist them by being a member of the team that would infiltrate the wooded area before the raid and assist with the surveillance of the house and farm before the Team arrived to secure the property. He explained that as the Team arrived and began to secure the house and suspects, we would then become a perimeter team responsible for the protection of the SWAT team as they focused upon the house and suspects throughout the property. After the entire farm was secured and all suspects involved were arrested and brought to the holding area, we would then continue to provide security for the search teams as they completed their investigative activity on and around the farm. This was the first time that I had formally acted as direct support to the Jackson FBI SWAT Team during an actual operation. It would be the first of many opportunities that I would have, for almost two decades that followed, to work closely with these exceptional men during dozens of high risk operations. From this beginning of my association with their Team until now, I have always been honored and very proud to work with and train with the members of the Jackson FBI SWAT Team. Heroes all!!!

Obviously, I accepted the request and set about preparing accordingly. After the meeting, Eddie and I travelled back to our offices and made arrangements for all necessary manpower and other resources needed to support the raid that would occur early the next morning. After all was set at the GDO, I went home and performed my own equipment checks and verified all my gear was present, ready and functional.

Early… Early the next morning, I travelled to a prearranged location in a remote part of Harrison County far away from Doobie's farm and met with the other Agents involved in the operation. After a short final briefing, I entered a van with the rest of the team going into the woods and departed for the farm. We were followed by all the other vehicles carrying the other teams that were assigned the various responsibilities at the farm. At a point about a mile from the farm, the other teams slowed and turned into a predesignated holding area and parked their vehicles out of sight from the road.

Our van continued to an area near the farm that was not visible from the house or entrance to the farm property. With all the van's lights turned off, our driver slowed quietly and stopped at the specified point along the road as planned. We all quickly and quietly exited the van and only partially closed the doors so as not to make any loud noises in our departure. As the van slowly pulled away, we walked quietly into the dark woods. We carefully made our way to our assigned positions well within the wooded area that partially surrounded the main farm house. Within minutes we were all set up and ready…

We were "at the office".

After notifying the "Entry Teams" that we were in place and operational, we watched and listened for any activity around the house and farm. Just after daylight, we began to observe movement as several individuals exited the house and began moving about the property. As their activity increased, we knew that it was about time for the flight. Keeping the Entry Teams aware of everything that was occurring at the farm, they too knew that it was nearly time for the big event.

During a covert "drive-by" of the farm road by an undercover Agent in a vehicle that looked as though it could belong to the next door neighbor, the Agent observed two cars that were immediately identified as the "Security" for the air drop. The Agent recognized the vehicles! The vehicles were parked on the road that ran in front of the farm and at opposite ends of the farm's boundaries. Confirming that these cars were present, we knew that they were aware that the drop was about to occur. Within minutes, the distant sound of large airplane engines could be heard from the Southeast. With the Entry Teams slowly approaching the farm but still out of sight, Arrest Teams also were making their way toward the "Security Team".

Some of the vehicles and ATV's seized at the farm

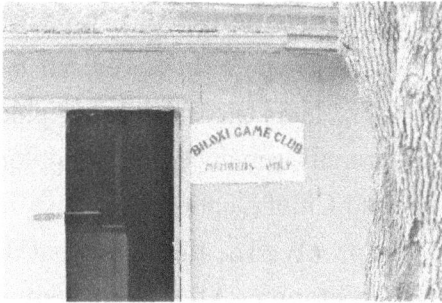

*"Biloxi Game Club"... front door of one
building located on farm. Various forms of
criminal activity were conducted at the farm
which was the site of the "cocaine drop"*

As the huge twin engine "Smuggling" plane made its first pass over the farm, the Arrest Teams descended upon the two "Security" vehicles and arrested the vehicles' occupants. The Entry Teams drove swiftly to the area in front of the farm house and quickly secured the house and arrested Doobie and his crew. As the Arrestees were brought to the holding area, we would all have confirmed what we had been told, but hoped was not true. The Security Team was comprised of the Harrison County Sheriff Leroy Hobbs and his Chief Deputy Billy McDonald. I had known the Sheriff for more than a decade and worked with him many times when he was a younger honest Cop. Even though the operation would be a great success, it was a sad day for Law Enforcement on the Gulf Coast.

Throughout the subsequent search of the farm, numerous vehicles, ATV's, and other items were seized. A large number of marijuana plants were seized from outdoor patches on the farm and were subsequently destroyed after evidentiary samples were taken to the Crime Lab. Many other items of evidence associated with numerous crimes were found on the property including a large arena which had been constructed many years earlier for the purpose of conducting large "Game Bird" or "Cock Fight" contests. It had been heavily used and was still fully functional.

About a week after the arrests, all suspects were afforded a preliminary hearing during which they were all bound over to the Grand Gury. They were later tried and either pled Guilty or were convicted. They were all sentenced to long terms in prison... including the Sheriff and Chief Deputy!

And the air drop... Well... that was what the DEA and FBI call a "Reverse" sting operation. After being approached by Doobie and crew to help them expand their drug operations through a huge acquisition of cocaine, Brian had convinced the outlaws that he could accomplish the transaction by means of an air drop over their farm. The large aircraft that flew over the farm at exactly the correct time was owned and operated by a well known organization within our Government... It was only a "prop". The outlaws had conspired to accomplish an elaborate smuggling operation that was never to actually occur! The entire operation was a well-planned and creative investigative response to a band of notorious bad guys by brilliant investigators and an undercover Agent named Brian Maas! The upper echelon of the famed and notorious *Dixie Mafia* had proven that *even they* were not immune to a well-known but sometimes fatal temptress... Greed!!!

That same temptress had likewise transformed old friends into dangerous foes.

Jay and Sam on an ATV seized during the raid on the farm

Fred standing in the "Arena" inside the "Game Club"

The Ace in the Hole

D uring late 1983, the Agents of the GDO developed a source who proved to be very valuable in our ongoing attempts to infiltrate the heroin and dilaudid dealers along the Coast. The source who we'll call Tony, had lived on the Coast all his life and had been involved in the use and distribution of drugs for many years. Tony had decided due to a series of unfortunate events which he had experienced, to change his ways and make a sincere effort to "right his many wrongs". One might say that Tony was highly motivated to cooperate in our war on drugs! Working with Tony, Agents had been introduced to many well known local drug dealers from whom the Agents of the GDO had purchased numerous "exhibits" of various drugs. One could say that Tony was *making a difference*.

Over a period of several months, we had interviewed Tony many times and had constantly been able to help him refresh his memory concerning various dealers with whom he had historically been partnered. During one of these visits, Tony had mentioned that he knew a well-connected supplier of heroin on the Coast and that he could introduce an Agent to the dealer, who we'll call "Ben". Tony was certain that Ben would be willing to expand his market by selling quantities of Heroin to our Agent. Infiltrating the close knit heroin users and dealers on the Coast had been very difficult historically. If one was not a known addict among the other addicts and dealers, one simply did not buy heroin from their guarded suppliers. It just wasn't accepted!

For several weeks while surveilling Agents watched and documented, our UC Agents, aided by Tony, bought package after package of heroin from Ben who by now we knew was a major supplier of heroin in the Gulfport area. Eventually, we began winding down our efforts with Ben. We knew that we had made ample purchases from him to insure that his Heroin dealing days were about to fade into his past as he aged comfortably and well guarded in the care of our State Penitentiary for many moons. His heroin career was coming to an end! While meeting with Ben during one of our final purchases from him, he mentioned to another associate who was present, that he had heard that "Ace" had a new shipment of dilaudid.

Ben went on to tell our UC Agent that he should get Tony to *hook him up* with Ace if he, the UC, should desire some dilaudid. The UC Agent assured Ben that having Tony connect us with Ace would be a priority. Through this incidental conversation, we had just learned that our friend Tony had somehow forgotten to inform us that he knew Ace. Because of Ace's position of significance among the criminal element along the Coast, this oversight was puzzling to us all. We decided that we should have another visit with Tony! After a short but productive meeting, Tony had been thoroughly reminded of the vast benefits of a fully successful partnership between us. At this juncture, his memory had been adequately stimulated... He now recalled his relationship with Ace.

Over the next several months, after an introduction by Tony, the Agents of the GDO made numerous "hand-to-hand" undercover purchases from a notorious career criminal who was also another member of the... "Dixie Mafia". Another member of the infamous group of travelling criminals was about to have a career altering experience. It would also be career ending!

Because of the significance that Ace represented within the hierarchy of Coastal Outlaws, we wanted to make sure that when we ended our investigative efforts involving Ace, we would also end his criminal career. Therefore, we contacted the District Attorney's Office and spoke to one of the Assistant District Attorneys who regularly worked with us in the prosecution of our cases. Over the years, ADA's like Dickey Smith, Herman Cox, and others, had successfully prosecuted many of our cases and were always a great source of advice and legal counsel. With all case documents in hand, we met with Herman and explained our investigation regarding Ace.

While very complimentary of our efforts thus far, Herman made several suggestions that he felt would insure the unquestioned successful prosecution of this notorious outlaw. Herman suggested that we make every effort to document future purchases from Ace through the use of audio and video recordings. We explained to Herman that due to Ace's criminal "savvy" and the fact that he often employed counter-surveillance during transactions, it had been impossible to "record" any of our previous purchases. I told Herman I would see what we could do.

Over the next few months, other Agents and I conducted a thorough assessment of the total environment in which Ace operated. Knowing how much recordings enhanced our ability to convict alleged drug violators, we had wished that we could better document all of the previous cases against Ace. It had just proved to be too dangerous for our Agents to actually "wear" recording devices on their person during the transactions. We decided to pursue other more difficult but equally valuable resources to provide a means of recording future transactions with Ace.

Another problem which had developed was that Tony had, shall I say, fallen from grace. His trustworthiness had been seriously challenged by a series of unfortunate events and we had taken him "off-line". Because of his current status with our group, we feared that he might also have compromised the Agents who had previously made purchases from Ace. Due to the threat that Ace and his associates posed, we could not take a chance on sending the same Agents back to Ace for additional purchases. Not having a "source" for new introductions of Agents to Ace, we were at a standstill.

Hoping that we could develop another source, I continued my efforts to find a technical solution to our need for better documentation of Ace performing his evil deeds. Having worked with the DEA Technical Services Unit for several years, I contacted one of their "Tec's" and asked what they might do to assist with our dilemma. As always, Lee Stone was more than anxious to help. He told me that they had recently acquired a "system" that was exactly what I needed.

To protect the still viable integrity of the system and its descendants, I'll just say that it was a remotely installed transmit/receive video system that was, and is, almost completely "invisible" to untrained observers of such technology. When placed covertly into the operational environment, this system can transmit live video of the Target Location back to a dedicated observation post where the video signal can be viewed and recorded. In 1985, this was quite a miracle machine. We'll just call the system our "eyeball". Knowing now that we had the needed resources for the video documentation of any future encounters with Ace, the only other desirable asset that we had not yet procured was a means to record audio during future transactions. I was still working on that.

Within a short while, in *Narc years*, fate once again reared its generous head and I received a call from another fellow Officer. This time it was an Investigator with the Mississippi Highway Patrol. The Investigator told me that he had a source who claimed that she could purchase drugs from... Yep, I know, you're ahead of me... Ace. Within a very short time, I met the Investigator and interviewed the source. We'll call her Pam. After the interview, I knew that we were about to need the "eyeball".

By the next day, Lee and I had talked and he was making plans to assist us through the Gulfport DEA Office and with the assistance of DEA Agent Woody Wilson. After Woody made all the proper requests in writing, with several "carbon copies", to all the required approvers of such endeavors along his chain of command, we had approval for Lee to go forth and install our "eyeball". Since this was no small task, I summoned several resources from close friends and contacts along the Coast who provided all the needed support.

Within a few days, the "eyeball" was installed, the observation post was functional and we were "on the air". Knowing that we still needed that "audio" recording resource that was mentioned earlier, I went to work on that. I again met with Pam and acquired from her a *purse* that she commonly used to transport all her "possibles". I took it to a work area in which I had built and modified many previous articles during similar investigations, and went to work. I dissembled the purse and built a hidden compartment inside for the purpose of implanting an audio transmitter. Routing the antenna into one side of the shoulder strap and the microphone into the other side, I reassembled the purse and tested the set-up. It worked perfectly. We were in business. In the absence of a full blown "rip down, tear apart" search of the purse, our secret would be safe.

I took the purse back to our new source and told her that before each transaction, we would turn the device on and she could carry it with her to make her purchase from Ace. Afterwards, we would meet her and deactivate the device until the next transaction. She took the purse, looked in it, turned it inside out, and asked *"What are you talkin about?"* My "install" had passed its first test.

With all technical resources in place, it was time to get the show on the road. We tested all of our equipment and everything was working perfectly. From several blocks away in a semi controlled environment, we could see Ace's business perfectly on the monitor that displayed the video images being captured by the "eyeball". During a dry run, Pam had driven to the front of Ace's office while we did an audio test. We could hear every word as she gave us several verbal "test" articulations intended to represent a spontaneous conversation with Ace. One could say that "technically" we were ready!

Stretching the operation out over the next several months, we observed and recorded multiple transactions between Pam and Ace in which Ace sold various quantities of drugs to our source. With audio and video recordings of each transaction, we again went back to visit with Herman at the D.A.'s Office and again sought his council. He seemed both amazed and extremely pleased with our efforts and our work product. He explained in highly technical legal terms that…

"Ace's Goose Was Cooked"!!!

Meeting several more times with Herman over the next week or so, he assembled necessary paperwork and legal documents that he assured us would make the arrest of Ace and the seizure of his property fool proof. After assembling all needed court orders, we were ready to remove Ace from the community and his life of crime. Assembling Agents and Officers who had helped and contributed to the investigation, we all went to visit Ace at his "used car lot".

Upon our arrival Ace was simply overcome by events. Again we witnessed "sensory overload" in its purest form. Ace was immediately arrested without incident. He was given his rights and informed of his charges. He was served with a pre-filed *notice of forfeiture* for his business and all the vehicles on the lot. The business was searched as was he. Additional drugs were found in his car which was parked in front of his office. A large quantity of U.S. currency was seized

Ace's ""Continental" being searched and seized. Pat Sullivan takes photos at left while Mickey Ladner records video on right. Jay is in striped shirt

from his car and business. A local Locksmith, with whom I had made previous arrangements, arrived and re-keyed all locks on all doors of his business while Ace watched. As Ace sat on the bricks which established a low, perimeter wall around the front of his office, Officers who had attempted to make cases against him dozens of times for several decades, watched as we systematically dissembled

Agent Dean Shepard finishes compiling the inventory of items and property seized during search of Ace's car lot. Fred stands in rear near a very unhappy "Ace"

Ace's criminal career. The look on Ace's face was one that I've seen many times before and since his arrest. It is a look of ultimate defeat when one knows his luck just ran out... for good!

The next day Ace's cases were presented to a Harrison County Grand Jury led by Assistant DA Herman Cox. He was indicted on all charges presented. Later convicted, he was sentenced to many years in the penitentiary and was incarcerated for his crimes. Like his former friend and associate Ellis, Ace died before he could complete his time in jail. Although Ace had been sentenced by a completely different Judge, I am sure Rip would be satisfied that Ace had *done all he could* to pay back society for the untold hardship and suffering that he had imposed on countless victims through his life of crime along the Gulf Coast!

Another criminal icon was off the streets for good.

The Agents and Officers went back to work!

Let's Take a Break

Shortly after I was promoted to Lieutenant and placed in charge of the Gulfport District, I decided that I wanted to do something each year to get the Agents and their families together to relax and visit. Gayle and I had the perfect location at our rural home. It was far from any neighbors and very remote. Here, both "Topside" and

"Deep Undercover" Agents could meet and feel secure that they would not be in danger of physical harm or compromise. Although these Agents worked together daily on the streets making drug cases, they seldom had a chance to socialize together due to the concerns for safety and compromise. Our home provided the perfect location for a party.

For many years, an old friend and I had occasionally gotten together for visits. On some of these occasions we had assembled assorted hardware, household commodities, adult refreshments and large sacks of an indigenous species of edible crustaceans for which the above hardware was needed to accomplish what was known throughout Louisiana and Mississippi as a…

"Crawfish Boil"!

My old friend, being from Louisiana, possessed more than adequate skills and experience in these outings. He had generously agreed to act as somewhat of a manager in the activities required to actually, shall I say, *get the bugs on the table*. Known by fellow consumers throughout his area of normal travel and by all his family and friends, this culinary legend was recognized as the best dang crawfish boiler that ever dirtied a pot in the Irish Channel. Yes indeed… It was, and is, my old partner and lifelong friend… Harold Richard!!!

Once we had a general estimate of the number of pounds of crawfish needed for our estimated crowd, he would order the correct number of sacks. On the big day Harold would pick them up from the seafood company and bring them to our country residence. He would also bring his boiling hardware and other items needed to perform his tasks for the day. It was a sight to behold!

Originally, Gayle and I just wanted to do this "Something Special" for the Agents in the GDO. So, the first year… that's who was invited. We boiled about one hundred pounds of Crawfish and provided all the trimmings. Any adult beverages that were desired, were the responsibility of the individual guests. With perfectly boiled Crawfish, corn on the cob, boiled potatoes and plenty of paper towels, we spread the boiled delicacies onto the tops of three 4'X8' pieces of plywood laying on top of three sets of well placed homemade wooden *saw horses*. With ice chests all about, we had a party right there in our front yard. The adults ate and drank and the children played all across the fenced yard. The Agents and families all loved it and to say the least, it was a grand success!

Within a few days after the event, I was receiving calls from Agents all across the State who were distraught! As they called, the questions and comments were almost identical. They went something like this... "I thought we were friends..." "I can't believe after all we've been through, you had a party and didn't invite me...". Trying to do something special for my guys, I had insulted the rest of the Agents throughout the State. I promised each caller that I still admired their friendship... and promised to do better next year. This was still the 1980's... we had not become "comfortable enough" yet to openly comment on how much we "*Loved*" each other... Not cool yet...!

The next year, I tried to make amends. The peak season for crawfish was approaching and plans were again made for what would be the second annual "*Buck and Gayle's Crawfish Boil*". As the time drew near, Harold and I talked and calculated quantities once again. Having personally invited every Agent in the State this year, the numbers had grown for those expected to attend. Because of the numbers involved, I wanted to make sure that I minimized the waste involved in the process of throwing the party because Gayle and I again planned to "pay the tab" for the event.

Arriving early on the big day, Harold immediately recognized that I had purchased extra cooking pots and propane cookers as well as more plywood and saw horses. All related commodities had also been acquired in larger numbers. This year, Harold boiled over two hundred pounds of the cherished "mud bugs" and all the trimmings likewise increased proportionately. During the course of the day we had over fifty humans engaged in merriment across

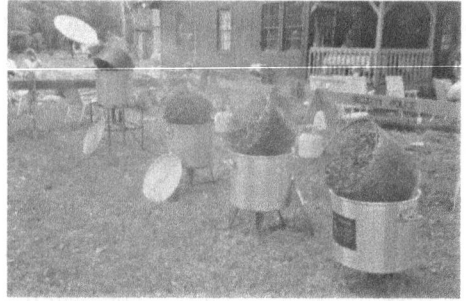

"Pots and Mo-Pots" draining the water from recently boiled mud-bugs ... bout to eat...

our front yard and the second "*Buck and Gayle's*" event was a slam dunk success!

Also present this year were some other close friends who became the sustainers of this and many future "after the party-parties". As the crowd would dwindle each year, a core group would remain and help make sure that the merriment did not end too abruptly. We all felt that after such a wonderful day of visiting and happiness we should make every effort to extend the party for as long as possible... or as long as we were physically able to do so. Therefore... our group would gather around a common spot in the yard or on a porch and *remain festive* until the wee hours of the following morning.

The plywood table tops would be "cleaned" and taken off the saw horses and thrown on the ground to make a large temporary dance floor. The speakers attached to the ever present Marantz stereo system would blare out a wide variety of country music. As the music played we would visit and dance by the moonlight until, as we say where I'm

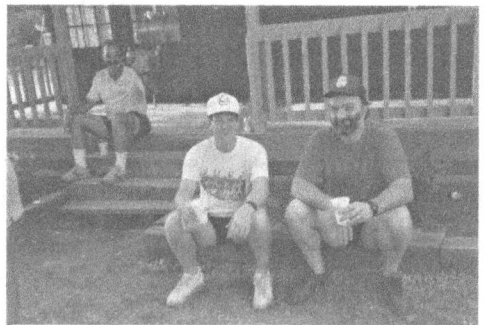

Harold and Fred on "crossties" and Harold's brother Glen is on the steps in front of Buck and Gayle's house during "Crawfish Boil"

from, "*We just couldn't go no mo*!" At that variable and unpredictable point in time, we would all mutually agree that we should reluctantly close out the current year's "Party". Some years it took several attempts to come to a unanimous agreement that the time had arrived, so we'd party a little while longer and then "vote" again.

This group consisted of what was, by that time, some of our closest and dearest life long friends. There, of course, was Harold and his wife Cathy, Jay Moore and wife Marsha, Billy Pickens and wife Sandy and Gayle and me. The nights that we spent dancing on that plywood are some of our most treasured memories with some of our most treasured and trusted friends.

Those were some *"Good ole Days"*!!!

Recovering from the festivities and the *clean-up* over the following days, I began to receive calls once again from unhappy uninvited friends. This year, those with their heads hung low were all of my friends from other Departments across the Gulf Coast! The numbers of sad faces had grown significantly. Knowing that financial resources for the expansion of the "Buck and Gayle" event were already somewhat stretched, I changed my approach to the planning of the next year's get together. I told everyone in advance that for a minimal fee, I would furnish everything from mud bugs to refreshments.... Including all trimmings and condiments. I promised that all the guest had to do was show up, eat, drink and leave under their own power. My plan and offer was met with universal endorsement and great enthusiasm!!!

As the time drew nigh, invitations went out, money and names came in, a guest list was made, supplies and needed items were purchased and Harold ordered the required number of "sacks" of crawfish. I purchased more boiling pots and propane cookers and before one could say *"Buck and Gayle"* three times, it was the day of the party. As Harold rolled into the yard and pulled into his cook area, I could see that familiar smile on his face. Getting out of the car he looked with amazement at the yard and how it was covered with items in preparation for the crowd.

This year, we boiled over four hundred pounds of crawfish, and proportionate quantities of taters, corn and now, for the first year, mushrooms. There was a dispenser in the yard that contained enough kegs of adult beverages to accommodate the entire

Plywood tables with hundreds of pounds of "bugs" ready to eat. Enjoying the day in the foreground are Circuit Judge R.I. "Rip" Prichard, and Picayune PD Narcotics Agent Jim Luke

crowd. We had eight plywood/sawhorse tables (dance floors), and trash cans everywhere. It was about to be what we often refer to as a "Happenin"! By the end of the day, with over one hundred humans in attendance, our front yard was seeing some wear! Harold cooked for several hours to accommodate the demand around the tables, and I regularly swapped kegs to insure that no cup ran dry. When the last guest had departed, the crawfish and all related edible items had departed also. There wasn't enough food left for a snack. Once again the annual event had been a huge success.

Over the next several years, *Buck and Gayle's boil* grew in fame and the crowds grew in direct relation. At the sixth annual event, we had almost three hundred guests from Law Enforcement Agencies all across the Nation. From San Francisco PD, to Dade County Sheriff's Office, and from Chicago PD to Texas DPS, we learned that there weren't many Cops that wouldn't drive for days to eat Mr. Harold's crawfish on plywood tables, under the Live Oak tree in Buck and Gayle's front yard.

We also wound up with US Attorneys, Judges, Attorneys General, District Attorneys, and many other criminal justice officials from across the south in attendance. Billed as a Law Enforcement and Criminal Justice event, we kept it "*secret*" so these brave and dedicated Heroes could continue to have a day to relax and unwind with their friends and families in a safe secure environment provided by Buck and Gayle! It was more than worth the effort for us all!!!

Cook area protected by barricades, with five "cookers" going at once. Harold and his "assistants" including Lynda's husband Eddie (right side of photo) could boil almost 300 pounds of bugs per "cookin". Note parking area, tents, porta-toilets...

At the peak year, Harold boiled almost two thousand pounds of crawfish, we had two hundred pounds of potatoes boiled and twenty dozen ears of corn cooked in Mr. Harold's magic seasoning pots. A local Distributor of adult beverages parked their portable "Keg & Tap" truck in the yard and told me to call when the party had ended. We had six porta-toilets in the front yard, two *GP-Medium* military tents, a security guard at the gate taking up specially printed tickets, and ten plywood tables with matching fifty gallon trash cans. There was a special table set up where Gayle, her sister Lynda, and Sandra Pickens handed out pre-paid *"Buck and Gayle" famous Tee-shirts* with the current year's Logo. There was an eighteen wheeler Mardi Gras float in the yard compliments of the *"Ambassador of Vishna"*, who's day job was acting as DEA Agent Woody Wilson. Last but certainly not least, there was a local highly respected singing celebrity, *Frank Basket*, providing live entertainment on our front porch. As I looked out over the crowd at about three o'clock that afternoon, after the last of three helicopters had just lifted off from our front yard, I knew exactly how Waylon Jennings felt when he sang...

"Don't yall think this outlaw thing's done got outa hand...?"

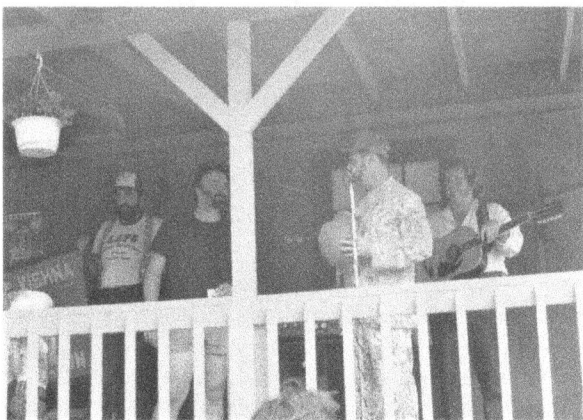

DEA Agent Woody Wilson (aka: Ambassador of Vishna) with Frank Basket on stage, as they present the award for the Best Crawfish Boil of the Year to Buck and Gayle... I guess an orange "Pith Helmet" seemed an appropriate award...

Back at the Office

Back on duty, after each year's *crawfish throw-down*, and while still craving the smell of more of Mr. Harold's Cajun delicacies,

Mike Tyson (facing camera) monitors and assists other Agents and Cadets as they begin burning thousands of marijuana plants seized from a rural farm in southeast Mississippi

we would move back into another year of dealing with outlaws until the next party came along. There was the almost always present duty of destroying the most recent marijuana patch like the 13,265 plants seized in Green County by MBN Agents and members of the Green County Sheriff's Office. As late as October of some years we were still participating in seizures of outdoor "grows". As in the above instance, we often pulled and destroyed plants for several days while guarding the patches from would be thieves during the nights. In this case, the patch was so large that we summoned Cadets from the ongoing MBN Recruit class in Jackson, to help pull and destroy the thousands of plants found on the property. Our newest "Narclets" got a firsthand taste of some of the

MBN Agents and Cadets "harvesting" marijuana plants in a multi-acre outdoor grow in southeast Mississippi

dirtier and less glamourous duties associated with being an MBN Agent.

Still demanding much time were other corollary duties such as training. Enjoying the opportunity to constantly meet new Officers, Deputies, and citizens, I accepted every offer to provide training, special presentations, and speeches to Agencies and groups all across the Gulf Coast. Teaching my *Officer Survival Classes* took me from the smallest of Departments to much larger groups like the Security Officers at NASA located at the Stennis Space Center in Hancock County. With the Space Center located on the deep water channel of the East Pearl River, I also taught Counter Smuggling for the NASA group. From speeches for Church groups to Booby Trap classes for the DEA's "Domestic Cannabis Eradication Program" or *DCEP* schools, the presentations always yielded the opportunity to share information that might help save Heroes' lives and take outlaws off the streets.

Then… while weaving through events that to an outsider might seem repetitive, a bump in the highway would cause just enough vibration that we would take a detour from our normal routes and become involved in another exciting series of events. Two such detours immediately come to mind.

Detour #1... The Party Pad

The *first detour* was an investigation that led to the arrest of a well known "Lady" from Hancock County who had developed quite an enterprise over the years preceding our story. We'll call her "Ella". For many years she had maintained a well hidden and cleverly disguised "Retreat" on the property behind her rural home. This "getaway" was frequently visited by many well known "officials" and businessmen from across the Gulf Coast and was a favorite location to relax with like minded friends and acquaintances. Here these patrons could enjoy their privacy and indulge in various types of gaming while being entertained by soft music and extremely friendly employees who were determined to insure that the guests' every wish was administered properly by delicate companions.

It was the perfect "Party Pad".

The "Party Pad"

Unknown to her regular patrons however, Ella had decided to... branch out. While the everyday business was being conducted by Ella and her staff, she had cultivated sources for an entirely new "Product Line". Unfortunately, the new product was controlled by State and Federal law and was considered contraband. She had ventured into the business of buying and selling multi-ton quantities of marijuana. Even more unfortunate for Ella, she had been infiltrated by one or more individuals who were not corrupt and would not stand by while Ella pursued the distribution of her new product line. They knew it just wasn't right!!!

Upon gaining information regarding Ella's new ventures, Agents and Deputies from MBN, DEA, US Customs and the Hancock County Sheriff's Office swooped down upon her kingdom late one afternoon and disrupted her prosperous and highly protected empire. Her long established empire had been toppled and the "Party Shack" had been shut down! During the search of her property, fruits of her new product line were seized from a rental truck which had just arrived from the McAllen, Texas, area. It contained over 5,000 pounds of marijuana wrapped securely within burlap and plastic in a form with which we had become very familiar by now. The bales were of the most recent generation and were perfectly squared and tightly compressed.

Former Sheriff Ronnie Peterson and Fred sit on
bales of marijuana in the back of the rental truck
used to bring tons of marijuana to the "Party Pad"

Ella was arrested and later pled guilty to multiple felonies. The patrons who had become very nervous and feared that Ella might start "naming Names" to save her tender hide, had lost their *rendezvous hideout* and were forced to find entertainment elsewhere along the Coast. Although Ella had become another victim of Greed…

to my knowledge, Ella never "sang".

Detour #2… Camp Safe

The *second detour* was an Investigation with which we were asked to assist in another part of Hancock County. This time the Hancock Sheriff's Office had conducted a lengthy investigation into a group in the Pearlington area. Alvin Ladner who was the Chief Investigator for the SO at that time had received information from a local resident along the Pearl River that a suspicious group had rented and occupied a large camp on the edge of the Pearl and had been acting very suspiciously since moving in.

Smugglers' camp on East Pearl River. Note vastness of area downstream from the camp at the end of the gravel road.

Watching the group and the camp for several months, Alvin had determined that the group was in fact involved in marine smuggling. In watching them move about, Alvin had identified several of the members of the group as previously arrested smugglers from the Florida area. With this knowledge and the fact that the group had all the Boats, vehicles and manpower staying at the camp that were needed to support a large smuggling operation, Alvin knew that it was only a matter of time until the group's "boat and load came in"… he, as usual, was right.

Seeing indicators that a load had arrived, Alvin obtained a search warrant for the camp and associated property. After asking for additional manpower from US Customs, MHP, and MBN, Alvin and his Deputies executed the warrant. During the search that followed, one of the most significant smuggling groups ever arrested in Hancock County was arrested by Alvin and his team. As a result of the search and Alvin's Investigation five outlaws were arrested, 28 firearms were seized, as were two large open water vessels, three vehicles and a total of 5,010 pounds of marijuana. The many bales of marijuana were found in every area of the camp, vehicles and outbuildings on the property. Their load had definitely come in!

Bales seized from various "storage areas" in and around camp

While searching the camp and property, an old friend and MHP Investigator, T.P. Naylor "kicked" a pile of bricks stacked loosely in the front yard. The bricks had been stacked in a manner to support a small piece of plywood that lay on top of the column of bricks. On top of the plywood was a "flower pot" with a blooming decorative flower. It was beautiful! As the pot, plant, plywood and bricks fell in response to T.P.'s "Kick", a two foot tall, not too cleverly hidden floor safe was revealed. Still shocked by his discovery, T.P.

reached down and twisted the handle on the safe. It easily turned and T.P. opened the safe. Inside the unlocked, poorly hidden safe sitting unattended in the front yard, T.P recovered over $236,000.00 cash. As T.P. pulled stack after stack of cash from the safe, both the outlaws and the "good guys" lost our breath! My old buddy T.P. had just "hit the jackpot"!!!

The "Jackpot's recipient" in this story, however, was still subject to the ruling of a Circuit Judge and to be determined at a later date. At this point in time the money was immediately placed into

MHP Investigator   T.P. Naylor pulls hundreds of thousands of dollars from a "floor safe" in the front yard of the camp

large plastic evidence bags and sealed and witnessed by T.P. and other Officers. It was then transported to a local Bank where the Bank's Staff counted the money with the Bank's counting machines in a highly controlled environment. Once counted, the money was again placed into evidence bags and sealed. Once sealed, the bags were initialed by all present who had observed the counting process. Then the funds were stored in a vault at the offices of the Agency which actually made the seizure. In this case, the vault belonged to the Hancock County Sheriff's Office. The seizure process was meticulous and strictly followed prescribed policies and the law.

Standing in the front yard of the camp that day, I was struck with a thought. Looking at the familiar faces of the Law Enforcement Officers present during the search, I realized that those Officers were moving about performing the highly technical tasks of searching, locating, seizing and cataloging a large volume of important evidence. Having first served an extremely high risk warrant on an elevated camp occupied by numerous heavily armed and dangerous felons, these guys made it *all* look far too easy. As I had seen many dozens of times in the past during the execution of dangerous warrants by these Officers, their knowledge, expertise, courage, and attention to detail was unsurpassed.

These were not just Heroes...

They were *"Professional Heroes"*!!!

While there were dozens of similar occupied camps all around the area in which Alvin had identified these outlaws, other than knowing a few "marked patrol cars" were at the camp down the road, even the closest neighbors had no idea what dangerous bad guys had just been removed from amongst them. Likewise, they had no idea what bravery had been demonstrated by unknown Heroes who had walked quietly and unnoticed among them.

Hardly anyone noticed anything!!!

SWAT Narcs?

Not long after the Pearlington seizure, I was approached by several Agents including Jay Eubanks regarding an opportunity that supported a concept that had been the desire of many Agents in the MBN for several years. Because we were constantly dealing with extremely dangerous and heavily armed felons, we had long asked for the opportunity to form a SWAT or High Risk Warrant Team within the MBN. While we had several Agents who had previously been on similar teams within other Departments, we did not have a team of our own.

Each time there was a preplanned operation involving dangerous characters, several of the same Agents with applicable skills would be summoned to assist in the operation. While this had always sufficed in the past, and these Agents were more than willing to provide themselves and their skills for these events, we all knew that this "*ad hoc*" team was no match for a well trained, well equipped, and properly structured SWAT Team.

The current "*opportunity*" was that the FBI was about to conduct an iteration of their one week basic SWAT school on the Keesler Air Force Base in Biloxi. This was an opportunity to at least acquire some up to date competently presented training from a respected group of Instructors. It was also to be taught by some of the FBI's Jackson SWAT Team members so I would be among Instructor friends throughout the week long school.

After a series of discussions and a fair amount of friendly *arm bending* at Headquarters, three other Agents and I were approved to attend the SWAT school that was to occur in mid-September of 1984 at Keesler. With the school approaching, we all gathered the required equipment and supplies for the course. Assembling clothing, protective gear, ammunition, weapons and such, we readied ourselves for the activities that lay ahead. Finally, we were geared-up and ready to go to work.

Showing up early on a Monday morning, we were introduced to all the Instructors and the Keesler Security Police Officers who would oversee the use of their classrooms, ranges and other facilities during the school. It was the first of many times that I would work with the excellent Staff of the Keesler Security Police including Mike Allen and Tim McKaig. They proved to be the best of Hosts and would become lasting friends and partners in the training of SWAT Officers for many years!

Throughout the week, we attended formal classroom presentations, practical exercises and scenario based exercises that

addressed and exposed us to numerous Tactical Skill Sets that were integral to being a member of a SWAT Team. We practiced basic team movement, entry and clearing techniques, firearms proficiency, Sniper Team applications, mechanical breeching, rappelling, and other topics. Each block of

Bowen Johnson, FBI SWAT Instructor and close friend for many years, demonstrates "inverted" rappel techniques during a SWAT Class

instruction was reinforced with practical exercises in which the students had the opportunity to practice the topics covered in the classroom.

At the end of the week all of the topics and exercises were combined in a final scenario in which we were required to execute a warrant on a structure within the housing area of Keesler. The exercise was made more realistic with the presence of role players who were provided by the Security Police. At the conclusion of the scenario, our Instructors critiqued our performance and made suggestions for improvements. Back at the classroom, we were given a written exam, and the course was complete. After storing all equipment and cleaning the training areas, it was time for graduation. Along with the FBI Instructors, the Jackson Resident Agent gave a brief speech

and then helped with the distribution of our Certificates. We were now

Gene Waldrop (Chief of Police, Madison, MS) coaches Jay Eubanks atop a fifty foot tall tower, as Jay goes through the rails to begin his "first ever" rappel. I was standing to the right "enjoying the show"…

official graduates of the prestigious FBI SWAT School.

Although I knew that the skills learned and those revisited during the school would help me and the other Agents in all of our future warrants, I had no concept of how the training and the liaisons created during the course would impact the many years that followed

Fred receives his FBI SWAT certification from Special Agent in Charge, Weldon Kennedy of the Jackson Division, as Special Agent Bowen Johnson watches. Within a few years, Weldon was promoted to "Deputy Director" of the FBI.

as I progressed through my career. The ride still continues. Along with Agents Jay Eubanks, Ken Coleman, and Lee Porter, we had become the first MBN Agents to graduate from a SWAT School for the purpose of employing these skills while performing our official duties as Agents. Although we all knew that we were a *LONG* way from actually having our own SWAT Team, we at least had been able to receive much needed training that would increase the safety of our Agents Statewide.

It was long overdue!!!

Within a month, I would be responding to requests from other Agencies for tactical related training. Armed with tactical skills learned while a member of the NOPD, Picayune PD, MBN, and the most recent SWAT School, I assisted the Jackson Police Department with their SWAT school later in September. From this foundation, I would attend dozens of tactical operations, planning and management courses for the next ten years and would teach SWAT related programs for well over thirty-five years. Meeting untold Heroes and Giants within the national and international Tactical communities throughout those years has been among the most rewarding experiences of my entire life!

My ride with Heroes was about to be expanded beyond my wildest dreams!

An Association of Like Minded

Another unique opportunity was afforded me in early 1985. I was contacted by several well known Agency Leaders from throughout the State and asked to attend a meeting at the Mississippi Law Enforcement Officers' Training Academy near Jackson. The meeting was being organized for the purpose of creating a statewide Tactical Association. The intent was to create an organization which would promote the sharing of tactical expertise and training among the various Departments' tactical units and teams across the State. This would expand the knowledge needed to manage the high risk events being conducted by these Departments and enhance the skills of these teams' members. The ultimate goal of this effort was to increase these team members' likelihood for *Safety and Success* in all of their high risk operations.

Within weeks, the meeting was conducted and the *Mississippi Tactical Officers' Association* was born. Among the *State's Tactical Leaders* who met to create the MTOA were Billy Pickens, Steve Ford, L.M. Davis, Gene Waldrop, Bob Tinsley, Andy Waller, Joe Hart, Bowen Johnson, Bill Jones, Tom Long, me, and dozens of others. That first meeting was literally a *"Who's Who"* of Mississippi's SWAT leadership in the 1980's. It was a great honor just to be among these men and be a part of creating an organization which would become an Icon within the Tactical Community throughout the Nation for the next several decades!

At a subsequent meeting in Jackson, elections were held and a "Staff" was elected to manage the direction and activities of the MTOA. It was decided that there would be one statewide "President's" position and a *Northern* and *Southern* "Vice President's" position. There would be five "Board of Directors" members elected from the north half of the State and five from the south half. Finally, there would be one statewide "Secretary/Treasurer" who would manage all of the Association's financial affairs. In all, there would be fourteen members of what would become the "managing Staff" of the MTOA. Among those elected for the first one year term were two of my oldest and closest friends and partners. Steve Ford would officiate as the MTOA's first President and Billy Pickens was elected as Secretary/Treasurer. The Association could not have started out with better leadership!

Over the next year the MTOA held quarterly meetings and began to establish itself and its reputation. Various members provided blocks of instruction during the meetings and the Association began to take shape. At the first *annual* meeting on March 19, 1986, I was elected to the position of President and was to hold that position for the next ten years. By my side for the entire decade, was my trusted friend from Columbus, Billy Pickens who served for well over a decade as both Secretary/Treasurer and Vice President during different terms. Numerous other Tactical Legends from across the State also served in various positions within the Staff at different times during the ten years that followed. It was to be one of the most demanding and rewarding rivers that I ever rode during my career. As always, the other *trail breaking cowboys* with whom I rode this river, helped make it all possible! They are all among the greatest of Heroes in Mississippi's history of SWAT training, operations, and innovation.

MTOA Staff and other Instructors (including John Plaster) during an early MTOA annual Conference and Competition.

Another Hero is Born

In early 1986, I had another experience which would forever be noted as one of my "Life Altering Events"! On January 20, our daughter Freddye Nicole was born. As with my son Chad, upon the birth of Freddye, my life would never be the same. Just as Chad had filled a unique spot in my life that only my son can make complete, Freddye had now created and permanently occupied a position in my fabric that only she could make whole. How tattered I must have

Freddye Nicole with Daddy. There aren't many people whom I have ever allowed to paint my fingernails... my "Punkin" heads that short list of "1"!

appeared before these Heroes blessed my life! I'll always hope and pray that I might mean half as much to them as they have both meant to me since the first days that I held each of them many years ago!

Going Tactical

B lended with other responsibilities, I began to receive more and more requests from Agents and Officers from other Agencies to assist with "Tactical" related events. It became very common to be called upon to assist with the planning of high risk search warrants, arrest warrants, surveillances and other similar operations being conducted by MBN and by other Agencies. Over the next several years, I had the great opportunity to support Officers in our area with a wide variety of other enforcement situations including bank robberies, hostage situations, barricaded suspects, dignitary protection details, and "round-up" operations.

After each of these events, the Officers involved would be assembled for an informal debriefing. In these talks, we would discuss the event, how it was planned, and how we all performed. It was one of the best opportunities that I ever experienced to identify mistakes or problems and then "fix" the problem before it eventually got someone hurt. During these debriefings, we also always discussed the performance of our equipment. Because our lives often depended upon a particular piece of equipment and its performance, we all wanted to discuss what worked and identify the items which did not work.

Having been fortunate enough to have used and tested many categories of equipment over the years, I also frequently found myself offering advice on a wide variety of tactical gear ranging from weapons to clothing and from lighting devices to load bearing equipment. It was a responsibility that I took very seriously.

Having personally purchased a great deal of the specialty equipment that I used over the years, I knew how quickly one could spend a lot of money only to find that the purchased equipment simply did not work. I wound up over the years, with what I still refer to as *"The Box"*. It's that cardboard receptacle in the back of every Cop's closet that is full of *junk*. It's overflowing with expensive items that once looked like the coolest thing on the planet, when observed in a movie or magazine, but when purchased, quickly saddened the buyer because it simply didn't do the job *"as advertised"*.

Offering advice on equipment that could help save a hero's life became and still is a great honor. It is a concept that still permeates our training environments. We frequently acquire various items of equipment and inject them into the most realistic training environments that we can create. By allowing the students to "test" the equipment in this fashion, they can see for themselves whether the equipment works or doesn't work. It also allows them to make these determinations in a safe environment... not when their life depends upon the equipment working!

In the mid 1980's, this process led to the creation of our company,

Southern Tactical Supply.

Starting out selling only equipment that I had personally tested and proven reliable, we quickly branched into manufacturing. We produced a variety of holsters, belts, and load bearing equipment that soon became popular with SWAT Teams and individual Officers across the Country. Each Item was developed around the concept of "Does *it work and is it durable?"* In all the years that we manufactured hundreds of specialty items, none were ever sent back for replacement or repair! In developing a piece of equipment, I would draw *what I wanted* on the nearest paper tablet and Gayle would work her magic on her *Heavy Duty Industrial Sewing Machine* that we had purchased "secondhand". It was a lot of fun and when I handed a new piece of equipment that we had made, to a purchasing Officer, I knew he or she could bet their life on what I had just delivered to them! It was very rewarding!

Still running the Gulfport District, the other Agents and I continued to make cases and look for ladders. Along with the usual speeches to Civic groups and numerous training responsibilities, we continued to make drug case after drug case on significant drug dealers all along the coast and purchased a variety of drugs in varying quantities almost every day. The Gulfport Agents always led the State in numbers of cases, quantities of drugs seized, and quality of cases and violators. Certainly, the geographic area that we occupied had some impact upon the availability of such drugs and violators. However, I will always maintain that the MBN *Agents* who worked in the Gulfport Office, had the greatest impact on the quality of cases that were made and their record of successful prosecutions.

Having worked with hundreds of highly qualified and dedicated Agents and Officers from all across the nation, I still consider these men and women to be among the most capable, bravest and most professional of all those with whom I ever worked. Other than the names that I have presented herein, there were many other Agents who either were assigned to the GDO full time or were assigned only temporarily. Because I do not know the status of each of those Heroes today, I have kept their identity anonymous. They, their families, and I know who they are and they should all know that *riding the river* with each of them was a privilege that I will never forget. Day after day, week after week, and year after year they willingly went into harm's way and performed the most dangerous of Law Enforcement tasks. They all contributed their valuable skills each day to apprehend and convict drug dealers and other outlaws who were constantly preying upon our communities, our citizens and particularly our youth!

They were so good at their job that they often…
"made it look too easy"!!!
In many cases they made it look so easy that
they were never adequately appreciated for what they did…!!!
*I appreciated their dedication and their sacrifices more than they
will ever know!*
***It was a great honor to lead these Heroes as the Commander of the
Gulfport District Office!***

You Can't Always Pick What You Get

L ooking back is always a lot clearer than trying to look ahead.
Hindsight is always more accurate than trying to anticipate
future events. If we look objectively back at our previous actions and
their results and evaluate the outcome honestly, we should never
make the same mistake twice! Sometimes however, we don't control
the circumstances that control us. Such is the world in which most
career Law Enforcement Officers find themselves.

By "career" Officers, I'm referring to those who recognize
being an enforcer of the laws and protecting their fellow citizens as a
"*Calling*". Being a Cop is not simply what they do, it is what they
ARE! They are not "on the job" only to find the next opportunity for
their own advancement, nor are they there to enrich themselves
financially. They are Cops because they want to be a "protector".
They want to take dangerous outlaws off the streets of their
communities. These Heroes are truly the *Centurions* of our time.
These brave souls make conscious decisions each day which place
them in harm's way so that others around them can remain safe.
There are no greater Heroes than these!!!

Cops *recognize* Cops. They also recognize those imposters
who sometimes infiltrate their ranks. Through only minimal
interaction, Cops can determine those who are on the job for all the

right reasons and identify those who are present only for some form of personal gain. Cops know instinctively upon whom they can rely when the chips are down. When given the opportunity, the brave will assemble with the brave. Unfortunately, in the real world, these courageous, dedicated Officers don't always have the opportunity or the authority to select by whom they stand. This is sadly true especially when it comes to the area of selecting the "Boss" who leads the Department by whom both the Cops and the imposters are employed!

By this time, I had worked for the Mississippi Bureau of Narcotics for almost ten years. Experience now revealed that the path down which the MBN was to travel within any given four year "political cycle" was controlled exclusively by a series of *political promises, commitments, and decisions which resulted in the Governor's appointment of a new Director and Deputy Director*. I, like most career Agents, have never been involved in that decision process, but every Agent who ever worked for the MBN has been affected by the process and the ultimate decision.

We had to live with it!

The Law Enforcement environment is a unique world by any definition. Unlike most professions controlled by "profits and losses", which are driven by statistics and academically derived "Probabilities" for success, the Cop's world is driven by the rules of "Possibilities"! Officers can never only be prepared for those events which will "Probably" occur, they must be prepared every moment, of every hour, of every day, for what might *"Possibly"* happen!!! This would be daunting enough if the outcome for misjudging "Possibilities" was just a lower dollar figure on a "bottom line", but in the Cop's world, the penalty for misjudging can very likely be the difference between life and death for the Officer and for others. In the Cop's world, the ability to consistently and accurately predict "Possibilities" is literally the key to survival!!!

The Cop's world is also governed by *guidelines* that create a matrix of formulas with which Officers must also evaluate their every action. They must insure that the most likely results of their next action meets all of the criteria that will allow that action to be deemed *"correct, legal, and appropriate"* after the action is initiated and completed. This matrix is composed of several components over which the Officers have little, if any, control. These are, however, elements of every decision that they make while doing their job… decisions which often must be made in micro-seconds while the Officer operates in life threatening situations and environments.

To explain, Officers must always abide by and act in accordance with all local, State, and Federal Laws. All of their decisions must be *Legally Sound* and capable of withstanding extreme "Legal" scrutiny by the most competent of Attorneys. They must also comply with all "Court Decisions" which directly or indirectly affect the Officers' enforcement actions, tools, and techniques. Finally, they must abide by all Agency *"Policies and Guidelines"* as set forth in their Department's *Operational Manual.*

While most Officers are familiar with the rules pertaining to the enforcement of our drug laws, most are only familiar with the *"policies and regulations"* of their own Departments. For example, a Deputy from the Lowndes County Sheriff's Department would most likely not be familiar with the policies of the Vicksburg Police Department. Most often the Policies governing any given Department will have many similar regulations but many of the Agencies' guidelines would likewise be quite different. In the case of the MBN, our policies were vastly different from most other Agencies due to our structure and mission.

Most Agents and employees who had been employed by the MBN for many years were not only familiar with the Agency's policies and guidelines, but also were familiar with *WHY* those policies and guidelines were created and established. Having this unique insight enabled the Agents and especially the Supervisors to manage other employees and direct them in a manner that would insure that the goals of the MBN were met. This insight also helped minimize or eliminate mistakes which could endanger the Agents, other Officers with whom we worked, civilians within any given operational environment, and even the Outlaws as we developed cases against them and ultimately arrested them.

The MBN Manual was a very important instrument within the Agency. Many of the regulations enumerated within the Manual were written and incorporated into the Manual because of mistakes, mishaps, or wrongdoings perpetrated by or upon Agents as they performed their enforcement duties throughout the years since the MBN was created in 1971. It was a *roadmap of experience* that helped us to avoid making the same or similar mistakes from which we had historically already learned valuable and sometimes costly lessons. It helped us to prevent the reliving of tragedies that we had already previously endured. Our Manual was one of our most valuable assets. Adhering to its "General Orders" helped insure safety and success. Straying from its structure and its guidelines was most often a formula for disaster!

As new Directors and Deputy Directors were appointed over the years, some sought insight from and were guided by our Manual. Some ignored the Manual almost completely and made-up their own rules as they rode the trail toward the next election cycle and ultimately the next Bosses to fill their current seats. I'll allow the reader to imagine under which category of administration the MBN, its employees, and the State prospered most.

I have observed that the most successful of all Directors were those who could listen well. They tended to seek the advice of Agents, Supervisors, and other employees who had been in the MBN for years and knew how to get the job done. These Bosses listened carefully, compiled information regarding a situation and then made sound decisions that yielded a high probability for success. These were very wise and honest leaders who had the best interest of the Agents and the MBN in mind, and in their hearts!

It also became painfully obvious that in some instances we were the unwitting recipients of Directors and Deputy Directors who had no intention of listening to the experienced personnel within the Agency nor concerning themselves with the "written word" of our Manual. Often these Administrators listened only to those who would willingly support anything that the Boss suggested in order to achieve some personal advantage that the "parrot" employee desired. In many instances the previous actions of these same "Parrots", while working "in the field", were the catalyst for the creation of a *new* "General Order" within the Manual designed and written to prevent the same disaster from occurring again. This category of Bosses and "Parrots" were almost exclusively driven by personal motives that ultimately benefited only them!

The lesson soon became obvious. Whenever decisions are made for personal gain, the results are almost always disastrous, and there are always victims. Conversely, when decisions are made exclusively for the good of ALL concerned as well as the Agency, everybody wins and there are no victims! The problem for the career Agent and employee was and still is that *we never got to choose our Bosses.* We had to survive in the environment created by a decision that was made every four years by someone called a Governor. Even with the best of intentions, the Governor might choose Bosses that become "millstones" for the Agency and its personnel.

With that glimpse into the political atmosphere created by the ***political appointment*** of the MBN Bosses, I will add that it is an unbelievably stressful profession being a sworn Officer in today's world. Going to work each day knowing that death might literally wait around the next corner is enough to cause all but the bravest of the brave to seek a new career path and alternate job opportunities.

The men and women who remain in Law Enforcement for an entire career are truly special people and world class Heroes. It is a travesty that these Heroes are frequently victims of internal and external *political decisions* that dramatically affect their likelihood for *safety and success*.

Within the MBN, as with most other Agencies across the Nation, we were blessed with some of the best leaders ever to wear the Badge and we were also cursed with some of the worst! We never knew what brand of Boss would roll down the tracks and into the MBN Station next...

For the "career" Agent, it was the *"luck of the draw"*!!!

In the years that were to follow, we were to see many changes within the MBN... some good, and some not so good! The one consistently positive factor was the many world class Heroes with whom I rode! Unknown to me then, my ride was just getting started along a river still filled with challenges, excitement, dangers, and adventures.

I was yet to meet hundreds of incredible Heroes who would impact my life forever along a river that would twist and turn through a career path that was as unpredictable as it would be rewarding! Many uncharted miles lay ahead...

The story had just begun!!!!!

Author's Note

When I first began compiling thoughts and notes for this book several years ago, my wish was that I might create a factual account of my life, and career. Critical to the accurate depiction of my story was an explanation of my interaction with many of the most important people in my life, and some of the most memorable events which have occurred during my fifty year Law Enforcement career. To accomplish those goals, I felt that I needed to "start from the start" and first explain why I ever even had an interest in becoming a "Cop". Starting with stories of my youth and those who had the greatest influences on me, I moved through the history of becoming a Cop, and along the continuing journey that actually BECAME my life.

The greatest motivator in the entire process from concept to reality has been to chronical my life, and experiences in a manner that my family, and especially my grandchildren, will know and possibly benefit from many life lessons that I learned while *riding the river* with some of America's greatest Heroes. *For my grandchildren*, I embarked upon this journey of documentation.

For most of my career, my family knew little or nothing about what I was involved in during the course of my official duties. Either because I was working undercover or involved in investigations and operations which were of a highly sensitive nature, they were constantly under a protective umbrella. They knew little about what I did "on the job" and very few people who knew them, knew *exactly* what Fred (or Dad) did for a living. While my son and daughter heard snapshots of some of the stories in the book, most of the stories were never talked about "within our family". Now, many years after these events occurred, hopefully my family and friends can enjoy and benefit from these stories.

After I had written most of the stories, I wanted to challenge my memory regarding the details in each story and insure that my recollection was accurate. I was able to contact and talk with many of the Heroes in most of the stories and in talking with each of them, it was as though the events depicted in most of the stories had just occurred "last week". With them, I relived many of the stories presented herein and was able to reinforce, and in a few instances, correct my memory of dozens of events that we shared together over the course of knowing each other and working together for decades. Visiting with each of these Heroes became a treasure which I did not anticipate when I started writing the book.

As I wrote for more than a year, I also searched through boxes and lockers to find hundreds of photographs of the events depicted in the book. I found numerous photos related to many of those events and dozens of other significant stories. As I compiled and sorted photos, and assigned them to the stories that they represented, I began to realize that the "size" of my book was growing to an unpredictably high number of pages.

By the time that I had actually finished writing the text of the book, it had increased to a total "page count" which many of my fellow Authors, *gasped at* (lost their breath) when they heard the figure. The solution was one which I had no enthusiasm for! It was, however, agreed with by everyone with whom I discussed my options from a publishing stand point. *The book needed to be broken into two volumes.* This was probably one of the hardest decisions that I have ever had to make. Finally, after several months of head scratching and soul searching, I concluded that I could either reduce the number of stories in the book or the number of photos (or both), or… I could leave all the stories and photos intact, and separate the book into two "volumes". That is what I have decided to do.

Because the photos represent such a valuable aspect of the book, and help visually explain many of the stories, I believe that they are each a very necessary contributor to the readers' understanding of many of the stories. Because each of the stories play an important part in the overall "timeline" of the book, I felt that each story needed to be told. To avoid the necessity of *extra support* under the shelves of the bookstores which would display copies of a "one volume" version of my book, my best option was to divide the book into two near equal, but more "portable" volumes.

The point at which I selected to "divide" the book, is a significant intersection along the timeline of my career. It represents a point at which I was about to switch totally from an "Enforcement" role into a position of "Operational Support". While continuing to participate in hundreds of ongoing high level investigations and operations, I was no longer the Agent who "made the cases" but one who *supported* the Agents who were making the cases and arresting those outlaws upon whom the cases were to be made.

For more than a decade, I would hold positions including Task Force member, Counter Smuggling Group Commander, SWAT Commander, Special Operations Group Commander, Director of Training and Academy Director, and Director of Special Projects. While holding these positions, I had the opportunity to participate in and manage numerous complex investigations conducted by Agents throughout the State. I also managed hundreds of High Risk Operations throughout the State in which notorious Outlaws were tracked down and arrested during many of the most dangerous operations ever conducted by our Agency.

The switch from enforcement to support was probably one of the most difficult transitions that I ever made during my career! For many years, I had most often been the "first guy through the door" during hundreds of search warrants and arrests. I now realized that from this point forward, I would no longer be that *first guy*... I would be the Guy sitting outside or in a command post *"sending my guys through those doors"*! The responsibility associated with the decisions which must be made while occupying this level of Command can only be appreciated by one who has shared such positions and decisions!

It is very "Sobering"!!!

The trail along the many rivers that lay ahead throughout our State and Nation would hold hundreds of opportunities to ride and work with more Heroes than I could have ever imagined! It was to be quite a ride and quite a story!!!

I sincerely hope that you have enjoyed "Volume I" of my story, and I also hope that in the near future, you will equally enjoy "Volume II", where......

"The Story Continues"

Acknowledgements

During the process of writing this book, I had the support of many people. Among them was my beautiful wife of forty years, Gayle. She spent hours, days, weeks, and months reading and proofing each day's "entries" as I typed and *mis-typed* the many pages that are now the two volumes of "our" book! Her love and loyalty has always been unwavering! Whether proofing the book or sitting at home endless hours while most of the stories in the book actually unfolded in real time, she has been my "Rock" for more than four decades! She is my best friend and greatest Hero!!!

Also, my son Chad and my daughter Freddye, assisted with the proofing of the book and likewise endured many years of Dad's being "gone" from home. As young children, I remember them both standing in driveways watching with tears in their eyes as Dad drove away for another day, or week, or month on the road doing whatever Dad did… Upon each return, I was met with the most loving of arms and smiles offered by two of my greatest Heroes… my Buddy, and my Punkin!!!

Without a few special people, the book would still contain unforgivable grammatical errors, "type-o's", misspelled or misused words, and other errors that are almost impossible to detect without a "Team" of dedicated proof readers and editors. Among them were my sister-in-law Lynda Stinson, Jim Luke, Harold Richard, Steve Mallory, Jim Kelly, John Plaster, Kent McDaniel and a VERY SPECIAL lady and much loved Aunt… Martha Brown. Having been an educator for decades, with specialties in "English" and "Grammar", Martha coached me through corrections in structure and language errors, and all the time made me feel like my *Boo-Boo's* "weren't that bad"…

Thank you Sweetheart!
Your *"Teddy Bear"* loves you very much!!!

A special thanks is extended for a contribution provided by two new friends… Sharilyn and Michael Glover. As the current owners of the home and property along the Pearl River that belonged to Papa Mac and Mama Nina during my teenage years, they generously allowed Gayle to take photos of me standing upon the exact spot *on the river's edge*, where Papa Mac and I "target practiced" with his shotgun, rifles, and pistol more than a half century earlier while I was…

"Growing up at Walkiah Bluff".

Also throughout the writing of the book, many of the Heroes in the stories were highly supportive of my efforts. Among them were Charlie Faught, Gene Fields, Harold Richard, Dave Henley, Tommy Casey, Paul Melancon, Rudy Melancon, Bill Derbyshire, David McCann, Billy Roth, Bruce Rogers, Steve Ford, Sam Owens, Jay Eubanks, Jim Kelly, Charlie Spillers, Jerry Dettman, Steve Mallory, Jim Luke, Billy Pickens, Don Frierson, Mike Tyson, Brenda Smith, Freddy Drennan, Rhett Magnon, Mark Helton, and Jim Catalano.

Throughout the years, many Heroes mentioned in the book have passed away. Even since I started writing this book we've lost additional heroes. For their tremendous contributions to my life and career, I will be eternally grateful! Each one touched my life in a special and unique way and without their individual presence in my life, my journey along the rivers that we rode would have been much less exciting, less rewarding, and in many cases…

Less survivable!!!

About the Author

Fred Gray Macdonald III retired as a Captain with the Mississippi Bureau of Narcotics in April of 1999 ending a twenty-five year career with that agency. During his time with the MBN, he held many positions including Enforcement/Undercover Agent, Technical Services Commander, District Commander, Federal Task Force Agent/Deputy US Marshal, Counter Smuggling Unit Commander, SWAT Commander, Special Operations Group (SOG) Commander, Director of Training, Class 1 Academy Director, and Branch Director for Special Projects. During his time with the MBN, Fred successfully initiated, participated in, and/or managed hundreds of the most complex and high level investigations ever conducted by the State's Drug Enforcement Agency. From long term undercover operations spanning multiple states, to planning for and managing complex SWAT operations involving some of the most dangerous criminals ever arrested in Mississippi, Fred spent many years on the "front lines" of Law Enforcement. His fifty year Law Enforcement Career has also included employment with the Mississippi Highway Patrol, Pearl River Sheriff's Department, New Orleans Police Department, and the Picayune Police Department.

Throughout his career, he provided training to members of local, state, and federal agencies as well as every branch of our military. Fred was the Managing Instructor for the Officer Survival Program at the Harrison County Law Enforcement Academy for more than ten years. He has provided instructional programs for the Law Enforcement Television Network (LETN), and has published articles in the National Tactical Officers' Association (NTOA) quarterly magazine as well as other periodicals. After helping create the Mississippi Tactical Officers' Association (MTOA) in 1985, Fred served as President for ten years, and managed all of the training and annual competitions conducted by the MTOA.

Since 1992, Fred has conducted his High Risk Event Planning System, and Tactical Training Programs contractually throughout the Nation. Along with his T.I.G.E.R. Training Group he has trained thousands of Law Enforcement Officers and Military members from every corner of our Nation and from other countries. Fred has received dozens of awards and commendations for his enforcement, management, and training accomplishments, from local, state, and federal agencies as well as from specialty units within the military, and from NASA.

Acronym Legend

ABC	Alcohol Beverage Control (State Enforcement Agency)
ASIA	Air Smuggling Investigations Association
ABI	Alabama Bureau of Investigation
ATF	Alcohol Tobacco and Firearms (Federal Enforcement Agency)
CB	Citizens Band (Radio)
CI	Confidential Informant
CO	County
CLU	Central Lock Up (Jail at NOPD)
CPD	Columbus Police Department
CPR	Cardio Pulmonary Resuscitation
DC-3	Large Twin-Engine Aircraft
DCEP	Domestic Cannabis Eradication Program
DEA	Drug Enforcement Administration (Federal Enforcement Agency)
DPS	Department of Public Safety (State Enforcement Agency)
ECMS	Electronic Counter Measures Sweep (Check for "Bugs")
FBI	Federal Bureau of Investigation (Federal Enforcement Agency)
FBO	Fixed Base Operator (The Control Office/Officer at a Small Airport)
GDO	Gulfport District Office (Gulfport Office of the MBN)
GPD	Gulfport Police Department
HDO	Hattiesburg District Office (Hattiesburg Office of the MBN)
JPD	Jackson Police Department
JPSO	Jefferson Parish Sheriff's Office
LEA/LEAA	Law Enforcement Assistance Administration
LSD	Lysergic Acid Diethylamide (Hallucinogenic Drug)
LSP	Louisiana State Police
MBN	Mississippi Bureau of Narcotics
MHP/MHSP	Mississippi Highway Patrol

MLEOTA	Mississippi Law Enforcement Officers Training Academy
NOPD	New Orleans Police Department
NVD	Night Vision Device
OJT	On the Job Training
OP	Observation Post (Surveillance Position)
OSF	Official State Funds ("Buy Money")
PCP	Phencyclidine – A psychedelic drug ("Angel Dust")
PPC	Picayune Police Department
R-5	Region 5 (Original Designation for Gulfport Office of the MBN)
SO	Sheriff's Office
SWAT	Special Weapons and Tactics
T's & Blues	Substitute for Heroin, Talwin or "T's" (Pentazocine), and Pyribenzamine (Blues) a first generation antihistamine
THC	Tetrahydrocannabinol
U/C	Under Cover (Covert Officer, Investigation, or Condition)
USM	University of Southern Mississippi

Name Index

The following is a list of the individuals mentioned within the book *"I Rode With Heroes, Volume I"*. Their names are followed by the page numbers in which each name appears.

www.ingramcontent.com/pod-product-compliance
Lightning Source LLC
Chambersburg PA
CBHW051848090426
42811CB00034B/2258/J

9 781734 088809